Contents

AutoCAD for Windows

A. Yarwood

Longman Scientific & Technical
Longman Group Limited
Longman House, Burnt Mill, Harlow
Essex CM20 2JE, England
and Associated Companies throughout the world

Copublished in the United States with
John Wiley & Sons, Inc., 605 Third Avenue, New York, NY 10158

First Published 1995

British Library Cataloguing in Publication Data
A catalogue entry for this title is available from the British Library

ISBN 0-582-23935-4

Library of Congress Cataloging-in-Publication Data
Yarwood, A. (Alfred), 1937–
    AutoCAD for Windows/A. Yarwood
        p.   cm.
    Includes index.
    ISBN 0-582-23935-4. – ISBN 0-470-23406-7 (Wiley)
    1. Computer graphics.   2. AutoCAD for Windows.   I. Title.
T385.Y392   1994
620'.0042'02855369–dc20   94-9030
                                                                            CIP

ISBN 0-470-23406-7 (USA only)

Set in Melior 10/13pt
Produced by Longman Singapore Publishers (Pte)
Printed in Singapore

List of plates

Colour plates are between pages 112 and 113.

Preface

This book was written for the use of students in colleges and for those in industry who are beginning to learn how to use AutoCAD in the Windows environment. AutoCAD is the most widely used CAD system in the world, with more than 50% of all the CAD workstations throughout the world equipped with AutoCAD software. Windows has become the leading Graphical User Interface (GUI) system in the world. AutoCAD for Windows combines the excellence of the world leading CAD software with the increasingly popular interface supplied by Windows. This combination allows drawings in AutoCAD to be constructed with the aid of tool icons, together with the speed of operation of Windows and other GUI features of the AutoCAD/Windows systems.

AutoCAD for Windows is a *user-friendly* CAD program, but is very complex. A book of this size cannot possibly hope to explain all the command systems, variables, GUI features and interchange systems between AutoCAD and Windows. There is, however, sufficient detail in the pages of the book to enable students and those wishing to get to grips with working in AutoCAD to become reasonably expert in its operation. It is hoped that the contents of the book will encourage readers to undertake further research and exploration of the possibilities with this quite remarkable CAD package. Among the systems in the software not described are the numerous set variables for controlling the way in which drawings can be constructed; some of the commands which are not commonly used when constructing drawings; the AutoLisp files; The ADS (Autodesk Development System) files.

The contents of the book are primarily aimed at those using AutoCAD on a PC (Personal Computer), but its contents are equally suitable for those working on other computer set-ups for which an AutoCAD package is available.

Early chapters deal with 2D (two-dimensional) drawing. These are followed by chapters dealing with methods of constructing 3D (three-dimensional) drawings. Later chapters deal with the construction of

3D solid model drawing with the aid of AME (Advanced Modelling Extension). The final chapter contains a short description of the rendering of a couple of solid models in AutoCAD Render. Two appendices follow, the first a very short description of some of the facilities offered by the Windows software and the second a short glossary of computing terms. A number of colour plates include screen shots of some of the variety of graphics windows possible with the software, together with examples of simple solid models which have been rendered with the Render command systems.

All drawings in the books were constructed in AutoCAD for Windows loaded into a PC computer built by Dart Computers of Romsey and fitted with an Intel 486 DX2 operating chip. A 210 Mbyte hard disk was fitted in the PC, together with a video card capable of running an SVGA (Super Video Graphics Array) monitor with a resolution of 1024 by 768 pixels and in 256 colours. The version of Windows used was Windows 3.1. The screen dumps in the book were taken with the aid of the screen-dump package Hijaak for Windows, published by Inset Systems. Both drawings and screen-dump illustrations were printed with the aid of a Hewlett Packard Laserjet printer.

As this book was going into print, a new AutoCAD extension AutoVision was released, which can if desired be purchased to replace AutoCAD Render in AutoCAD for Windows or AutoCAD Release 12. Renderings produced with the aid of AutoVision can be taken directly into the rendering package Autodesk 3D Studio. AutoVision works in a very similar manner to 3D Studio and can, with the use of the CD-ROM included in the AutoVision package, produce renderings of a very large range of materials and finishes.

Salisbury 1994   A. Yarwood

Acknowledgements

The author wishes to acknowledge with grateful thanks the help given to him by members of the staff of Autodesk Ltd.

Trademarks

The following are trademarks registered in the US Patent and Trademark Office by Autodesk Inc.:

Autodesk®, AutoCAD®, AutoSketch®, Advanced Modelling Extension® (AME).

The following are trademarks of Autodesk Inc.:

ACAD™, DXF™, AutoCAD Device Interface™ (ADI), AutoCAD Development System™ (ADS).

IBM® is a registered trademark of the International Business Machines Corporation.

MS-DOS® is a registered trademark, and Windows ™ is a trademark of the Microsoft Corporation.

A. Yarwood is a Registered Applications Developer with Autodesk Ltd.

Registered Developer

CHAPTER 1

Introduction

Advantages of using a CAD software package

The abbreviation CAD stands for Computer Aided Design. Some will say that it stands for Computer Aided Drawing (or Draughting), but a first-class CAD software package such as AutoCAD for Windows is not just a drawing tool. It is a designing tool.

1. CAD software can be used to produce any technical drawing which can be produced "by hand";
2. Drawings can be produced much more quickly with CAD than when working "by hand" – as much as 10 times faster when used by skilled CAD operators;
3. Drawing with CAD equipment is less tedious than working "by hand" – in particular, the adding of features such as hatch lines and the drawing of notes and other lettering is easier, much quicker and more accurate;
4. Drawings, or parts of drawings, can be copied, scaled, rotated, mirrored or moved with ease, without having to re-draw the drawing or part of drawing;
5. Drawings or parts of drawings can be rapidly inserted into other drawings, without having to re-draw the insertion;
6. The same detail need never be drawn twice because it can be copied or inserted into another drawing with ease. A basic rule when drawing with the aid of CAD is:

    Never draw the same thing twice;

7. New details can be added to a drawing, or details within a drawing can be easily altered without having to make any mechanical erasures;
8. Skilled operators can automatically dimension drawings with accuracy, greatly reducing the possibility of dimensional error;
9. Drawings saved to files on disk allows the saving of storage space;

10. Drawings can be plotted and/or printed to any scale required by the user without the need for re-drawing;
11. With AutoCAD for Windows, solid drawing data can be exchanged with other computer devices such as CAM (Computer Aided Manufacturing).

AutoCAD for Windows

AutoCAD for Windows works as a graphics window in the GUI (Graphical User Interface) system of Windows and has all the systems of AutoCAD Release 12 with the following additional features:

1. Can be configured from within an AutoCAD graphics window. The following configuration details can be changed:
   (a) A choice of:
       (i) A method of command selection from icons in a movable toolbox, or/and:
       (ii) A method of command selection from on-screen menus;
   (b) Whether or not a toolbar is included at the top of the graphic window. This toolbar:
       (i) includes icon buttons to toggle Snap, Ortho and PSpace on/off; buttons for Layer control and name; icon buttons to bring File Save As and File Open dialogue boxes into the window;
       (ii) can be configured to add icon buttons for selecting commands of the operator's own choice;
   (c) The colours for the various parts of the graphics window;
   (d) The font and its height for use in the on-screen menu and in the command line;
2. An Aerial View window can be added to the AutoCAD graphics screen in which zoomed and/or panned areas of a large drawing will be highlighted to show the operator exactly in which area of a drawing he/she is working;
3. Up to three sessions of AutoCAD can be run at the same time in separate graphics windows, allowing switching from one window to another and, in particular, copying of detail from one drawing to another;
4. Drawings can be copied to the Windows Clipboard, for insertion into other applications such as word-processor or desktop publishing programs. Text from a word processor, or data from a database can be pasted into an AutoCAD graphic window via either the Clipboard or the Windows Packager program;
5. The DDE (Dynamic Data Exchange) system allows data to be sent to a spreadsheet or added to a drawing from a spreadsheet. Changes

in a drawing can be automatically updated to a spreadsheet or vice versa;

6. Help is context-sensitive. When the F1 key is pressed, help for the command or dialogue box in use appears in a Help window.

Equipment required to run AutoCAD for Windows

Hardware

Fig. 1.1 shows a typical hardware set-up for running AutoCAD for Windows:

1. An IBM compatible 386 or 486 PC or an IBM PS/2;
2. If 386 or 486SX, then a 80387 or 80487 math coprocessor is required. The 486DX series chips have inherent math coprocessors;
3. At least 8 megabytes (Mb) RAM memory, preferably more. Running more than one AutoCAD graphics window at any one time requires a further 4.5 Mb of memory for each window;

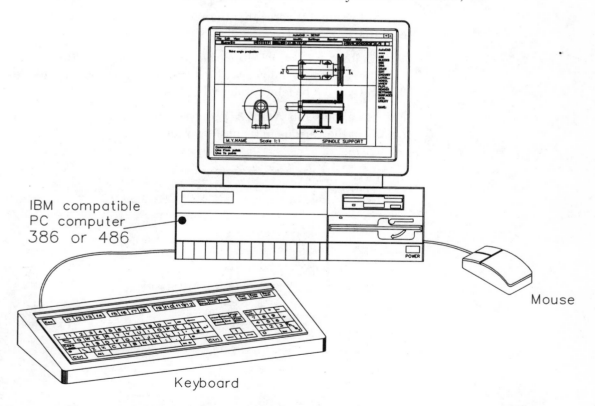

Fig. 1.1 A typical PC set-up for running AutoCAD for Windows

4. Hard disk requirements to obtain maximum performance are:
    (a) All AutoCAD for Window files, including the Advanced Modelling Extension, require 37 Mb hard disk space;
    (b) A minimal AutoCAD (mainly without AME) can run on 12 Mb of hard disk space;
    (c) A permanent Windows swap file of 32 Mb.
5. A floppy disk drive is necessary if you are loading AutoCAD for Windows for the first time;
6. A VDU (Visual Display Unit or monitor) which is at least of VGA standard (Visual Graphics Array) or better – e.g. SVGA (Super Video Graphics Array). But note that AutoCAD for Windows operates in the Windows VDU settings;
7. A mouse. A digitizing tablet can also be used;
8. A plotter or printer;
9. The AutoCAD hardware lock ("dongle") fitted into the parallel port socket. AutoCAD for Windows will not run without the hardware lock.

Software

The following software other than AutoCAD for Windows software is essential:

1. Windows 3.1, which must be run in Enhanced Mode because AutoCAD for Windows will not run in real or standard modes;
2. MS-DOS 3.3 or later, preferably MS-DOS 5.0 or later.

Fig. 1.2 shows the AutoCAD for Windows graphics window with details of the various parts of the windows.

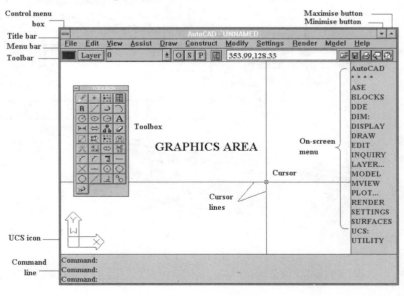

Fig. 1.2 Details of the parts of an AutoCAD for Windows graphics window

Different graphics window configurations

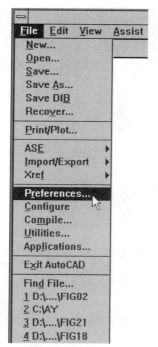

Move the mouse so that the cursor is over the word **File** in the **Menu bar**. The cursor changes to an arrow. Press the left-hand button of the mouse and release it – this is known as a *left-click*. A *pull-down* menu appears (Fig. 1.3). *Left-click* on **Preferences**... in the menu. A *dialogue box* appears in the graphics window (Fig. 1.4). This dialogue box is the **Preferences** box and is the medium through which the AutoCAD for Windows graphics window is configured. Fig. 1.7 shows the graphics window configured to have no toolbox and no toolbar.

Fig. 1.3 The **File** pull-down menu with **Preferences...** selected

Fig. 1.4 The **Preferences** dialogue box

The toolbar

Right-click on any one of the empty icon boxes in the toolbar. The box highlights and the **AutoCAD Toolbar Button** dialogue appears (Fig. 1.6). *Left-click* on the circle to the left of **Image**, *left-click* on the name of the command you wish to see represented by an icon in the toolbar. *Left-click* on **OK** and the icon appears in the selected icon box in the toolbar. Now, to call any one of the commands you place in the toolbar, *left-click* on its icon. In this manner you can customize your own toolbar. If the **Save to ACAD.INI** box in the **Acad Toolbar Button** dialogue box is checked – i.e. with diagonals across the box – when you leave AutoCAD, the toolbar you have customized will reappear when AutoCAD is recalled. One advantage of making up your own customized toolbar is that you can, by reducing the number of lines in the Command prompt lines to zero, use nearly all the graphics window for drawing. Fig. 1.5 is an example of a toolbar configured to the

Fig. 1.5 A customized toolbar with the icons for the commands Line, Pline, Arc, Circle, Ellipse, Trim and Extend

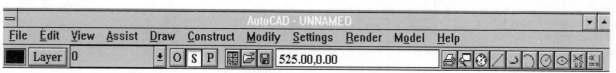

Fig. 1.6 The **AutoCAD Toolbar Button** dialogue box

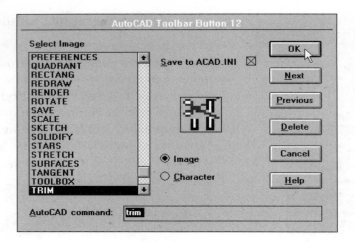

operator's own wishes. This method of customizing the graphic window is only really suitable for simple constructions because of the limitations of the number of commands that can be fitted into the toolbar.

Note the other icons and buttons in the toolbar as they always appear, whether customized to the operator's wishes or not. As shown in Fig. 1.5, from left to right they are:

Layer colour box – shows the colour used for constructions in the layer being worked on at the time. More about layers on page 25;

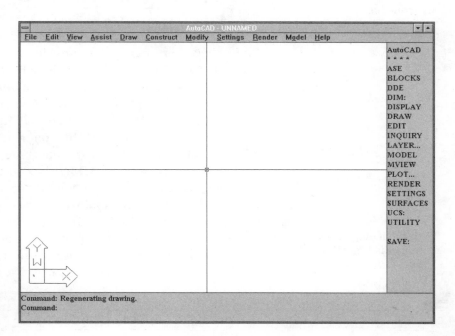

Fig. 1.7 The AutoCAD for Windows graphics screen with the toolbox and toolbar deselected in the **Preferences** dialogue box

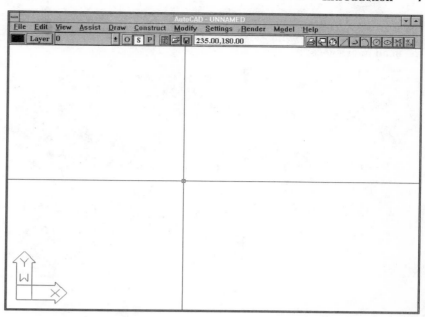

Fig. 1.8 The AutoCAD graphics screen with a customized toolbar and with no Command prompt lines

Layer button – *left-click* on this and the **Layer Settings** dialogue box appears;

Layer name box – *left-click* on this button and a pull-down menu appears with the names of the layers available;

Ortho button – *left-click* and **Ortho** is set on: all lines etc. can only be drawn horizontally and vertically in the graphics window;

Snap button – *left-click* and **Snap** is set on: lines etc will snap onto snap points on the screen depending upon the snap setting;

Paper Space button – sets PSpace when required – see page 160;

Toolbox icon – *left-click* and the toolbox appears. *Right-click* and the **AutoCAD Toolbar Button** dialogue box appears, for adding further command icons to the toolbox;

The Open Drawing icon – *left-click* to bring up the **Open Drawing** dialogue box;

Save As icon – *left-click* to bring up the **Save As Drawing** dialogue box;

Coordinates window – this window shows the position of the cursor in coordinate units – see page 11;

Plot – *left-click* to bring up the **Plot Configuration** dialogue box;

Zoom icon – *left-click* to start a zoom window – see page 95.

How to start AutoCAD for Windows

When **Windows 3.1** is started, the monitor screen will show the Windows **Program Manager** (Fig. 1.9). *Double-left-click* on the **acad**

Fig. 1.9 The Windows 3.1
Program Manager showing
the **acad** icon selected

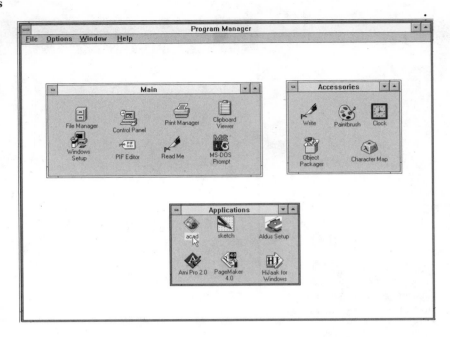

icon and after a few seconds' delay the **Program Manager** screen is
replaced by the AutoCAD for Windows graphics window. Note that
there are a number of different acad icons apart from the one illustrated
in Fig. 1.9.

Methods of calling commands

There are a number of different methods for calling commands in
AutoCAD for Windows. The chosen method depends upon the selected configuration. Taking the methods available in all possible
configurations, and with the drawing of an arc as an example, the
following methods are available:

1. Entering arc at the keyboard, followed by pressing the Return
   (Enter) key or by a right-click. The command line changes to:

   Command: *enter* arc *right-click* (or *Return*)
   ARC Center/<Start point>: *left-click* at required start point in the
      graphics window
   Center/End/<Second point>: *left-click* at required second point
   End point: *left-click* at required end point.

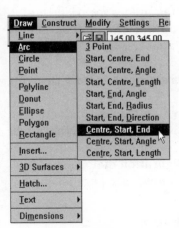

Fig. 1.10 The **Draw** pull-
down menu and the **Arc**
pull-down menu

2. Instead of entering arc, enter an a followed by *Return* (*or right-
   click*);
3. *Left-click* on **DRAW** in the on-screen menu. The **DRAW** menu

replaces the AutoCAD menu. *Left-click* on **ARC**: in the **DRAW** menu. The **ARC** menu appears. Unless a different order of drawing the arc is required, the command line shows the same prompts as before;

4. *Left-click* on **Draw** in the **Menu bar**. *Left-click* on **Arc** (Fig. 1.10). The **Arc** pull-down menu appears. *Left-click* on the desired method of drawing the arc from this menu and follow the prompts which then appear at the command line;

5. *Left-click* on **Settings** in the *Menu bar* (Fig. 1.11) The **Settings** pull-down menu appears. *Left-click* on **Menu Bitmaps** in the menu;

6. *Left-click* on **Draw** in the **Menu bar**. The pull-down menu which now appears shows icons instead of words (Fig. 1.12) *Left-click* on the **Arc** icon. The **Arc** pull-down menu appears. *Left-click* on the method by which the arc is to be drawn and follow prompts at the command line;

7. *Left-click* on the **Arc** icon in the **Toolbox** and follow the prompts at the command line (Fig. 1.13);

8. If the graphic window is customized with an **Arc** icon in the toolbar, *left-click* on that icon and follow the prompts at the command line.

Note: It will be seen from the above that regardless of which method of calling a command is chosen, the command line will show prompts indicating the actions that need to be taken by the operator. Because

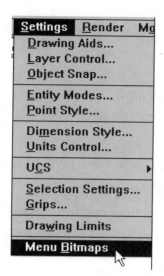

Fig. 1.11 The **Settings** pull-down menu

Fig. 1.12 **Bitmap** icons appearing in place of commands in words.

Fig. 1.13 The **Toolbox** showing **Arc** selected

of this it is probably advisable for those new to AutoCAD for Windows to ensure when setting parameters in the **Preferences** dialogue box, that **3 lines** are selected for the **Command Prompt**.

The Help dialogue box

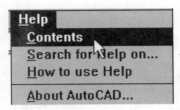

Fig. 1.14 The **Help** pull-down menu

Left-click on **Help** in the **Menu bar**, followed by a *left-click* on **Contents** in the pull-down menu (Fig. 1.14). The **AutoCAD Help** dialogue box appears, showing icons for the various parts of the **Help** contents (Fig. 1.15).

If the key **F1** is pressed, a **Help** dialogue box appears with help for the command, dialogue box, variable etc. which was being used at the time of pressing **F1**.

At this stage it is a good idea for a beginner to look through the help screens by *left-clicks* on the names in green showing in the **Help** dialogue box.

Setting up an AutoCAD graphics window

For the time being we will work in an AutoCAD graphics window configured in the **Preferences** dialogue box as shown in Fig. 1.16. The

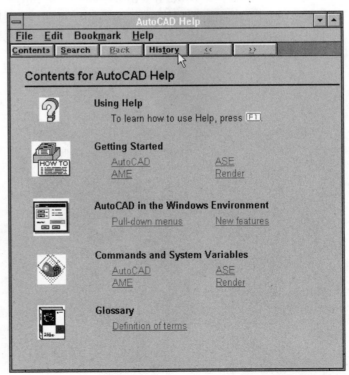

Fig. 1.15 The **Help Contents** dialogue box

Fig. 1.16 The **Preferences** dialogue box after a *left-click* on the **Fonts...** button, bringing up the **Fonts** dialogue box

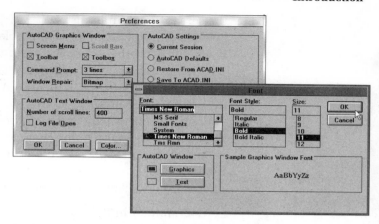

text for the window can be set as shown in the **Fonts** dialogue box, after a *left-click* on the **Fonts...** button in the **Preferences** dialogue box. These settings – **Toolbox** and **Toolbar** selected, **Screen Menu** not selected and with the **Command Prompt** with **3 lines** – result in a screen such as that shown in Fig. 1.17.

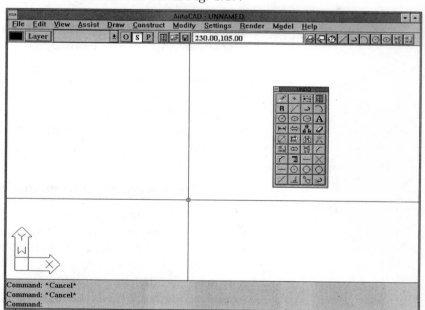

Fig. 1.17 The AutoCAD graphics windows as used for the work in the remainder of this chapter

The AutoCAD coordinate system

When working in AutoCAD, the graphics window is divided both horizontally and vertically into equal-size spaces by a coordinate system, in which the position of any point horizontally on the screen can be stated in terms of **X** and the position of any point vertically on the screen stated in terms of **Y**. Any point on the screen can then be given in terms of **X** and **Y**, usually referred to as *x,y*. Later in this book it will be seen that another coordinate **Z** can be used to state the position of any point in front of or behind the screen. The number of coordinate spacings available in an AutoCAD window is set by using the command **Limits**.

Look at the coordinate numbers box window in the toolbar. This is the window in which numbers are constantly changing as the cursor is moved around the screen under the movements of the mouse. The **Limits** of the window coordinate system numbers are set by entering figures from the keyboard when **Limits** are called for, as follows:

> **Command:** limits (entered at the keyboard) *right-click*
> **ON/OFF/<Lower left corner><0.00,0.00>:** *right-click* – to accept these figures
> **Upper right corner<420.00,297.00>:** *right-click* – to again accept these figures
> **Command:**

If the **Upper right corner** coordinates were not as given, then enter 420,297 from the keyboard. These figures set the AutoCAD window to coordinates units corresponding to the millimetre sizes of a A3 sheet of drawing paper – which is 420 mm by 297 mm.

After setting **Limits**, enter **zoom** at the keyboard followed by a *right-click* then an **a** followed by a *right-click*. This sets the AutoCAD window to the required coordinate limits. If a drawing constructed in the window is then printed or plotted full size, each coordinate unit length will print or plot as 1 mm long.

Some terms used when drawing in AutoCAD

Entity – any line, arc, circle or other such feature which can be moved, copied erased or acted upon as a single unit;

Object – has a similar meaning to the term *entity*;

Command – the order given to start an action in a CAD system – to start a drawing or other form of action;

Tool – a command displayed on screen in an icon form, either in the **toolbar** or **toolbox**;

Coordinates – the basis for determining the position of any point in space, in terms of *x* and *y* for two-dimensional drawing and in terms of *x*, *y* and *z* for three-dimensional models;

Left-click – press the left-hand button of a mouse or a similar button of other selection devices;

Right-click – press the right-hand button of the selection device;

Double-left-click – press the left-hand mouse button twice in rapid succession;

Select – move the window cursor over a name, button or other feature by moving the mouse, followed by a *left-click*;

Pick – has a meaning similar to *select*, to select a point or objects on the screen;

Return – press the **Return** key of the keyboard. The same as an **Enter** key. Has an action in AutoCAD similar to that of a *right-click*, but not always.

Drawing with tools selected from the toolbox

In the examples of drawings in this chapter all commands will be by the selection of icons from the toolbox. When a command tool is selected from the toolbox:

1. The name of the command represented by the icon appears in the title bar of the toolbox;
2. A series of prompts appears at the command line at the bottom of the screen to guide the operator through the operations necessary to construct entities with the selected tool.

As an example, *left-click* on the **CIRCLE** icon in the toolbox:

1. The name CIRCLE appears in the title bar of the toolbox;
2. The following appears at the command line:

> **Command:** _circle 3P/2P/TTR/<Center point>: either *pick* a point on screen, or enter *x,y* coordinate figures followed by a *right-click*;
> **Diameter/<Radius>:** either *pick* a point on screen, or enter *x,y* coordinate figures followed by a *right-click*;
> **Command:**

The prompts for this command (tool) have the following meanings:

> **3P** – *pick* or enter coordinates for three points through which the circle will pass;
> **2P** – *pick* or enter coordinates for two points through which the circle will pass;
> **TTR** – pick points on other entities in a drawing to which the circle is to be tangential;
> **<Radius>** – with all command prompts, the prompt in brackets states the prompt which is currently in operation.

Note: If a prompt such as **3P** is required, enter 3p at the keyboard. Further prompts then appears guiding the operator through the methods by which the 3p circle will be constructed.

Absolute coordinate construction – Example 1

To construct the drawing in Fig. 1.18:
Left-click on the **LINE** icon in the toolbox

> **Command_line From point:** *enter* 100,200 *right-click* (or *Return*)
> **To point:** *enter* 250,200 *right-click* (or *Return*)
> **To point:** *enter* 250,150 *right-click* (or *Return*)
> **To point:** *enter* 350,150 *right-click* (or *Return*)
> **To point:** *enter* 350,100 *right-click* (or *Return*)
> **To point:** *enter* 100,100 *right-click* (or *Return*)
> **To point:** *enter* close (or c) *right-click* (or *Return*)
> **Command:**

Left-click on the **CIRCLE** icon in the toolbox

> **Command:** _circle **3P/2P/TTR/<Center point>:** *enter* 150,150 *right-click*
> **Diameter/<Radius>:** *enter* 30 *right-click*
> **Command:** *right-click* (to bring back the circle prompts)
> **CIRCLE 3P/2P/TTR/<Center point>:** *enter* 150,150 *right-click*
> **Diameter/<Radius>:** *enter* 15 *right-click*
> **Command:**

Left-click on the **ELLIPSE** icon in the toolbox

> **Command_ellipse**
> **<Axis endpoint 1>/Center:** *enter* 210,180 *right-click*
> **Axis endpoint 2:** *enter* 210,120 *right-click*
> **<Other axis distance>/Rotation:** *enter* 225,150 *right-click*
> **Command:**

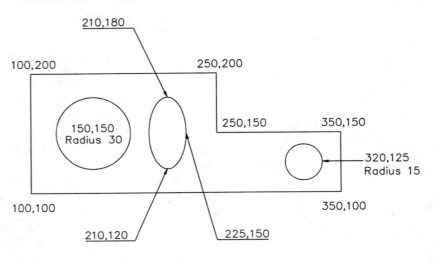

Fig. 1.18 Absolute
coordinates

Relative coordinate construction – Example 2

To construct the drawing in Fig. 1.19:

Left-click on the **PLINE** icon in the toolbox

> **Command_pline From point:** *enter* 100,250 *right-click*
>
> **Arc/Close/Halfwidth/Length/Width/<Endpoint of line>:** *enter* w (Width) *right-click*
>
> **Starting width <0.00>:** *enter* .7 *right-click*
>
> **Ending width <0.70>:** *right-click* (to accept)
>
> **Arc/Close/Halfwidth/Length/Width/<Endpoint of line>:** *enter* @200,0 *right-click*
>
> **Arc/Close/Halfwidth/Length/Width/<Endpoint of line>:** *enter* @0,–150 *right-click*
>
> **Arc/Close/Halfwidth/Length/Width/<Endpoint of line>:** *enter* @–200,0 *right-click*
>
> **Arc/Close/Halfwidth/Length/Width/<Endpoint of line>:** *enter* c (Close) *right-click*
>
> **Command:** *right-click*
>
> **PLINE**
>
> **From point:** *enter* 160,175 *right-click*
>
> **Current line width is 0.70**
>
> **Arc/Close/Halfwidth/Length/Width/<Endpoint of line>:** *enter* a (Arc) *right-click*
>
> **<Endpoint of arc>:** *enter* s (Second) *right-click*
>
> **Second point:** *enter* 200,215 *right-click*
>
> **Endpoint:** *enter* 240,175 *right-click*
>
> **<Endpoint of arc>:** *enter* s (Second) *right-click*
>
> **Second point:** *enter* 200,135 *right-click*
>
> **Endpoint:** *enter* 160,175 *right-click*
>
> **<Endpoint of arc>:** *right-click*
>
> **Command:**

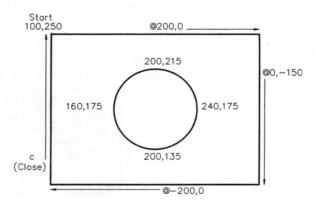

Fig. 1.19 Relative coordinates

Note: The sequence showed a method of drawing a circle when drawing with the **PLINE** command.

Notes on drawing using the relative coordinates method

1. The symbol @ must be placed in front of each set of relative coordinate numbers;
2. **+ve** x coordinates are horizontally to the right;
3. **−ve** x coordinates are horizontally to the left;
4. **+ve** y coordinates are vertically upwards;
5. **−ve** y coordinates are vertically downwards;
6. If the x coordinate is **0**, the next position is vertically up or down;
7. If the y coordinate is **0**, the next position is horizontally left or right.

The Object Snap tools from the toolbox

Fig. 1.20 shows the bottom two rows of icons in an AutoCAD toolbox. These show the eight **Object Snap** tools. Place the cursor, under mouse control, over each in turn. These tool icons will display the names:

ENDPOINT	INTERSECTION	MIDPOINT	CENTER
QUADRANT	NEAREST	PERPENDICULAR	TANGENT

in the order as shown in Fig. 1.20 in the toolbox title bar when the cursor is placed over each icon in turn.

An example of using Object Snap tools from the toolbox

Fig. 1.21 shows plines, a circle and an arc drawn with the aid of the Object Snap tools. Plines have been drawn with the aid of the **Object Snap** tools:

from the top **endpoint** of the vertical pline – point A;
to the top **quadrant** point of the circle – point B;
to the **centre** of the arc – point C;
to the right hand **endpoint** of the horizontal pline – point D;
to the **centre** of the circle – point E;
to the **intersection** of the horizontal and vertical plines – point F;

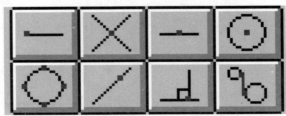

Fig. 1.20 The Object Snap tools from the **Toolbox**

Fig. 1.21 An example of a drawing using the **PLINE** tool and the **midpoint OBJECT SNAP** tool

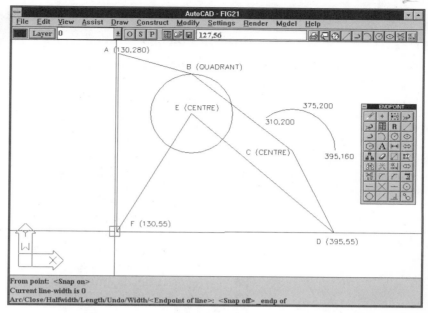

Exercise

Using **PLINE**, **PLINE arc** and the **Objects Snap** tools, copy the drawing shown in Fig. 1.21, using the coordinate points given.

Object Snaps from the AutoCAD on-screen menu

Left-click on ******** immediately below the word **AutoCAD** in the on-screen menu (Fig. 1.22). Any one of the **Object snaps** can be selected from the on-screen menu which appears after a *left-click* on ********.

Accurate drawing in AutoCAD

It will be seen from the above that accurate drawing can be achieved in AutoCAD with the aid of:

1. Setting **Grid** to show grid points on the screen to assist in positioning entities;
2. Setting **Snap** to ensure that points selected on screen with the aid of the mouse snap to snap points as set;
3. Entering **absolute** coordinates for points in a drawing at the command line;
4. Entering **relative** coordinates for points in a drawing at the command line;
5. Positioning points relative to entities on the screen with the aid of the **Object Snaps**;

```
AutoCAD
* * * *
 HELP
CENtre
ENDpoint
INSert
INTersec
MIDpoint
NEArest
NODe
PERpend
QUAdrant
QUICK,
TANgent
NONE
CANCEL:
U:
REDO:
REDRAW:
__LAST__
SAVE:
```

Fig. 1.22 Object Snaps from the AutoCAD on-screen menu

Keyboard key short-cuts

Switching **Snap** or **Grid** off (or back on again) can be done by:

> **Command:** snap (*entered* at keyboard) *right-click;*
> **Snap spacing ON/OFF/Aspect/Rotate/Style <5.00>:** off (*enter*)
> *right-click*
> **Command:**

Snap is no longer working – it is off.

A much quicker method is to press the function key **F9** which "toggles" **Snap** on/off. Other short-cut key strokes are:

F1   **Help** – context-sensitive – gives help for the action being taken;
F2   Toggles the AutoCAD **text screen** on/off;
F4   Toggles a **Tablet** on/off – if a graphics tablet is in use;
F5   Toggles between **Isoplane Top/Isoplane Right/Isoplane Left** – for isometric drawing;
F6   Toggles **Coords** on/off;
F7   Toggles **Grid** on/off;
F8   Toggles **Ortho** on/off;
F9   Toggles **Snap** on/off.

In addition, pressing the **Ctrl** key and another:

Ctrl/C   Cancels the last command;
Ctrl/I   **Help**;
Ctrl/T   **Tablet**;
Ctrl/E   **Isoplanes**;
Ctrl/G   **Grid**;
Ctrl/O   **Ortho**;
Ctrl/B   **Snap**;
Ctrl/D   **Coords**.

Switching between applications in Windows

One very important keystroke pair is **Alt/Tab** – press the **Alt** key and the **Tab** key at the same time. If several applications are running in Windows at the same time – say AutoCAD, a word-processor and a desktop publishing program – an operator can switch between these applications by pressing this pair of keys. In this manner a drawing from AutoCAD can be "pasted" into the Windows Clipboard, and from the Clipboard pasted into a page being produced in a desktop publishing program, or into a letter being written on a word-processing program. This short-cut is invaluable if using AutoCAD to produce illustrations to be pasted into documents produced in other applications.

Questions

1. What do the letters CAD stand for?
2. List the advantages of using a CAD system.
3. Can you think of any disadvantages in using a CAD system?
4. What is the meaning of the abbreviation GUI and how does it apply to AutoCAD for Windows?
5. How is the AutoCAD for Windows graphics window configured?
6. Can AutoCAD for Windows be run on a 286 PC?
7. What is the minimum size of RAM memory for AutoCAD for Windows to run on a PC?
8. List the different ways in which commands can be called in AutoCAD for Windows.
9. What happens when the following keys are pressed: **F1**; **F2**; **F6**; **F7**; **F8**; **F9**?
10. What is meant by the term coordinates?

Exercises

Set **LIMITS** to 420,297; **GRID to 10; SNAP** to 5 and copy the three drawings connected with the following three exercises. **PLINE** width can be 0.7.

1. With the commands **LINE** and **CIRCLE** and using the absolute coordinates method of drawing, copy Fig. 1.23.
2. With the commands **PLINE** (including **Arc**) and using the relative coordinates method of drawing, copy Fig. 1.24.
3. Fig. 1.25 is a three-view orthographic projection in First angle of a FORK CONNECTOR. Make an accurate copy of the projection using the command **PLINE** (including **Arc**).

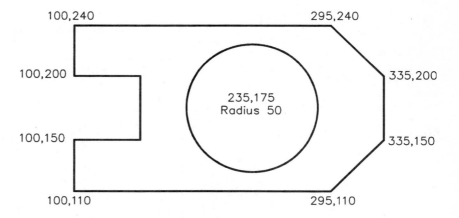

Fig. 1.23 Exercise 1

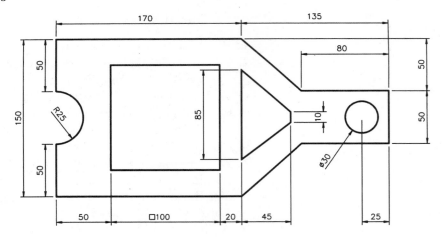

Fig. 1.24 Exercise 2

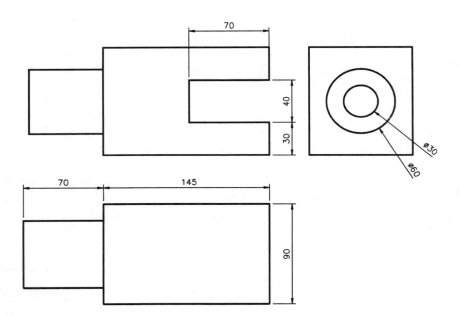

Fig. 1.25 Exercise 3

CHAPTER 2

Configuration, dialogue boxes

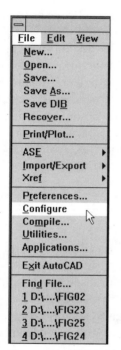

Fig. 2.1 **Configure** from the **File** pull-down menu

Configuration on start-up of AutoCAD for Windows

The start-up for AutoCAD for Windows is a *double-left-click* on the **acad** icon in the Windows **Program Manager**. The AutoCAD graphics window appears after a short period of time once AutoCAD files have been loaded into memory. Features, such as the way in which AutoCAD reacts with the VDU screen (the video display), the digitizer which is to be used (mouse etc.), the plotter or printer to which AutoCAD drawings are to be sent for plot/printing and the operating parameters for AutoCAD, can be configured from inside the graphics window by a *left-click* on **Configure** in the **File** pull-down menu (Fig. 2.1). An AutoCAD **text screen** appears showing details of the current configuration (Fig. 2.2). The details are completed on pressing the *Return* key. Press the *Return* key a second time and a numbered list

Fig. 2.2 The AutoCAD text screen showing configuration details

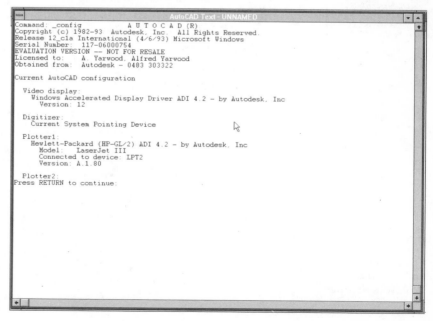

```
0.   Exit to drawing editor
1.   Show current configuration
2.   Allow detailed configuration

3.   Configure video display
4.   Configure digitizer
5.   Configure plotter
6.   Configure system console
7.   Configure operating parameters
```

Fig. 2.3 Configurations which can be amended within AutoCAD for Windows

appears of configurations which can be carried out once a figure has been entered from the keyboard followed by *Return*. These configuration possibilities are shown in Fig. 2.3. Thus, with the **Preferences** option considered in Chapter 1 and the **Configure** option, AutoCAD for Windows can be completely configured ready to commence drawing. There are, however, further details to consider – the type of video driver in use, the keyboard set-up and the mouse in operation are those in which Windows itself is running. Other settings which are determined by the Windows settings are some of the colours within the AutoCAD graphic window, although, as shown in Chapter 1, some of these colours can be set in the **Preferences** dialogue box. AutoCAD for Windows is thus dependent upon many of the settings made for Windows.

The Windows settings

Fig. 2.4 The **Windows Setup** from the Program Manager

Left-click on **Windows Setup** in the **Program Manager** (Fig. 2.4). The Windows Setup dialogue box appears, displaying the settings in which Windows is running. If one wishes to alter these settings, *left-click* on **Options**, followed by a *left-click* on **Change System Settings...** in the pull-down menu which appears. The **Change System Settings** dialogue box appears (Fig. 2.5). Windows settings can be changed from

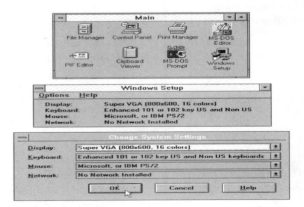

Fig. 2.5 The **Windows Setup** and **Windows** and **Change Windows Settings** boxes

selections made in this dialogue box – but have the original set of Windows floppy disks available, because settings can only be made from files found in the original disks (or their backups).

Dialogue and other boxes

In Chapter 1, as with the example of the **Preferences** dialogue boxes, parameters for drawing in the AutoCAD graphics screen can be set in dialogue boxes. If three full stops follow the name of a command in a pull-down menu or in an on-screen menu, a *left-click* on the name results in a dialogue box appearing in the graphics window. As an example, *left-click* on **Open...** in the **File** pull-down menu and the **Open Drawing** dialogue box (Fig. 2.6) appears in the graphic window.

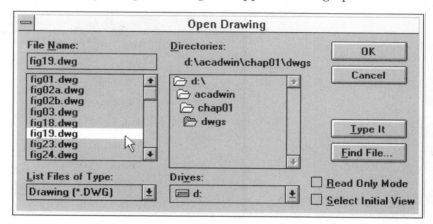

Fig. 2.6 The **Open Drawing** dialogue box

Fig. 2.7 The **Settings** pull-down menu

Settings

A *left-click* on **Settings** in the **Menu bar** brings down the **Settings** menu (Fig. 2.7). Most of the commands in this menu are followed by three full stops. Therefore, selecting any one of these results in a dialogue box coming up on screen. Practically all drawing settings can be made from these dialogue boxes. There are other dialogue boxes, e.g. **Print/Plot...** can be seen in the **File** pull-down menu and the **Render** menu shows a number of others. A few settings require keyboard entry, an example being the setting of type of line to be used. Take the dialogue box settings available from the **Settings** menu in turn.

Drawing Aids

Left-click on **Drawing Aids...** in the **Settings** menu. The resulting dialogue box is shown in Fig. 2.8. In this dialogue box **Modes** has check boxes to the left of the mode names. A *left-click* in a box either brings up a cross or clears the cross. In the example given (Fig. 2.8), **Solid Fill** and **Highlight** are on and **Ortho**, **Quick Text** and **Blips** are off. It is worthwhile experimenting with these modes to test what happens when they are selected to be on or off. Personally I prefer setting **Ortho** when required by pressing the **F6** key of the keyboard, and I do not like **Blips** appearing on screen as I construct drawings in AutoCAD, but other operators may prefer different settings from mine. **Snap** and/or **Grid** can be set on or off by *left-clicks* in the boxes against the names. Again I prefer setting these with the aid of the **F7** and **F9** keys. The unit size of **Snap and Grid** are set by entering figures in the respective boxes. **Isometric Snap/Grid** settings will be described later in the book (page 98).

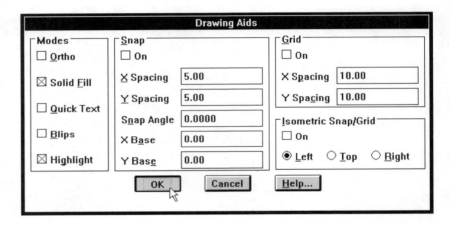

Fig. 2.8 The **Drawing Aids** dialogue box

Layer Control

A *left-click* on **Layer Control...** in the **Settings** menu brings up the **Layer Control** dialogue box (Fig. 2.9). In any form of CAD drawing, layers are important. When constructing engineering drawings, I construct features such as drawing outlines on one layer, centre lines on another, hidden detail on a third, text on a fourth and dimensions on a fifth. In architectural drawing, features such as each floor of a multistorey building would be drawn on its own layer, electrical circuitry in the building would be on other layers, plumbing on another set of layers, sewage on another set and so on. Each layer can be compared with a tracing in hand drawing. A layer in CAD can be turned off in the same way as a tracing from a series of hand drawings can be removed. Layers can be On, Off, Frozen, Thawed, Locked or Unlocked:

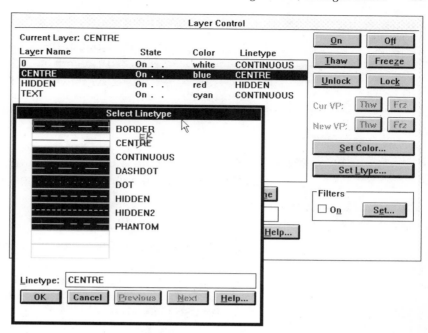

Fig. 2.9 The **Layer Control** dialogue box with **Select Linetype...** selected

On: details on the layer appear on screen;

Off: details on the layer are not seen on screen;

Frozen: the layer is turned off and cannot be turned on again until it is thawed;

Thaw: unfreezing a layer;

Lock: a locked layer can be drawn on, but entities on the layer cannot be edited, e.g. by being moved or erased;

Unlock: undoes the effect of locking.

The type of line and the colour to be used in a layer can also be set from this dialogue box. Before setting a linetype, however, the necessary linetype must first be loaded:

Command: linetype (*enter* at keyboard) *right-click*

?/Create/Load/Set: *enter* l (Load) *right-click*

Linetype(s) to load: *enter* centre,hidden *right-click*

The Select **Linetype** dialogue box appears. All that is needed is a *right-click*

Linetype CENTRE loaded.

Linetype HIDDEN loaded.

?/Create/Load/Set: *right-click* (to accept)

Command:

and the two linetypes are loaded ready to be selected in the dialogue box.

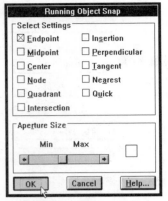

Fig. 2.10 The **Running Object Snap** dialogue box

Object Snap

Left-click on **Object Snap...** in the **Settings** menu. The dialogue box which appears (Fig. 2.10) gives a list of the Object Snaps which can be set to be on or off by *left-clicks* on the various check boxes. The **Aperture Size** can also be set by adjusting the slider control towards **Min** or **Max** to reduce or enlarge the size of the pick box associated with the Object Snap in use. As an example, if **Endpoint** is on, every time an entity is drawn a pick box of the size set in the dialogue box appears at the cursor. If the end of another entity on screen is within the area of the pick box, the new entity automatically snaps onto its end.

Entity Mode

Left-click on **Entity Modes...** and the **Entity Creation Modes** dialogue box appears (Fig. 2.11). By selection from **Layer...**, **Linetype...** or **Text Style...** settings for each of these entity types can be entered in another set of dialogue boxes. In Fig. 2.11, the **Select Text Style** and its dialogue box **Text Style Symbol Set** have been brought on screen by *left-clicks* on appropriate names within the dialogue boxes. Remember, however, that if settings such as layer colour have previously been defined in the **Layer Control** boxes, these will be overridden by further settings made in the **Entity Creation Modes** dialogue boxes.

Fig. 2.11 The **Entity Creation Modes** dialogue box with **Select Text Style...** and **Show All...** selected

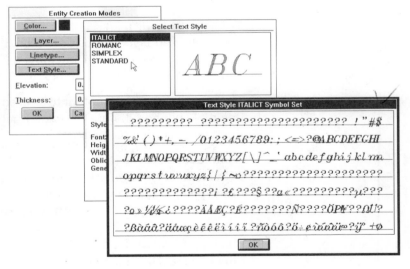

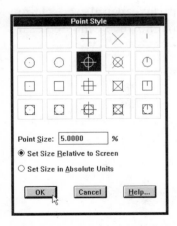

Fig. 2.12 The **Point Style** dialogue box

Point Style

Fig. 2.12 shows the **Point Style** dialogue box. The selection of a point style from this box determines what appears on screen in response to using the command **Point** from the **Draw** menu.

Dimension Style

There are a number of parameters which require setting when including dimensions within a drawing. More about dimensions in later pages (page 110). Fig. 2.13 shows the dialogue boxes appearing after a *left-click* on **Dimension Style...** in the **Settings** menu followed by another *left-click* on the **Features...** button in the **Dimension Style and Settings** box. The **Features** box shows all the settings which can be made, if thought fit, in the other dialogue boxes associated with the **Dimension Style and Settings** box.

Fig. 2.13 The **Dimension Styles and Features** dialogue box with **Features...** selected

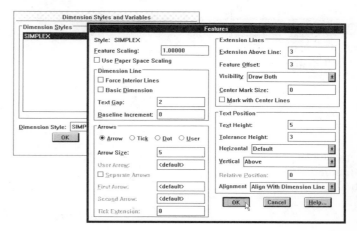

Units Control

The **Units Control** dialogue box, appearing with a *left-click* on **Units Control...** in the **Settings** menu, is shown in Fig. 2.14. The units in the box shown have been set to **Decimal** with a **Precision** of 0 – no figures after the decimal point. **Angles** have been set to show in **Decimal Degrees**.

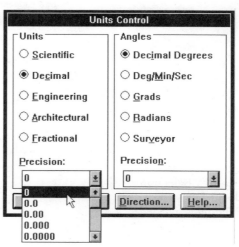

Fig. 2.14 The **Units Control** dialogue box with **Precision:** selected

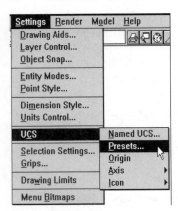

Fig. 2.15 The **Settings** pull-down menu with the **UCS** sub-menu

Fig. 2.16 The **UCS Orientation** dialogue box after selecting **UCS Presets...**

UCS

The UCS (User Coordinate System) will be explained in some detail later (page 146). Fig. 2.15 shows the UCS sub-menu which appears when the arrow cursor is moved over the name **UCS** in the **Settings** menu. Fig. 2.16 shows the **UCS Orientation** Dialogue box after a *left-click* on **Presets...** in the **UCS** sub-menu. The UCS is of particular importance when constructing three-dimensional solid models in AutoCAD.

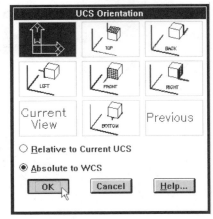

Entity Selection

The **Entity Selection Settings** seen on screen after a *left-click* on **Selection Settings...** in the **Settings** menu is shown in Fig. 2.17.

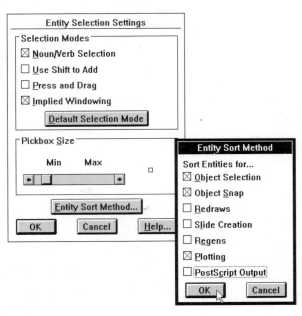

Fig. 2.17 The **Entity Selection Settings** dialogue box with **Entity Sort Method...** selected

Fig. 2.18 The **Grips** dialogue box

Grips

Fig. 2.18 shows the **Grips** dialogue box, after a *left-click* on **Grips...** in the **Settings** menu. If **Grips** are enabled, the ability to rapidly move, rotate, mirror, scale or stretch is possible by selecting one of the grip boxes which appear when an entity or group of entities is preselected in a drawing on screen.

Notes

1. Compare Fig. 2.6 with Fig. 2.8. The differences between the shadings in the two illustrations is because of different selections made in the **Color** window from the Windows **Control Panel** for the two illustrations;
2. Three full stops after a command name means that the name is associated with a dialogue box;
3. A letter in each of the commands in the **Settings** menu is underlined. If the underlined letter of the name is entered at the keyboard, the result is as if a *left-click* had been made on the name;
4. If **Drawing Limits** is selected from the **Settings** menu, a dialogue box does not appear but the command line changes to:

   Command: '_limits
   Reset Model space limits:
   ON/OFF/<Lower left corner><0.00,0.00>:

   and the limits must be entered from the keyboard in response to the prompts at the command line;
5. If **Menu Bitmaps** is selected from the **Settings** menu, the **Draw** and **Construct** pull-down menus show icons in place of names. See Fig. 1.12 on page 9.

Setting up a prototype acad.dwg file

Left-click on **File** in the **Menu bar**, followed by a *left-click* on **New...** in the pull-down menu. The **Create New Drawing File** dialogue box appears (Fig. 2.19). Note that the name of the **Prototype...** box is acad.

Fig. 2.19 The **Create New Drawing** dialogue box

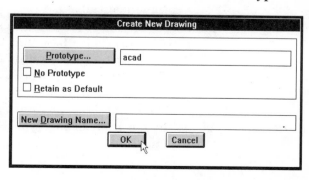

This prototype drawing file, *acad.dwg*, is normally held in the *acad\support* directory. On start-up it is the file which appears on screen complete with the settings with which it has been configured. The following procedure is for setting up an acad.dwg file as the prototype drawing file to be called to screen for the majority of the work throughout this book. Take care, however, because:

If others are working at the computer you are using, they may not wish to have the same prototype acad.dwg appear when *they* start up AutoCAD.

You can, if you wish and if others are using the computer, give another name to the prototype file when you wish to start a new drawing, thus avoiding the problem of causing others difficulty.

1. *Left-click* on **File** in the **Menu bar**;
2. *Left-click* on **New...** in the **File** menu. The **Create New Drawing** dialogue box appears. *Left-click* in the box next to **No Prototype,** followed by a *left-click* on **OK**;
3. At the command line:

    Command: *enter* limits *right-click*
    Command: '_limits
    Reset Model space limits:
    ON/OFF/<Lower left corner><0.00,0.00>: *right-click* (to accept)
    Upper right corner<12.00,9.00>: *enter* 420,297 *right-click*
    Command: *enter* z (for zoom) *right-click*
    All/Center/Dynamic/Extents/Left/Previous/Vmax/Window
    /<Scale(X/XP)>: *enter* a (for All) *right-click*
    Regenerating drawing.
    Command:

    The screen drawing limits are set to the A3 sheet millimetre sizes;
4. *Left-click* on **Drawing Aids...** in the **Settings** menu. In the **Drawing Aids** dialogue box:
    Modes: Check the **Solid Fill** and **Highlight** boxes. Check that both **Snap** and **Grid** boxes are on
    Snap: *Enter* 5 in the **X Spacing** box. The **Y Spacing** sets automatically
    Grid: *Enter* 10 in the X Spacing box. **Y Spacing** sets automatically. Check that both **X Base** and **Y Base** are each set at 0. *Left-click* on **OK**;
5. *Left-click* on **Units Control...** in the **Settings** menu:
    Check **Decimal** and **Decimal Degrees.** Set **Precision:** for both to 0;
6. *Left-click* on **Dimension Style...** in the **Settings** menu:
    Enter simplex in the **Dimension Style** box and a *left-click* on **OK**;
    In the **Dimension Style** dialogue box, *left-click* on **Dimension Lines....** In the dialogue box:

Dimension Line Color: red
Text Gap: 0
Left-click on **OK**;
In the **Dimension Style** dialogue box, *left-click* on **Extension Lines....** In the dialogue box:
Extension Line Color: red
Extension Above Line: 3
Feature Offset: 3
Visibility: Draw Both
Center Mark Size: 0;
Left-click on **OK**;
In the **Dimension Style** dialogue box, *left-click* on **Arrows....** In the dialogue box:
Arrows: check the **Arrow** box
Dimension Line Color: red
Arrow Size: 3
Left-click on **OK**
In the **Dimension Style** dialogue box, *left-click* on **Text Location....** In the dialogue box:
Dimension Text Color: red
Text Height: 4
Tolerance Height: 2.5
Horizontal: Default
Vertical: Above
Alignment: Align With Dimension
Left-click on **OK**
In the **Dimension Style** dialogue box, *left-click* on **OK**;

7. If it is OK to save your acad file as the main prototype file for all to use on the computer:
Left-click on **File** in the **Menu bar**
Left-click on **Save As...** in the **File** menu
In the **Save Drawing As** dialogue box (Fig. 2.20):

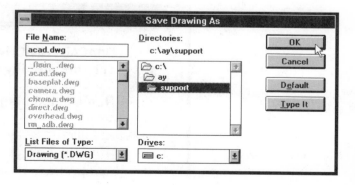

Fig. 2.20 The **Save Drawing As** dialogue box

Double-left-click on the name of the directory holding your
  AutoCAD files. In my case this directory name is **ay**
Double left-click on the sub-directory name **support**
Enter acad in the **File Name:** box
Left-click on **OK**

8. If you should save the prototype file to another name:
   In the **Save Drawing As** dialogue box:
   Double-left-click on **a:** in the **Drives:** list box
   Enter say myfile in the **File Name** box
   The file is then saved as *a:\myfile.dwg.*

To start a new drawing

In the **Create New Drawing** dialogue box, either:

1. If using the file *c:\acad\support\acad.dwg*, *left-click* on **OK**;
2. If using your own *a:\myfile.dwg*, place your disk in the a:\ drive of
   the computer and enter a:\myfile in the **Prototype** name box,
   followed by a *left-click* on **OK.**

A word of caution

Be careful when saving a drawing file. If you try to open a drawing
without having saved it first, a warning box (Fig. 2.21) will appear. If
you try to save a drawing to a filename of a file which already exists,
a second type of warning box will appear – the **Save Drawing As**
warning box (Fig. 2.22).

Fig. 2.21 The **Drawing
Modification** warning box

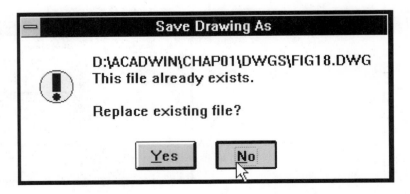

Fig. 2.22 The **Save Drawing
As** warning box

A note about moving dialogue and other boxes

To move a dialogue box, or any other type of box, move the cursor, under mouse control, until it is in the **Title bar** of the box you wish to move. The cursor cross-lines are replaced by a cursor arrow. Press and hold down the *left-hand* mouse button and under mouse movement move the box to its new position. This is of particular value for moving the toolbox, when it is in a position hiding a part of the graphics window you may be wishing to work in. Fig. 2.23 illustrates this action. This ease of movement of boxes is also of value when settings in dialogue boxes from within dialogue boxes are being made, because it allows the operator to move a second or even a third dialogue box into a position in the graphics window where information in all the dialogue boxes can be seen.

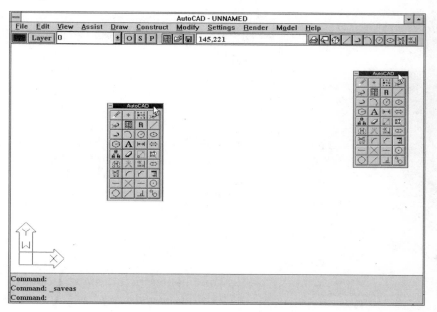

Fig. 2.23 Moving the **toolbox** to another position in the AutoCAD graphics window

Notes about layers

Layers can be set in one of several ways:

1. As previously shown (page 29) from the **Layer Control** dialogue box from the **Settings** menu;
2. By a *left-click* on the **Layers** button (Fig. 2.24) in the **toolbar** – this brings up the **Layer Control** dialogue box;
3. By a *left-click* on the **Layer colour** button in the **toolbar** followed by a *left-click* on **Layer:** in the **Entity Creation Modes** dialogue box which appears when the button is pressed. The **Layer Control** dialogue box then appears;

Fig. 2.24 The **Layer** and **Layer colour** buttons in the **toolbar**

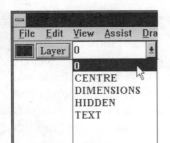

Fig. 2.25 The pull-down menu from the **Layer name** button

4. By a *left-click* on the **Layer name** button in the **toolbar** (Fig. 2.25) followed by a *left-click* on the Layer name required to be the current layer;
5. From the command line:

Command: *enter* layer *right-click*
?/Make/Set/New/ON/OFF/Color/Ltype/Freeze/Thaw/LOck/
    Unlock: *enter* s (for Set) *right-click*
New current layer<0>: *enter* centre *right-click*
?/Make/Set/New/ON/OFF/Color/Ltype/Freeze/Thaw/LOck/
    Unlock: *right-click*
Command:

Dd calls

Some dialogue boxes can be called to screen by entering the following at the command line from the keyboard:

ddim	Dimension Styles and Variables
ddgrips	Grips
ddlmodes	Layer Control
ddosnap	Running Object Snap
ddptype	Point Style
ddrmodes	Drawing Aids
ddselect	Entity Selection Modes
dducs	UCS Control
ddunits	Units Control

There are other dd calls, some of which will be discussed in later pages.

Questions

1. This chapter includes suggestions for the setting of parameters for a prototype *acad.dwg* file. Copy the following and add the settings:

Limits: Bottom left:
            Top right:
Layers: Names:
           Colours:
           Linetypes:
Dimension styles: Dimension lines:
                       Extension lines:
                       Arrow:

Snap:
Grid
Units:

2. If you were setting up a prototype file for an A4 sheet drawing, what would the settings be?

3. What are the main differences between configuring within AutoCAD for Windows and the settings needed for video and the graphics window colours?

4. Describe ways in which dialogue boxes can be called to the graphics window.

5. What is a warning box? Give two examples where warning boxes might appear in the graphics windows.

6. Describe several methods by which Layers and the parameters within layers can be set

7. What is meant by the abbreviation GUI? Why is GUI so important in the AutoCAD for Windows environment?

8. What happens when a command name followed by three full stops (...) is selected with a *left-click*?

9. In many instances, a letter in command names in pull-down menus is underlined. What is the purpose of this underlining?

10. If you are in the AutoCAD for Windows graphics window and you press the two keys **Alt** and **Tab** at the same time, what will happen?

CHAPTER 3

2D Drawing commands

Drawing commands

There are several ways in which the 2D (two-dimensional) drawing commands can be called:

1. By selection from the **Draw** pull-down menu (Fig. 3.1);
2. By changing the **Draw** command names into icons. This is done by a *left-click* on **Settings** in the **Menu bar**, followed by a *left-click* on **Menu Bitmaps** in the pull-down menu. The **Draw** menu names change to icons (Fig. 3.2);
3. By selection from the icons in the **Toolbox** (Fig. 3.3);
4. By selection from the **DRAW** on-screen menu (Fig. 3.4) a *left-click* on **DRAW in** the **AutoCAD** on-screen menu brings up the **DRAW** sub-menu with command names;

Fig. 3.1 Command names in the **Draw** pull-down menu

Fig. 3.2 Bitmap icons in the **Draw** pull-down menu

Fig. 3.3 The **Toolbox**

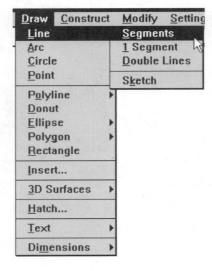

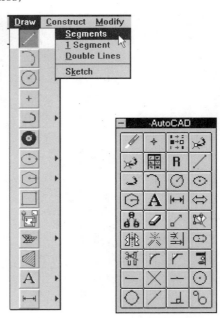

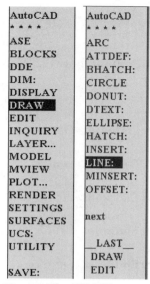

Fig. 3.4 The **DRAW** on-screen menu and sub-menu

5. By *entering* command names or their abbreviations from the keyboard at the command line. As an example, to draw lines:

> **Command:** *enter* line (or the abbreviation l) *right-click*
> **Line From point:** *enter* coordinates *right-click* – or *left-click* on a point in the graphics window
> **To point:** *enter* coordinates *right-click* – or *left-click* on a point in the graphics window
> **To point:** *enter* coordinates *right-click* – or *left-click* on a point in the graphics window
> **Command:**

6. By selection of any tool icons which have been added to the **Toolbar**.

2D drawing constructions using the icons

Whether the icons are chosen from the **Toolbox** the **Toolbar** or from the **Draw** pull-down menu they will be the same. When an icon is selected (*left-click* on the icon), if the command prompt lines are included in the graphics window the command name and its associated prompts will appear at the command line.

Lines

Fig. 3.5 The **Line** tool icon

Left-click on the **Line** icon (Fig. 3.5). Prompts appear at the command line:

> **Command:** _line From point: *enter* 100,100 *right-click*
> **To point:** *enter* 200,100 *right-click*
> **To point:** *enter* 200,200 *right-click*
> **To point:** *enter* 100,200 *right-click*
> **To point:** *enter* 100,180 *right-click*
> **To point:** *enter* 50,180 *right-click*
> **To point:** *enter* 50,120 *right-click*
> **To point:** *enter* 100,120 *right-click*
> **To point:** *enter* 100,120 *right-click*
> **To point:** *enter* c (close) *right-click*
> **To point:** *right-click*
> **Command:**

Plines

Fig. 3.6 The **Pline** tool icon

Left-click on the **Pline** icon (Fig. 3.6). Prompts appear at the command line:

Command: _pline
From point: *enter* 250,200 *right-click*
Current line-width in 0.
Arc/Close/Halfwidth/Length/Undo/Width/<Endpoint>: w (Width)
  right-click
Starting width<0>: *enter* 1 *right-click*
Ending width<1>: *right-click* (to accept 1)
Arc/Close/Halfwidth/Length/Undo/Width/<Endpoint>: *enter*
  @100,0 *right-click*
Arc/Close/Halfwidth/Length/Undo/Width/<Endpoint>: *enter*
  @0,–100 *right-click*
Arc/Close/Halfwidth/Length/Undo/Width/<Endpoint>: *enter*
  @–100,0 *right-click*
Arc/Close/Halfwidth/Length/Undo/Width/<Endpoint>: *enter*
  @0,20 *right-click*
Arc/Close/Halfwidth/Length/Undo/Width/<Endpoint>: *enter*
  @–30,0 *right-click*
Arc/Close/Halfwidth/Length/Undo/Width/<Endpoint>: *enter*
  @0,60 *right-click*
Arc/Close/Halfwidth/Length/Undo/Width/<Endpoint>: *enter*
  @30,0
Arc/Close/Halfwidth/Length/Undo/Width/<Endpoint>: *enter* c
  (Close) *right-click*
Command:

Circles

Fig 3.7 The **Circle**
tool icon

Left-click on the **Circle** icon (Fig. 3.7). Prompts appear at the command
line:

Command: _circle 3P/2P/TTR/<Center point>: *enter* 160,265 *right-click*
Diameter/<Radius>: *enter* 15 *right-click*
Command: *right-click* (brings back the Circle command)
CIRCLE 3P/2P/TTR/<Center point>: *enter* 230,265 *right-click*
Diameter/<Radius>: *enter* d (for Diameter) *right-click*
Diameter: *enter* 30 *right-click*
Command: *right-click*
CIRCLE 3P/2P/TTR/<Center point>: *enter* ttr *right-click*
Enter Tangent spec: *left-click* on first circle
Enter second Tangent spec: *left-click* on second circle
Radius: *enter* 25 *right-click*
Command:

Arcs

Fig. 3.8 The **Arc** tool icon

Left-click on the **Arc** icon (Fig. 3.8). Prompts appear at the command line:

> **Command_arc Center/<Start point>:** *enter* 130,80 *right-click*
> **Center/End/<Second point>:** *enter* 190,20 *right-click*
> **End point:** *enter* 260,80 *right-click*
> **Command:** *right-click* (brings back the Arc command)
> **ARC Center/<Start point>:** *enter* c (for Center) *right-click*
> **Center:** *enter* 325,80 *right-click*
> **Start point:** *enter* 325,20 *right-click*
> **End point:** *enter* 380,80 *right-click*
> **Command:**

Fig. 3.9 shows the results of the **Line**, **Pline**, **Circle** and **Arc** sequences given above.

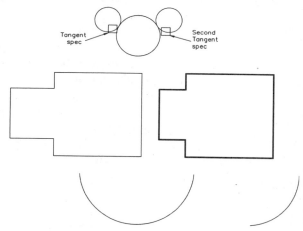

Fig. 3.9 The results of the **Line**, **Pline**, **Circle** and **Arc** sequences

Ellipses

Fig. 3.10 The **Ellipse** tool icon

Left-click on the **Ellipse** icon (Fig. 3.10). Prompts appear at the command line:

> **Command:** _ellipse
> **<Axis endpoint 1>/Center:** *enter* 70,230 *right-click*
> **<Axis endpoint 2>:** *enter* 170,230 *right-click*
> **<Other axis distance>/Rotation:** *enter* 30 *right-click*
> **Command:** *right-click* (brings back the Ellipse command)
> **ELLIPSE**
> **<Axis endpoint 1>/Center:** *enter* c (for Center) *right-click*
> **Center of ellipse:** *enter* 270,230 *right-click*
> **Axis endpoint:** *enter* 195,230 *right-click*

‹Other axis distance>/Rotation: *enter* 40 *right-click*
Command: *right-click* (brings back the Ellipse command)
ELLIPSE
<Axis endpoint 1>/Center: *enter* 220,230 *right-click*
<Axis endpoint 2>: *enter* 320,230 *right-click*
<Other axis distance>/Rotation: *enter* r (for Rotation) *right-click*
Rotation around major axis: *enter* 30 (degrees) *right-click*
Command:

Polygons

Left-click on the **Polygon** icon (Fig. 3.11). Prompts appear at the command line:

Fig. 3.11 The **Polygon** tool icon

Command: _polygon Number of sides<4>: *enter* 6 *right-click*
Edge/<Center of polygon>: *enter* 110,130 *right-click*
Inscribed in circle/Circumscribed around circle (I/C)<I>: *right-click* (to accept the I)
Radius of circle: *enter* 40 *right-click*
Command: *right-click* (brings back the Polygon command)
POLYGON Number of sides<6>: *enter* 8 *right-click*
Edge/<Center of polygon>: *enter* e (for Edge) *right-click*
First endpoint of edge: *enter* 195,95 *right-click*
Second endpoint of edge: *enter* 230,95 *right-click*
Command:

Donuts

Left-click on the **Donut** icon (Fig. 3.12). Prompts appear at the command line:

Fig. 3.12 The **Donut** tool icon

Command:_donut
Inside diameter<1>: *enter* 10 *right-click*
Outside diameter<1>: *enter* 50 *right-click*
Center of donut: *enter* 305,140 *right-click*
Center of donut: *enter* 305,75 *right-click*
Center of donut: *right-click* (to come out of the Donut command)
Command:

Text

Left-click on the **Text** icon (Fig. 3.13). Prompts appear at the command line:

Fig. 3.13 The **Text** tool icon

Command:_dtext Justify/Style/<Start point>: *enter* 70,60 *right-click*
Height<15>: *enter* 10 *right-click*

Rotation angle<0>: *right-click* (to accept the angle of 0 degrees)
Text: *enter* This is dtext *Return* (NOT a *right-click*)
Text: *enter* NOT text *Return Return* (i.e. twice)
Command:

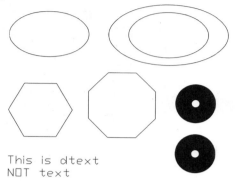

Fig. 3.14 The results of
using the tool icons **Ellipse**,
Polygon, **Donut** and **Text**

Hatch

Fig. 3.15 The **Hatch**
tool icon

When the **Hatch** icon (Fig. 3.15) is selected, a dialogue box **Boundary Hatch** appears. A *left-click* on the **Hatch Options...** button in the dialogue box brings up another dialogue box – **Hatch Options**. A *left-click* on the **Patterns... button** in this box brings the first of several **Choose Hatch Options** dialogue boxes, each brought to the screen one after the other by a *left-click* on the **Next** button in each **Choose Hatch Options** dialogue box in turn. Four of the **Hatch** dialogue boxes are shown in Fig. 3.16 and the results of following the routine of *left-clicks*

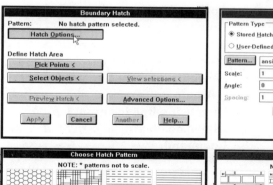

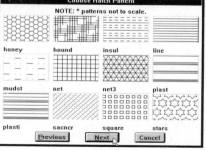

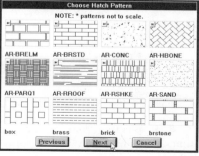

Fig. 3.16 Some of the
dialogue boxes associated
with **Bhatch**

on appropriate buttons in the dialogue boxes is given in four examples in Fig. 3.17.

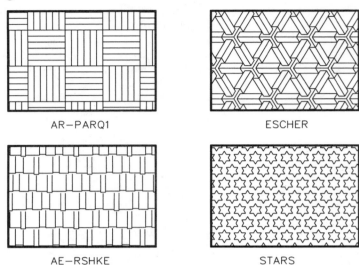

AR—PARQ1   ESCHER

AE—RSHKE   STARS

Fig. 3.17 Some examples of applied **Bhatch** patterns

Fig. 3.18 The **Dimensions** tool icon

Fig. 3.19 Selecting from the **Dimensions** tool icon

Dimensions

A *left-click* on the **Dimensions** icon (Fig. 3.18) in the **Draw** pull-down menu followed by another *left-click* on Linear in the sub-menu which appears, brings up a further sub-menu of linear dimensioning methods (Fig. 3.19). A *left-click* on **Horizontal** in this last sub-menu brings up the following prompts in the command line:

> **Command:-dim1**
> **Dim_horizontal**
> **First extension line origin or RETURN to select:** *left-click* on extension line origin
> **Second extension line origin:** *left-click* on second extension line origin
> **Dimension line location:** *left-click* at desired position
> **Dimension text<180>:** *right-click* or *enter* required figures
> **Command:**

Note: Only one dimension is placed when dimensioning with the aid of the dimension icon.

An example of dimensioning in this manner is given in Fig. 3.20, in which a horizontal, a vertical and an aligned dimension are shown.

Other tool icons

Four other tool icons are included in the **Draw** pull-down menu. These are shown in Fig. 3.21. The actions of two of these – the **Insert**

Fig. 3.20 Horizontal, vertical and aligned dimensions

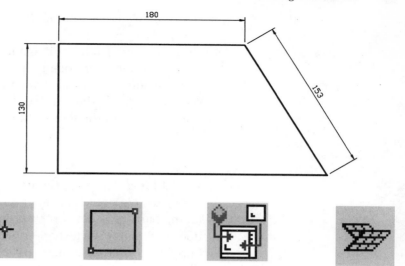

Fig. 3.21 The **Point**, **Rectangle**, **Insert** and **3D Surfaces** tool icons in the **Draw** pull-down menu

tool and the **3D Surfaces** tool – will be explained later (pages 127 and 151). Examples of the use of the **Point** and the **Rectangle** tool icons are illustrated in Fig. 3.22.

Notes

1. Different styles of points are set in the **Point Styles** dialogue box (see page 67);
2. The width of the plines forming a rectangle with the aid of the **Rectangle** icon is determined by the setting of the current pline width.

Questions

1. In how many ways can commands be called in AutoCAD for Windows? Can you name you own preference yet?

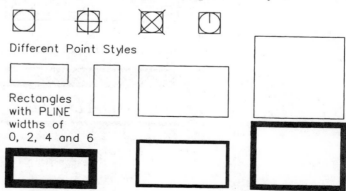

Different Point Styles

Rectangles with PLINE widths of 0, 2, 4 and 6

Fig. 3.22 Examples drawn with the **Point** and **Rectangle** tool icons

2. When using the **Circle** command, what does the prompt **TTR** mean?

3. If **dim** is entered at the command line or the **Dimension** tool icon is selected, dimensions of all types can be added to a drawing. What is the major difference between using these two methods?

4. What determines the width of the lines forming a rectangle when it is drawn with the **Rectangle** tool?

Exercises

1. With **3 Lines** set in the **Command Prompt** box in the **Preferences** dialogue box, practise using each of the **Draw** tools icons in turn, taking particular note of the prompts associated with the tools. It does not matter what shapes you draw.

2. Copy the three drawings given in Fig. 3.23 to the sizes and dimensions included with the drawing. Include the dimensions for Drawings 1 and 2.

3. Copy the four drawings given in Fig. 3.24 to the sizes and dimensions included with the drawing. Include the dimensions for Drawings 2 and 3.

4. Copy the three drawings given in Fig. 3.25 to the sizes and dimensions included with the drawing. Include the dimensions for Drawings 2 and 3.

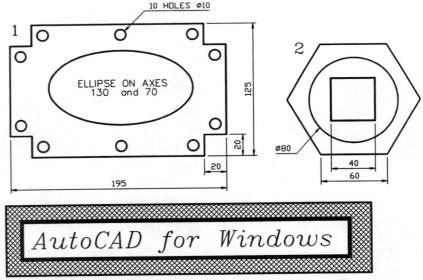

Fig. 3.23 Exercise 2

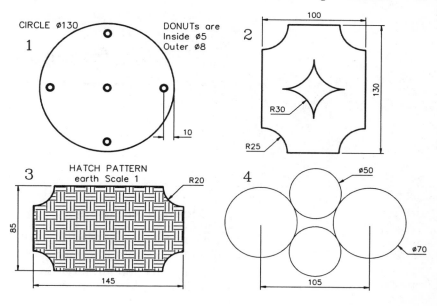

Fig. 3.24 Exercise 3

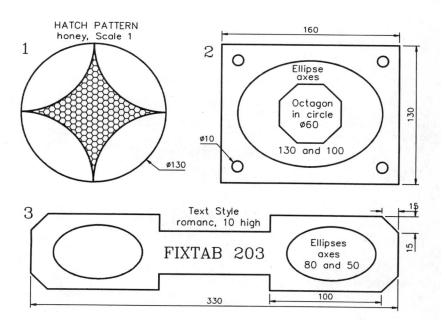

Fig. 3.25 Exercise 4

CHAPTER 4

2D Modify commands

Modify commands

As the name implies, the **Modify** set of commands is for modifying or editing entities or groups of entities in a drawing. In a manner similar to command selection for the **Draw** menus, there are several ways in which the **Modify** commands can be called:

1. By selection of command names from the **Modify** pull-down menu (Fig. 4.1);
2. By changing the **Draw** command names to tool icons – a *left-click* on **Menu Bitmaps** in the **Settings** menu and selecting from tool icons (Fig. 4.2);
3. By selection from the **Toolbox** (Fig. 4.3);

Fig. 4.1 Command names in the **Modify** pull-down menu

Fig. 4.2 Bitmap icons in the **Modify** pull-down menu

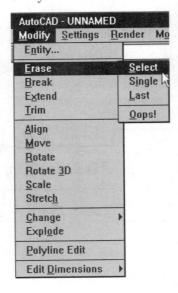

Fig. 4.3 The **Toolbox**

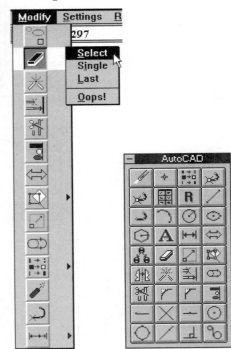

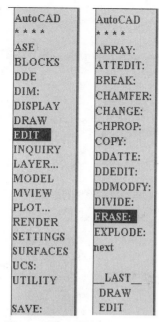

AutoCAD	AutoCAD
****	****
ASE	ARRAY:
BLOCKS	ATTEDIT:
DDE	BREAK:
DIM:	CHAMFER:
DISPLAY	CHANGE:
DRAW	CHPROP:
EDIT	COPY:
INQUIRY	DDATTE:
LAYER...	DDEDIT:
MODEL	DDMODFY:
MVIEW	DIVIDE:
PLOT...	ERASE:
RENDER	EXPLODE:
SETTINGS	next
SURFACES	
UCS:	
UTILITY	_LAST_
	DRAW
SAVE:	EDIT

Fig. 4.4 The **EDIT** on-screen menu and its sub-menu

4. By selection from the on-screen menus – **EDIT** and its sub-menu (Fig. 4.4);
5. By entering a modify command name at the command line, or in some cases the abbreviation for the command name. As an example to erase an entity:

Command: *enter* e (for erase) *right-click*
ERASE
Select objects: *pick* the entity to be erased **1 found.**
Select objects: *right-click*
Command: and the object disappears from the graphics window

6. By selection of the appropriate icon form the **Toolbar**.

Modifying 2D entities using the tool icons

There are **Modify** tools (commands) for both 2D (two-dimensional) and 3D (three-dimensional) drawing. The use of 3D **Modify** tools will come later in the book. In this chapter we are only concerned with the 2D **Modify** tools. As with the tools from the **Draw** menu, as a **Modify** is selected prompts will appear at the command line, if the command line is active (by choosing 1, 2 or 3 command line prompts in the **Preferences** dialogue box).

Note on the Modify tools

Entities can be modified singly or in groups with the **Modify** set of tools:

1. A single entity can be *picked* – that is, the pick-box which appears whenever a **Modify** tool is selected is moved on to the entity, followed by a *left-click;*
2. A group of entities can be selected in a **window** (abbreviation w) – all entities completely within the window are picked;
3. A group of entities can be selected in a crossing window (abbreviation c) – all entities crossed by the lines of the window are selected;
4. The last entity (abbreviation l) drawn is chosen for modification;
5. With **Erase** – and only with erase – the command **oops** will recall the erased entity or entities back to the graphics window.

Erase

Left-click on the **Erase** icon (Fig. 4.5). Prompts appear at the command line:

Command:_erase
Select objects: *pick* the entity to be erased *right-click*

Fig. 4.5 The **Erase** tool icon

Select objects: right-*click*
Command: and the object is erased

If erasing a group of entities with the aid of a window (Fig. 4.6), the prompts would be:

Command:_erase
Select objects: *enter* w (for Window) *right-click*
First corner: *pick* **Other corner:** *pick* **4 found**
Select objects: right-*click*
Command: and the entities within the window are erased

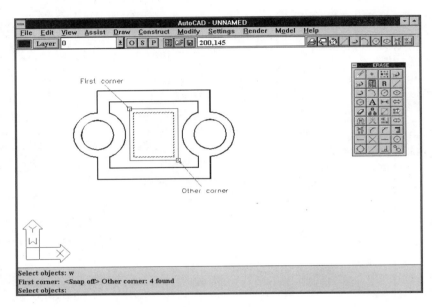

Fig. 4.6 **Erase** with a window

Fig. 4.7 The **Break** tool icon

Break

Left-click on the **Break** icon (Fig. 4.7). A sub-menu associated with **Break** appears (Fig. 4.8). The prompts at the command line for the selection as shown in Fig. 4.8, will be:

Command:_break Select objects: *pick* the entity to be broken
Enter second point (or F for first point): *pick* at a second point
Command: and the line breaks between the two points

Fig. 4.8 The sub-menu appearing when the **Break** icon is selected

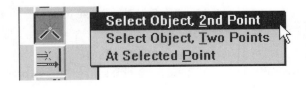

If an f (for First is *entered* in response to the prompt **(or F for first point)**:

> **Command:_break Select objects:** *pick* the entity to be broken
> **Enter second point (or F for first point):** f (for First) *right-click*
> **Enter first point:** *pick* the point on the entity
> **Enter second point:** *pick* the second point on the entity
> **Command:** and the entity is broken between the two points.

Notes
1. See Fig. 4.9;

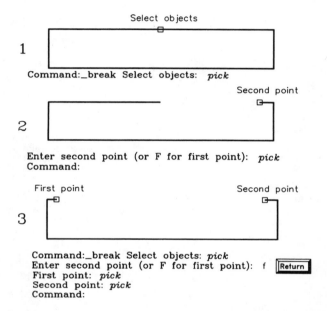

Fig. 4.9 The **Break** tool
– its command prompts
and the results of
Breaks

2. If breaking a circle or an arc, normal practice is to break anti-clockwise (counter-clockwise ccw) (Fig. 4.10);

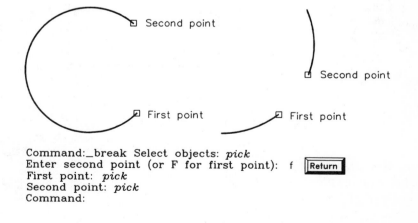

Fig. 4.10 **Break** used
with a circle or an arc

3. The third item in the sub-menu shown in Fig. 4.8, allows an entity to be broken into parts at a single point.

Extend

Fig. 4.11 The **Extend** tool icon

Left-click on the **Extend** icon (Fig. 4.11). Figure 4.12 shows the results of using this tool, together with the command line prompts which appear to guide the operator in extending lines and/or arcs.

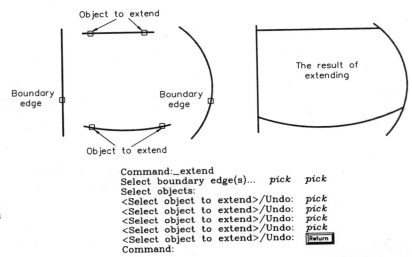

Fig. 4.12 The **Extend** tool - its command prompts and the results of extending

```
Command:_extend
Select boundary edge(s)...    pick    pick
Select objects:
<Select object to extend>/Undo:    pick
<Select object to extend>/Undo:    pick
<Select object to extend>/Undo:    pick
<Select object to extend>/Undo:    pick
<Select object to extend>/Undo:    Return
Command:
```

Trim

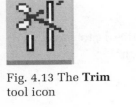

Fig. 4.13 The **Trim** tool icon

Left-click on the **Trim** icon (Fig. 4.13). Figure 4.14 includes both the command line prompts and a drawing showing the results of trimming to cutting edges.

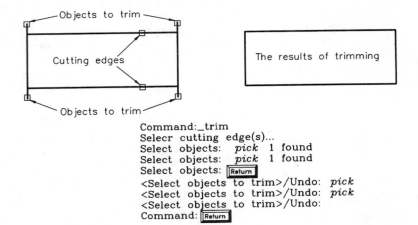

Fig. 4.14 The **Trim** tool - its command line prompts and the results of trimming

```
Command:_trim
Selecr cutting edge(s)...
Select objects:    pick   1 found
Select objects:    pick   1 found
Select objects:  Return
<Select objects to trim>/Undo:    pick
<Select objects to trim>/Undo:    pick
<Select objects to trim>/Undo:
Command:  Return
```

Move

Fig. 4.15 The **Move**
tool icon

Left-click on the **Move** icon (Fig. 4.15). Figure 4.16 shows both the command prompts associated with **Move** and the results of moving objects in the graphics window.

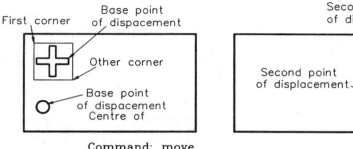

Fig. 4.16 The **Move** tool - its command line prompts and the results of a **Move**

```
Command:_move
Select objects: w  Return
First corner: pick  Other corner: pick  16 found
Select objects:   Return
Base point of displacement: pick          0,0
Second point of displacement: pick     40,-40  e.g.
Command:
```

Rotate

Fig. 4.17 The **Rotate**
tool icon

Left-click on the **Rotate** icon (Fig. 4.17). Figure 4.18 shows both the command prompts associated with **Rotate** and the results of scaling objects in the graphics window.

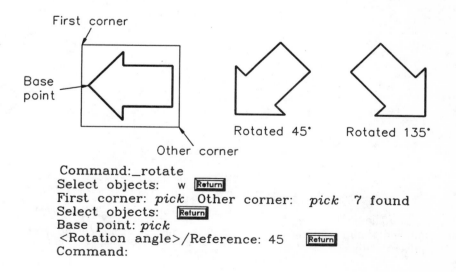

Fig. 4.18 The **Rotate** tool - its command prompts and the results of rotating

```
Command:_rotate
Select objects:   w  Return
First corner: pick  Other corner:  pick  7 found
Select objects:   Return
Base point: pick
<Rotation angle>/Reference: 45     Return
Command:
```

Scale

Fig. 4.19 The **Scale** tool icon

Left-click on the **Scale** icon (Fig. 4.19). Figure 4.20 shows both the command prompts associated with **Scale** and the results of scaling objects in the graphics window.

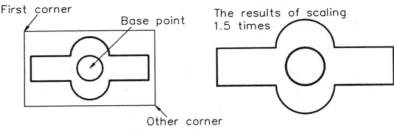

Fig. 20 The **Scale** tool – its command prompts and the results of scaling

```
Command: _scale
Select objects:  w Return
First corner: pick  Other corner:   pick 9 found
Select objects:   Return
Base point: pick
<Scale factor>/Reference: 1.5 Return
Command:
```

Stretch

Fig. 4.21 The **Stretch** tool icon

Left-click on the **Stretch** icon (Fig. 4.21). Figure 4.22 shows both the command prompts associated with **Stretch** and the results of stretching objects in the graphics window. Note the possible distortions when stretching arcs when the crossing window passes through the arc.

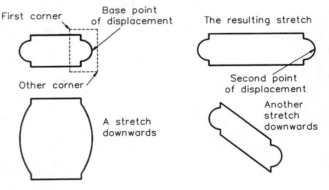

Fig. 4.22 The **Stretch** tool - its command prompts and the results of scaling

```
Command:_stretch
Selection of objects to stretch by window or polygon...
Select objects:_c
First corner: pick  Other corner: pick
Select objects:  Return
Base point of displacement: pick
Second point of displacement: pick
Command:
```

Fig. 4.23 The **Change** tool icon

Fig. 4.24 The sub-menu with the **Change** tool icon

Fig. 4.25 The **Change** tool - its command line prompts and an example of its use to change a linetype

Change

Left-click on the **Change** icon (Fig. 4.23). It will be seen that this results in a sub-menu appearing – Fig. 4.24. *Left-click* on **Properties** in this menu. Figure 4.25 shows both the command prompts associated with **Change** and the results of changing objects in the graphics window.

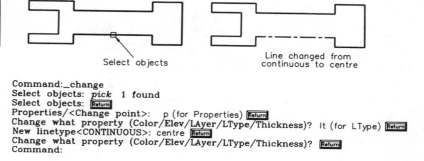

Select objects   Line changed from continuous to centre

```
Command:_change
Select objects: pick  1 found
Select objects: Return
Properties/<Change point>:  p (for Properties) Return
Change what property (Color/Elev/LAyer/LType/Thickness)?  lt (for LType) Return
New linetype<CONTINUOUS>: centre Return
Change what property (Color/Elev/LAyer/LType/Thickness)? Return
Command:
```

Notes on the Change tool

The Colour, the Elevation (see page 156), the Layer on which the entity to be changed has been constructed and the Thickness (see page 156) can be changed if the **Properties** prompt is chosen. To change the style of text, the **Change point** option must be chosen – Fig. 4.26.

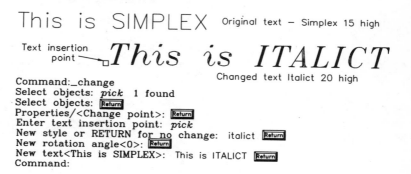

This is SIMPLEX   Original text – Simplex 15 high

Text insertion point → *This is ITALICT*

Changed text Italict 20 high

```
Command:_change
Select objects: pick  1 found
Select objects: Return
Properties/<Change point>: Return
Enter text insertion point: pick
New style or RETURN for no change: italict Return
New rotation angle<0>: Return
New text<This is SIMPLEX>:  This is ITALICT Return
Command:
```

Fig. 4.26 Changing text

Note: To change a text style in this manner, the new text style must already be loaded into memory and be of the required height.

Fig. 4.27 The **Explode** tool icon

Explode

Left-click on the **Explode** icon (Fig. 4.27). Some objects in AutoCAD are made up from a number of entities forming a **block**. One example is a hatched area. This is made up of a number of single entities but the whole area can be acted upon by one of the **Modify** tools as if it were a single entity. A *left-click* on **Explode** followed by a *left-click* on a hatched area would change the area into its single entities, each of which can then be acted upon by a **Modify** tool . Other examples which we will come across later in the book are **blocks**, which have been **inserted** into a drawing. Such blocks require exploding if they are to be modified in any way. Command line prompts associated with **Explode** are simple:

Command:_explode
Select objects: *pick* **1 found**
Select objects: *right-click*
Command:

Pedit

Left-click on the **Pedit** icon (Fig. 4.28). Pedit is short for Pline edit and the tool is for editing or modifying plines (polylines). The two examples given in Fig. 4.29 give some indication of the use of this tool. Plines can be modified as to their width; they can be joined together; their vertices can be moved; a curved pline can be de-curved; a previous editing can be undone.

Fig. 4.28 The **Pedit** tool icon

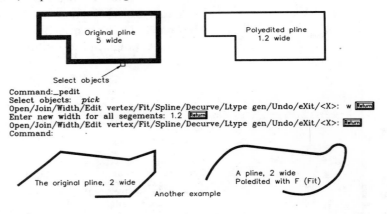

Fig. 4.29 The **Pedit** tool – its command line prompts and two example of its use

Dim

Left-click on the **Dim** icon (Fig. 4.30). Figure 4.31 shows the sub-menu for the **Dim** function and examples of its use for modifying dimensions are given in Fig. 4.32, together with the command line prompts associated with the tool.

Fig. 4.30 The **Dim** tool icon

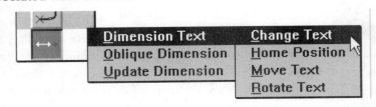

Fig. 4.31 The sub-menus from the **Dim** tool icon

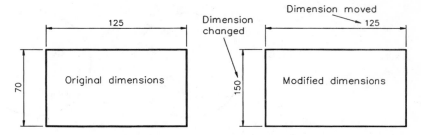

Fig. 4.32 The **Dim** tool –
its command line
prompts and examples of
it use

```
Command:_dim1
Dim_tedit
Select dimension: pick
Enter text location (Left/Right/Home/Angle): pick
Command:
```

Notes

1. When using the **Rotate** tool (command) you will have noticed that the angular rotation was ccw (counter-clockwise). This can be changed to operate cw (clockwise). *Left-click* on **Units Control...** in the **Settings** menu, then *left-click* on the **Direction...** button in the dialogue box. Note the **Counter-clockwise** and **Clockwise** circles.
2. There are some 3D tools in the **Modify** menu. Reference to these will be made in later chapter dealing with three-dimensional drawing (3D).

Questions

1. The **Modify** commands (tools) can be called for use in several ways. Make a list of these methods.
2. When using some of the **Modify** tools, the objects being acted upon can be selected in a window or a crossing window. What is the difference between these two methods of selection?
3. The term **Objects** frequently occurs in prompts seen at the command line in AutoCAD. What does the word mean?
4. What is the difference between **Erase** and **Break**?
5. In which direction should you use **Break** when breaking part of a circle or an arc?

Exercises

1. Draw 6 circles, each of diameter 100. Then break the circles as indicated in Fig. 4.33.
2. Fig. 4.34. With the aid of the **Pline**, set to 0.7 width, copy the two vertical lines and the two circles. Then add plines and arcs in a haphazard manner as shown in Fig. 4.34, but do not draw any of the

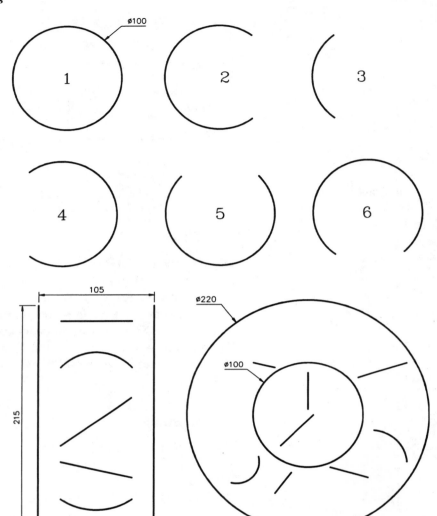

Fig. 4.33 Exercise 1

Fig. 4.34 Exercise 2

plines touching the lines or circles already drawn. Then with the **Extend** tool, extend the haphazard polylines to the vertical plines and the circles.

3. Fig. 4.35. Construct Drawing 1 – with **Polygon** and **Circle** tools from **Draw**. With the aid of **Trim** from **Modify** and **Hatch** from **Draw**, modify the drawing to obtain Drawing 2;

Construct Drawing 3 – with **Pline** and **Line** from **Draw**. With the aid of **Trim** from **Modify** and **Hatch** from **Draw**, modify the drawing to obtain Drawing 4;

Construct Drawing 6 with **Polygon** from **Draw**. With the aid of **Explode** and **Trim** from **Modify** and **Hatch** from **Draw**, modify the drawing to obtain Drawing 7. In this exercise ensure that **Snap** is set to 5 and **Grid** set to 10 and that both **Snap** and **Grid** are on. You may need to use the **Object Snap** tools to ensure accurate constructions.

4. Construct the arrow given in Fig. 4.36 nine times with the aid of the **Pline** tool. Then with **Rotate** from **Modify**, rotate each of the arrows to the angles given in Fig. 4.36.

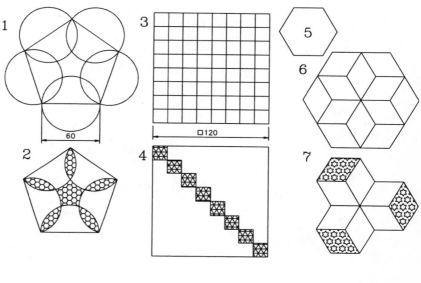

Fig. 4.35 Exercise 3

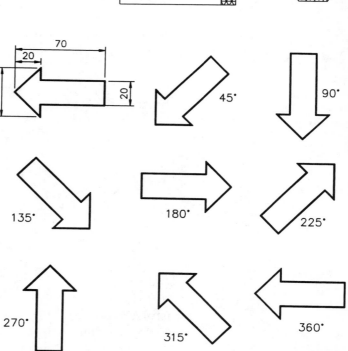

Fig. 4.36 Exercise 4

5. Make sure that **Snap** is set to 5 and on. Make sure that **Grid** is set to 10 and on. Construct Drawing 1 of Fig. 4.37 to the dimensions given. Then, with the aid of the **Trim** tool (Fig. 4.38), trim unwanted lines to produce Drawing 2 of Fig. 4.37.

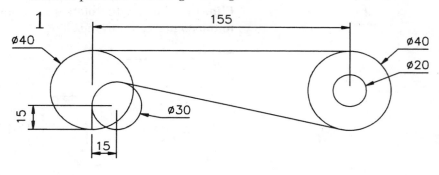

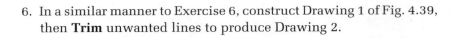

After using TRIM

Fig. 4.37 Exercise 5

Fig. 4.38 The **Trim** tool icon from **Modify**

6. In a similar manner to Exercise 6, construct Drawing 1 of Fig. 4.39, then **Trim** unwanted lines to produce Drawing 2.

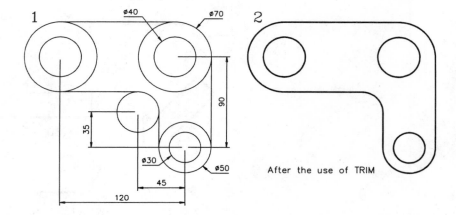

After the use of TRIM

Fig. 4.39 Exercise 6

7. Construct Drawing 1 of Fig. 4.40, using the **TTR** option of the **Circle** command when drawing the R200 circle. Trim unwanted arcs to produce the outline Drawing 2.

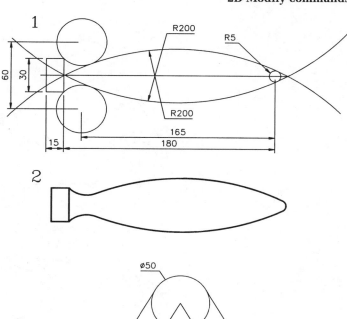

Fig. 4.40 Exercise 7

Fig. 4.41 Construction for front view of Exercise 8

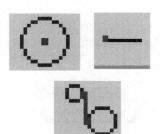

Fig. 4.42 The **Object Snap** tools **Centre**, **Endpoint** and **Tangent**

8. Construct the two-view Third angle orthographic projection given in Fig. 4.43. Details of the method of construction for the Front view are given in Fig. 4.41. To construct this view use the **Object Snaps Tangent**, **Endpoint** and **Centre** (Fig. 4.42). The equilateral triangle is constructed by using the relative coordinate method (page 13). The hatch pattern is **ansi31** at angle 0 and Scale 1.5.
   For this exercise you need to be working in the AutoCAD for Windows graphics window configured with **Layers** as described on page 25. This means that layers will need to be changed when adding hidden detail and centre lines to the views.

9. Construct the two-view Third angle orthographic projection Fig. 4.44. Note that the webs are not hatched, in conformity with the rule that in sectional views features such as spindles, nuts, bolts, webs, ribs and similar parts are shown as outside views.

10. Construct the three-view First angle orthographic projection given in Fig. 4.45.

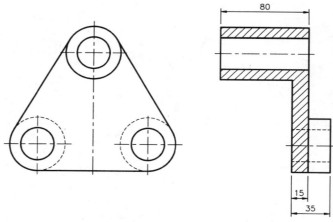

Fig. 4.43 Exercise 8

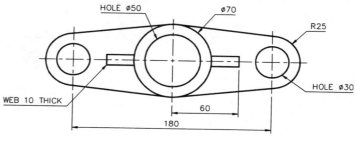

Fig. 4.44 Exercise 9

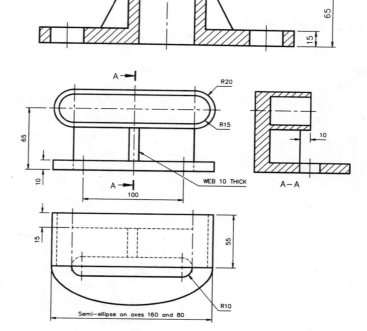

Fig. 4.45 Exercise 10

CHAPTER 5

2D Construct commands

Construct commands

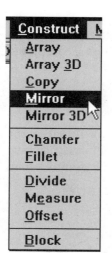

Fig. 5.1 Command names in the **Construct** pull-down menu

The **Construct** commands or tools are found in the **Construct** Pull-down menu – *left-click* on the name in the **Menu bar** – in either command name form (Fig. 5.1) or, after a *left-click* on **Menu Bitmaps** in the **Settings** menu, as tool icons (Fig. 5.2). They may also be found in **Toolbox** (Fig. 5.3), or in the **EDIT** on-screen menu and its sub-menus (Fig. 5.4). Thus, as with the **Draw** commands and the **Modify** commands, the **Construct** commands can be called in a variety of ways. Some of the **Construct** commands are for 3D constructions, but in this chapter we are only dealing with those associated with 2D constructions.

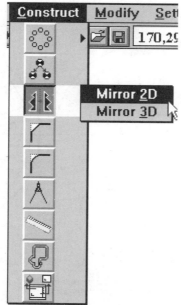

Fig. 5.2 Bitmaps in the **Construct** pull-down menu

Fig. 5.3 The **Toolbox**

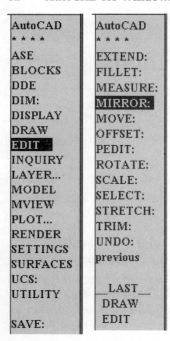

Fig. 5.4 The **EDIT** on-screen menu and its sub-menu

Fig. 5.5 The **Array** tool icon

Array

There are two forms of 2D array – entities or groups of entities can be arrayed in either:

1. A **Polar** fashion around a central point;
2. A **Rectangular** fashion in columns or rows vertically and horizontally.

Polar array

An example is given in Fig. 5.6. *Left-click* on the **Array** tool icon (Fig. 5.5). The prompts which then appear at the command line are included with Fig. 5.6.

A Polar array can be within a complete circle, or any part of a circle, depending upon the response to the prompt **Angle to fill:**. As an example, a response of 180 would result in the array being completed within a semi-circle.

Rectangular array

Figure 5.7 is an example of a **Rectangular** array and includes the prompts and responses associated with the array. Note the negative value of the -50 (the **Unit cell or distance between rows:**) figure. When setting up a rectangular array:

Fig. 5.6 An example of a Polar array, together with the prompts associated with the tool **Array**

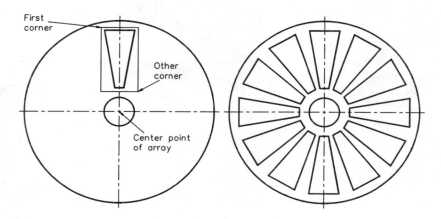

```
Command: _array
Select objects: w    First corner: pick  Other corner: pick
Select objects: Return
Rectangular or Polar array (R/P)<R>: P
Center point of array: pick
Number of items: 12
Angle to fill (+=ccw,−=cw)<360>: Return
Rotate objects as they are copied?<Y>: Return
Command:
```

+ve *x* is to the right horizontally;
-ve *x* is to the left horizontally;
+ve *y* is upwards vertically;
-ve *y* is downwards vertically.

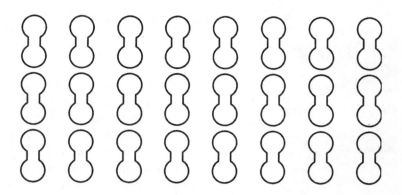

Fig. 5.7 A Rectangular array, together with the prompts and responses associated with **Array**

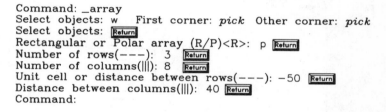

```
Command: _array
Select objects: w    First corner: pick  Other corner: pick
Select objects: Return
Rectangular or Polar array  (R/P)<R>:  p Return
Number of rows(---):  3  Return
Number of columns(||||):  8  Return
Unit cell or distance between rows(---):  -50  Return
Distance between columns(||||):  40 Return
Command:
```

Copy

Left-click on the **Copy** icon (Fig. 5.8). Examples of the use of the tool are given in Fig. 5.9.

Fig. 5.8 The **Copy** tool icon

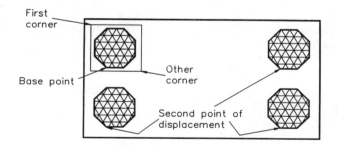

Fig. 5.9 The **Copy** tool – an example of its use for **Multiple** copy, together with associated prompts and responses

```
Command:_copy
Select objects: pick  First corner:  pick  Other corner:
Select objects:
<Base point or displacement>/Multiple:  m  Return
Base point:  Second point of displacement: left-click
Second point of displacement: left-click
Second point of displacement: left-click
Second point of displacement: Return
Command:
```

Note: In the given example the **Multiple** option has been chosen. If a single copy is required, do not respond with an m (for Multiple) to the prompt:

<Base point of displacement>/Multiple:

but respond with *left-click* at the required **Base point of displacement**.

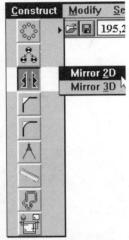

Fig. 5.10 The **Mirror** tool icon

Fig. 5.11 The **Mirror** sub-menu

Fig. 5.12 Two examples of the use of the **Mirror** tool

Mirror

Left-click on the **Mirror** tool icon in the **Construct** menu (Fig. 5.10). A sub-menu appears (Fig. 5.11). *Left-click* on **Mirror 2D** in the sub-menu and follow the prompts which appear at the command line. Two examples are given in Fig. 5.12: Drawing 1, a single action of the command, Drawing 2, two actions.

Mirrtext: Figure 5.13 shows the action of setting the AutoCAD set variable **Mirrtext**. There are two possible settings of this variable – 0

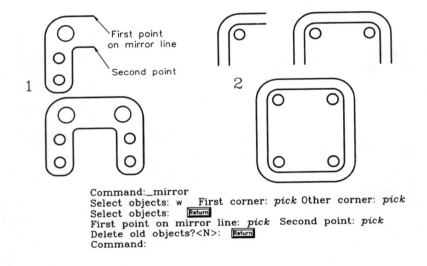

```
Command:_mirror
Select objects: w   First corner: pick Other corner: pick
Select objects:    Return
First point on mirror line: pick Second point: pick
Delete old objects?<N>:  Return
Command:
```

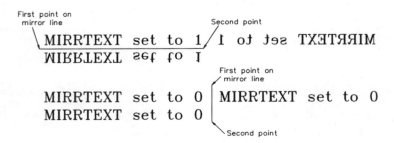

Fig. 5.13 The set variable **MIRRTEXT**

or 1. If set to 1, text is mirrored as one would expect – upside down or back to front. If set to 0, text is mirrored the correct way round. Thus if text is included with a drawing which is to be mirrored, it is best to set **Mirrtext** to 0 as follows:

Command: *enter* mirrtext *right-click*
New value for MIRRTEXT<1>: *enter* 0 *right-click*
Command:

and the variable is set to 0.

Chamfer

Fig. 5.14 The **Chamfer** tool icon

Left-click on the **Chamfer** tool icon in the **Construct** menu (Figure 5.14). Figure 5.15 gives examples of it use, together with the prompts appearing at the command line when it is called.

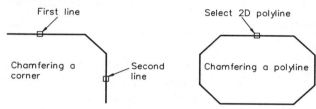

Fig. 5.15 The **Chamfer** tool – examples of its use and its associated prompts

```
Command:_chamfer Polyline/Distances/<Select first line>:  d  Return
Enter first chamfer distance<0>:  20  Return
Enter second chamfer distance<20>:  Return
Command:  Return
CHAMFER Polyline/Distance?<Select first line>: pick
Select second line: pick
Command:

              OR: if chamfering a polyline

CHAMFER Polyline/Distance?<Select first line>: p  Return
Select 2D polyline: pick
Command:
```

Fillet

Fig. 5.16 The **Fillet** tool icon

Left-click on the **Fillet** tool icon in the **Construct** menu (Fig. 5.16). Figure 5.17 gives examples of its use, together with the prompts appearing at the command line when it is called.
Note: With both the **Chamfer** and the **Fillet** tools:

1. If an attempt is made to chamfer or fillet two plines meeting at a point, the message appears:

   Cannot fillet polyline segments from different polylines. *Invalid*

2. If either **Chamfer** distances or **Fillet** radius are set to 0, lines not meeting at a point will be set to meet at their ends when either of

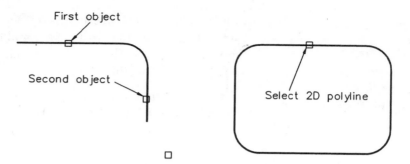

```
Command:_fillet Polyline/Radius/<Select first object>:  r  [Return]
Enter fillet radius<0>:  20  [Return]
Command:     [Return]
FILLET Polyline/Radius/<Select first object>:
Select second object:
Command:
```

Fig. 5.17 The **Fillet** tool –
examples of its use and its
associated prompts

the two commands is used. This facility is of value at times when one wishes to ensure that lines are meeting at a point.

3. Any one corner of a polyline can be chamfered or filleted by not responding with a p when the **Polyline/Radius/Select first object:** prompt appears at the command line.

Offset

Left-click on the **Offset** tool icon in the **Construct** menu (Fig. 5.18). Figure 5.19 gives examples of its use, together with the prompts appearing at the command line when it is called.

Fig. 5.18 The **Offset** tool icon

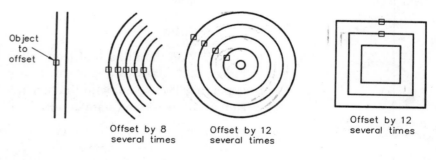

Object to offset

Offset by 8 several times

Offset by 12 several times

Offset by 12 several times

Fig. 5.19 The **Offset** tool –
examples of its use and
associated coommand line
prompts

```
Command:_offset
Offset distance or Through<Through>: 10  [Return]
Select object to offset:  pick
Side to offset?  pick
Select object to offset:  [Return]
Command:
```

Measure

Fig. 5.20 The **Measure** tool icon

Left-click on the **Measure** tool icon in the **Construct** menu (Fig. 5.20). Before using the tool, *left-click* on **Point Style...** in the **Settings** menu and select an appropriate **Point Style** from the dialogue box. Figure 5.21 shows a suitable selection. The purpose of **Measure** is to divide an entity into a number of segments and mark the segments with the selected **Point,** as illustrated in Fig. 5.22.

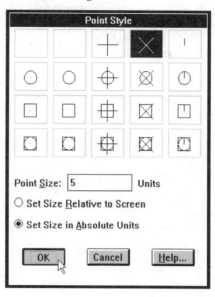

Fig. 5.21 Setting the **Point Style** for the **Measure** command

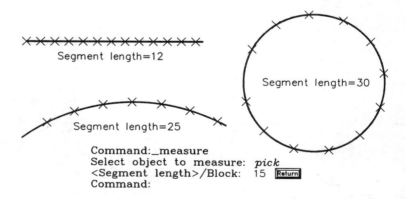

Segment length=12

Segment length=25

Segment length=30

```
Command:_measure
Select object to measure: pick
<Segment length>/Block:  15  Return
Command:
```

Fig. 5.22 The **Measure** tool – examples of its use and associated command line prompts

Note: If the **Block** prompt is accepted, a block from within the drawing (see page 124) can be used instead of points of the style selected from the **Point Styles** dialogue box. This may be of value when one wishes to repeat a small drawing, such as an icon at regular intervals along the length of an entity.

Divide

Fig. 5.23 The **Divide** Tool icon

Left-click on the **Divide** tool icon in the **Construct** menu (Fig. 5.23). Before using the tool, *left-click* on **Point Style...** in the **Settings** menu and select an appropriate **Point Style** from the dialogue box. In Fig. 5.24, a different **Point Style** was chosen from that chosen for the **Measure** tool examples in Fig. 5.22. Note the similarity between the **Measure** and the **Divide** commands. However, whereas **Measure** marks segments of given length along the entity, **Divide** divides the entity into the required number of divisions. In both commands a block can be inserted in place of the **Points**.

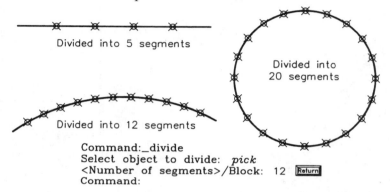

Fig. 5.24 The **Divide** tool – examples of its use and associated command line prompts

```
Command:_divide
Select object to divide: pick
<Number of segments>/Block: 12 Return
Command:
```

Examples of circles divided and with blocks in place of points are given in Fig. 5.25. In one example the blocks are aligned with the entity. In the second example, the blocks are not aligned with the entity.

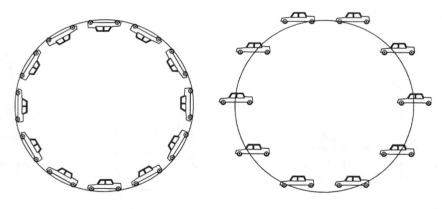

Fig. 5.25 Examples of blocks inserted into divided entities in place of points.

Block

Fig. 5.26 The **Block** tool icon

Left-click on the **Block** tool icon in the **Construct** menu (Fig. 5.26). An example of the use of **Block**, together with its command line prompts is given in Fig. 5.27. Blocks are defined within the drawing under

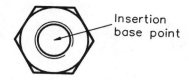
Insertion
base point

Fig. 5.27 The **Block** tool - an example of its use, together with its associated command line prompts

```
Command:_block Block name (or?): nut [Return]
Insertion base point: pick
Select objects:  w First corner: pick Other corner: pick
Select objects: [Return]
Command:
```

construction. If the **(or?)** prompt is answered with by entering a **?** a list of blocks already saved within the drawing will appear in an AutoCAD text screen. Blocks can be **Inserted** in a drawing (Fig. 5.28).

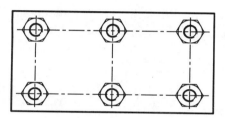

Fig. 5.28 An example of the use of the **INSERT** command

```
Command: enter insert [Return]
Block name (or?)<NUT>: [Return]
Insertion point: pick
X scale factor<1>/Corner?XYZ: 0.5 [Return]
Y scale factor (default=Z): [Return]
Rotation angle<0>: [Return]
Command:
```

Questions

1. Where can you find the **Construct commands/tools** in AutoCAD for Windows?
2. What is the difference between a **Polar** array and a **Rectangular** array?
3. What is the purpose of the **Multiple** option in the **Copy** command prompts?
4. What is the purpose of the set variable **MIRRTEXT**?
5. One of the prompts appearing when **Chamfer** is called is:

   Polyline/Distance/?<Select first line>:

   What is the purpose of the **Polyline** option in this prompt?
6. There are two methods for setting the **Offset distance** when using the **Offset** tool. What are these two methods?
7. Why is **Point Style** important in the use of the **Distance** and **Measure** tools?
8. What is the purpose of the **Block** tool?

Exercises

1. Construct the drawing in Fig. 5.29. There is no need to include any dimensions.

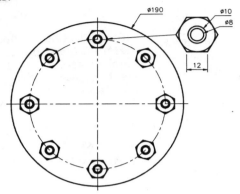

Fig. 5.29 Exercise 1

2. With the aid of the **Array** tool, construct the drawing in Fig. 5.30. Do not include any dimensions.

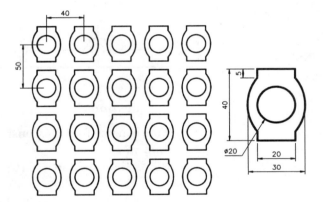

Fig. 5.30 Exercise 2

3. Using the **Array** tool, construct the drawing in Fig. 5.31. Work to any sizes you consider to be suitable.

Fig. 5.31 Exercise 3

4. With the aid of the **Copy** tool and using the **Multiple** option construct Fig. 5.32 to the dimensions given. Do not include any dimensions.

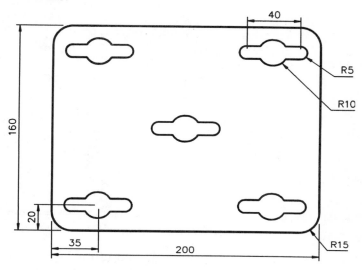

Fig. 5.32 Exercise 4

5. Fig. 5.33 is a three-view orthographic drawing of an angle bracket. Construct the drawing, including dimensions and the title block.

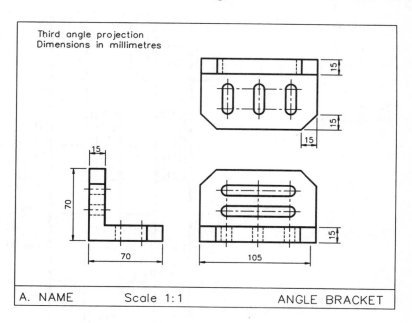

Fig. 5.33 Exercise 5

6. Using the **Divide** tool, construct the three drawings in Fig. 5.34, working to any sizes you consider suitable.

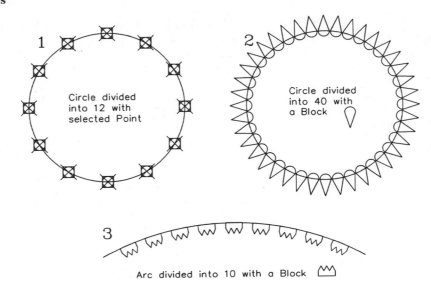

Fig. 5.34 Exercise 6

7. With the aid of the **Offset** tool and the **Hatch** tool (from **Draw**), construct Fig. 5.35. Do not include any dimensions

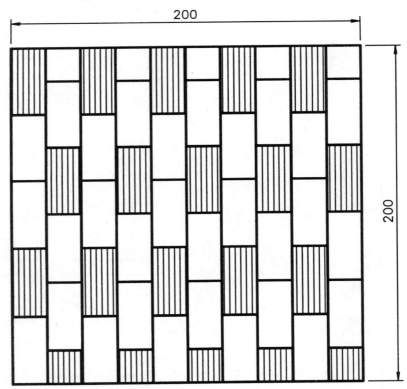

Fig. 5.35 Exercise 7

8. With the aid of the **Mirror** tool construct Fig. 5.36, working to any sizes you consider to be suitable.

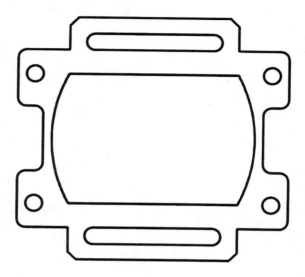

Fig. 5.36 Exercise 8

9. With the aid of the **Array**, **Mirror**, **Ellipse**, **Divide** and **Text** tools, construct Fig. 5.37, working to any sizes you consider to be suitable.

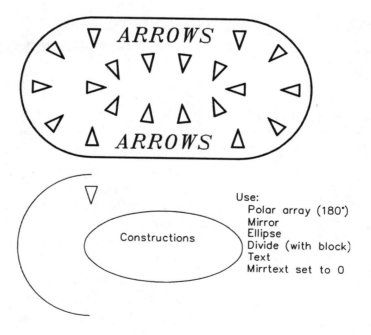

Fig. 5.37 Exercise 9

CHAPTER 6

Example 2D drawings

The acad.pgp file

In this chapter, instead of selecting the tool icons when calling commands, we will be *entering* abbreviations for command names at the keyboard. The AutoCAD for Windows software files are normally held in the directory *c:\acad*. There are several sub-directories of the *acad* directory, one of which is *acad\support*. A file *acad.pgp* will be found in the *acad\support* directory. This file, *c:\acad\support\ acad.pgp*, holds abbreviations for command names. It is easy to add further abbreviations to this file if you wish, but be careful if your computer is somewhat light on memory, because each added abbreviation uses some memory. To add abbreviations to the list already in the *acad.pgp* file, *left-click* on the MS-DOS editor in the Windows **Program Manager** window (Fig. 6.1).

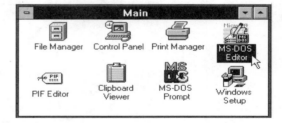

Fig. 6.1 The **MS-DOS Editor** icon in the **Program Manager** window

This brings the **MS-DOS text editor** on screen. Enter the file name *c:\acad\support\acad.pgp* and the text in the file appears (Fig. 6.2).

That part of the file which contains the 2D command names and their abbreviations is shown below. The abbreviations are those used on the computer I work on, which has 16 Mb of memory – sufficient to allow me to place a large number of abbreviations in the file.

Sample aliases for AutoCAD Commands
; These examples reflect the most frequently used commands.
; Each alias uses a small amount of memory, so don't go
; overboard on systems with tight memory.

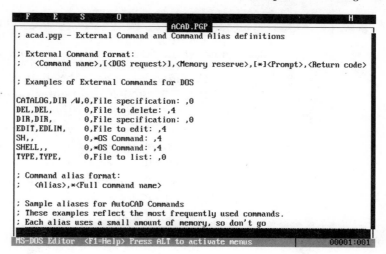

```
  F     E     S     O                                                          H
                                    ACAD.PGP
 ; acad.pgp - External Command and Command Alias definitions

 ; External Command format:
 ;    <Command name>,[<DOS request>],<Memory reserve>,[*]<Prompt>,<Return code>

 ; Examples of External Commands for DOS

 CATALOG,DIR /W,0,File specification: ,0
 DEL,DEL,      0,File to delete: ,4
 DIR,DIR,      0,File specification: ,0
 EDIT,EDLIN,   0,File to edit: ,4
 SH,,          0,*OS Command: ,4
 SHELL,,       0,*OS Command: ,4
 TYPE,TYPE,    0,File to list: ,0

 ; Command alias format:
 ;    <Alias>,*<Full command name>

 ; Sample aliases for AutoCAD Commands
 ; These examples reflect the most frequently used commands.
 ; Each alias uses a small amount of memory, so don't go
 MS-DOS Editor  <F1=Help> Press ALT to activate menus              00001:001
```

Fig. 6.2 The *acad.pgp* file in the **MS-DOS** editor

A,	*ARC
B,	*BREAK
BH,	*BHATCH
C,	*CIRCLE
CP,	*COPY
D,	*DISTANCE
DO,	*DONUT
E,	*ERASE
EL,	*ELLIPSE
EP,	*EXPLODE
EX,	*EXTEND
F,	*FILLET
L,	*LINE
M,	*MOVE
MI,	*MIRROR
O,	*OFFSET
P,	*PEDIT
PO,	*POLYGON
PL,	*PLINE
R,	*REDRAW
RO,	*ROTATE
S,	*STYLE
SC,	*SCALE
ST,	*STRETCH
T,	*TEXT
TR,	*TRIM
WB,	*WBLOCK
Z,	*ZOOM

When abbreviations are *entered* in place of a selection from the tool icons, the prompts associated with the command automatically appear at the command line. As an example, to draw a circle:

> **Command:** *enter* c (abbreviation for circle) *right-click* (or Return)
> **CIRCLE 3P/2P/TTR/<Center point>:** enter coordinates (or pick a point on screen)
> **Diameter/<Radius>:** *enter* the required radius figures (or *pick* a point on screen)
> **Command:**

As with all command prompts any prompt in brackets (< >) will be the current prompt.

Example drawings

The methods of constructing drawings follow prescribed sequences, which you can follow to produce the completed drawing. Please remember that there will be other methods in AutoCAD which would achieve the same constructions. All the commands used in this chapter will be in the form of abbreviations. Command prompts as they appear at the command line will be included.

Example drawing 1 – an engineering drawing

This drawing will be a third angle orthographic projection of a V-pulley. It can be constructed either:

1. Within a simple sheet layout such as that shown in Fig. 6.3, which is quite suitable for most student work; or:

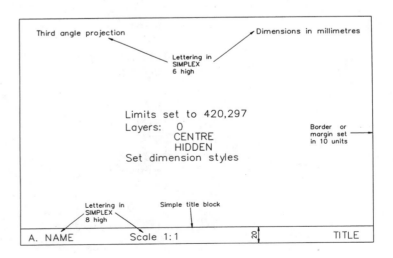

Fig. 6.3 A simple A3 sheet layout

2. Within a more complicated A3 sheet layout such as might be used in the design office of an engineering firm – Fig. 6.4.

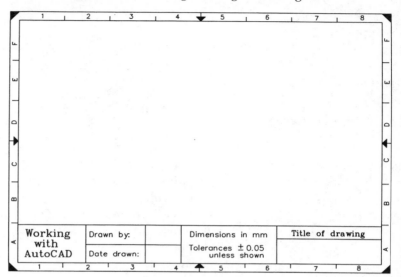

Fig. 6.4 An A3 sheet layout such as might be used in the design office of an engineering firm

It is not at all a bad idea to prepare an A3 sheet outline such as suggested in Figs. 6.3 and 6.4 and save it to a file name such as *A3SHEET.DWG*. When starting a new drawing *Left-click* on **File** in the **Menu bar** then *left-click* on **Open...** followed by another *left-click* on the name **a3sheet** in the **Open Drawing File** dialogue box. This will allow you to commence work straight away without having to draw border lines, title block etc. The settings for this sheet should be similar to those given on page 27 under the heading **Setting up a prototype acad.dwg file**.

The completed drawing in this example is shown in Fig. 6.12 on page 82. Although the drawing is shown constructed within the A3 sheet suggested in Fig. 6.4, it can just as well be constructed in the simpler A3 sheet layout suggested in Fig. 6.3.

Stage 1 – Fig. 6.5

1. *Left-click* on **Open As...** in the **File** menu. Open your a3sheet.dwg;
2. *Left-click* on the **Layer name** button in the **Toolbar.** *Left-click* on **CENTRE**;
3. Press **F9** to set **SNAP** on. Check that **S** is highlighted in the **Toolbar**;

Command: *enter* l (for LINE) *right-click*
Line from point: *enter* 65.175
To point: *enter* 225,175
To point: *right-click*
Command: *right-click*

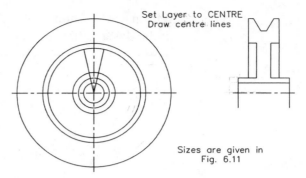

Set Layer to CENTRE
Draw centre lines

Sizes are given in
Fig. 6.11

Fig. 6.5 Stage 1 of Example
drawing 1

LINE From point: *enter* 145,225
To point: *enter* 145,95
To point: *right-click*
Command:
LINE From point: *enter* 280,175
To point; *enter* 340,175
To point: *right-click*
Command:

4. *Left-click* on the **Layer name** button in the **Toolbar.** *Left-click* on **0**;

   Command: *enter* c (for CIRCLE) *right-click*
   CIRCLE 3P/2P/TTR/<Center point>: *left-click* on 145,175
   Diameter<Radius>: *enter* 75 *right-click*
   Command: *right-click*
   CIRCLE 3P/2P/TTR/<Center point>: *left-click* on 145,175 repeat
      for circles of radius 50,45,20,15 and 10
   Command: *enter* l (for LINE) *right-click*

5. Draw the lines for the sides of the slot in the front view;
6. Draw the part end view as shown in Fig. 6.6 Sizes in Fig. 6.10 on
   page 81;
7. *Left-click* on **Save As...** in the **File** menu and save the drawing to a
   suitable filename, e.g. pulley. It is preferable to save to your own
   floppy disk in, say drive a:. The full filename of your saved drawing
   is then is *a:\pulley.dwg;*

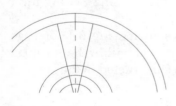

Fig. 6.6 The **Zoom** window
for **Trimming** the slot shape

Stage 2 – Fig. 6.7

1. **Command:** *enter* z (for Zoom) *right-click*
   All/Center/Dynamic/Extents/Previous/Window/<Scale(X/XP>:
   enter w (for Window) *right-click*
   First corner: *pick* **Other corner:** *pick*
   Command: – see Fig 6.6
2. Using the sequence:
   Command: *enter* tr (for TRIM) *right-click*

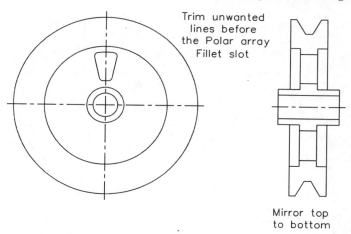

Trim unwanted
lines before
the Polar array
Fillet slot

Mirror top
to bottom

Fig. 6.7 Second stage of
Example drawing 1

Select objects: *pick*
<Select objects to trim>/Undo: *pick*
Trim the upper of the six slots in the front view to its shape;
3. **Command:** *enter* f (for FILLET) *right-click*
   FILLET Polyline/Radius/Select first object>: *enter* r (for Radius)
   right-click
   Enter fillet radius<0>: *enter* 3 *right-click*
   Command:
   FILLET Polyline/Radius/Select first object>: *pick*
   Select second object>: *pick*
   Command:
   and so on to add **Fillets** to the upper slot in the front view;
4. **Command:** *enter* mi (for MIRROR) *right-click*
   MIRROR Select objects: w (for Window) *right-click*
   First corner: *pick* **Second corner:** *pick*
   First point on mirror line: *pick* 280,175 **Second point:** *pick*
   340,175
   Delete old objects?<N>: n *right-click*
   Command:
   This will mirror the upper part of the end view to the lower part;
5. *Left-click* on **Save** in the **File** menu and save the drawing;

   Stage 3 – Fig. 6.8

1. **Command:** *enter* array *right-click*
   Select objects: *enter* w (for Window) *right-click*
   First corner: *pick* **Other corner:** *pick* (and window the slot in
   the front view)
   Select objects: *right-click*
   Rectangular or Polar array(R/P)<R>: *enter* p (for Polar) *right-
   click*

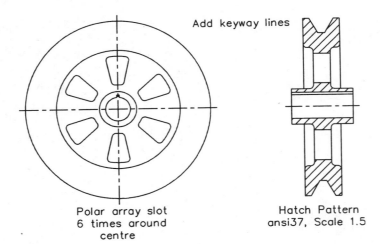

Add keyway lines

Polar array slot
6 times around
centre

Hatch Pattern
ansi37, Scale 1.5

Fig. 6.8 Stage 3 of Example
drawing 1

Center point of array: *pick* the point 145,175
Number of items: *enter* 6 *right-click*
Angle to fill (+=ccw,-=cw)<360>): *right-click* (to accept)
Rotate objects as they are copied?<Y>: *right-click* (to accept)
Command:

2. **Command:** *enter* l (for LINE) *right-click*
   and add the lines for the keyway in both front and end views;
3. **Command:** *enter* bh for BHATCH) *right-click*
   The **Boundary Hatch** dialogue box appears. By a series of *left-clicks*
   on appropriate buttons and features in the dialogue boxes of
   Boundary Hatch – Fig. 6.9 – add hatching to the end-sectional
   view. The **Hatch Pattern** is **ansi37** at **Scale** 1.5.
4. *Left-click* on **Save** in the **File** menu and save the drawing.

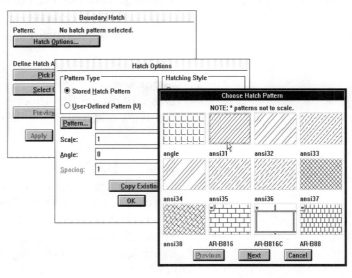

Fig. 6.9 The **BHatch**
dialogue boxes

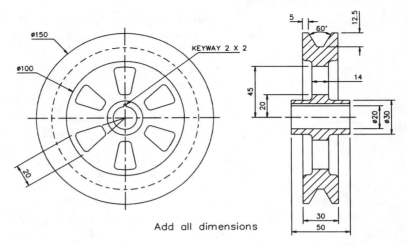

Fig. 6.10 Stage 4 of Example drawing 1

Add all dimensions

Stage 4 – Fig. 6.10

1. **Command:** *enter* s (for Style) *right-click*
   STYLE Text style name (or ?)<SIMPLEX>: *right-click* (to accept)
   Existing style. *double-left-click* on **simplex.shx** in the **Select Font Style** dialogue box which appears – Fig. 6.11

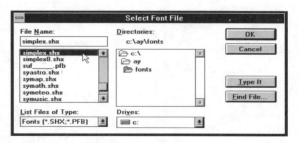

Fig. 6.11 The **Select Font Style** dialogue box

   Existing height Height<6>: *enter* 4 *right-click*
   Width factor<1>: *right-click* (to accept)
   Obliquing angle<0>: *right-click* (to accept)
   Backwards<N>: *right-click* (to accept)
   Upside down<N>: *right-click* (to accept)
   Vertical<N>: *right-click* (to accept)
   Simplex is the current text style.
   Regenerating drawing.
   Command:
    This will set the text style for adding dimensions;
2. **Command:** *enter* dim (Dimensions) *right-click*
   Dim: *enter* hor (for Horizontal) *right-click*
   First extension line origin: *pick* 285,160
   Second extension line origin: *pick* 335,160

Dimension line location: *pick* 340,70
Dimension text<50>: *right-click* (to accept)
Dim:
This enters the dimension of 50 in the end view. Other dimensions are entered in a similar manner with ver (for vertical), dia (for diameter), rad (for radius) or l (for leader) in response to the **Dim:** prompt.
3. *Left-click* on **Save** in the **File** menu and save the drawing;

Stage 5 – Fig. 6.12

My own preference when constructing engineering drawings of this type in AutoCAD is to draw all outlines as **Plines** of a thickness of 0.6 or 0.7 units when working in an A3 sheet graphics window. Other operators may prefer using lines instead of plines. The final drawing in this series for Example 1 – Fig. 6.12 – shows my preferred drawing with outlines drawn with Plines of 0.7 thickness. See page 34 on which there is a description of drawing line plines, circle plines and arc plines. This last drawing has been constructed in an industrial style drawing sheet.
Zoom: Use zoom (window or crossing) frequently when constructing the smaller details in any drawing in CAD.

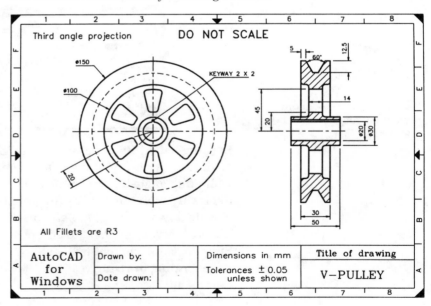

Fig. 6.12 The completed Example drawing 1

Example drawing 2 – a building drawing

Figure 6.13 is a three-view first angle orthographic projection of a design for a building. The stages in constructing the drawing were:

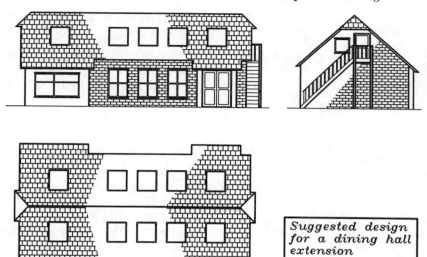

Fig. 6.13 The completed
Example drawing 1

Stage 1 – Setting Layers

1. *Left-click* on **New...** in the **File** menu. *Left-click* on **OK** in the **Create New Drawing** dialogue box;
2. Before commencing construction of the drawing, *left-click* on the **Layer** button in the **Toolbar**. In the **Layer Control** dialogue box which appears. Make two new layers – **Hatch** and **Hatch01**.

Stage 2 – Front elevation outline – Fig. 6.14

1. **Command:**
   PLINE From point: *enter* 65,180 *right-click*
   Arc/Close/Halfwidth/Length/Undo/Width/<Endpoint of line>: *enter* w (for Width) *right-click*
   Starting width<0>: *enter* 0.7 *right-click*
   Ending width <0.7>: *right-click* (to accept)
   Arc/Close/Halfwidth/Length/Undo/Width/<Endpoint of line>: *enter* @225,0 *right-click*

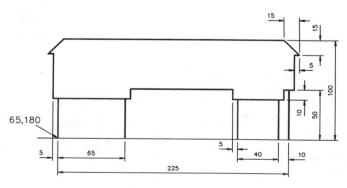

Fig. 6.14 Stage 2 of Example
drawing 2

Arc/Close/Halfwidth/Length/Undo/Width/<Endpoint of line>:
enter @0,50 *right-click*
Arc/Close/Halfwidth/Length/Undo/Width/<Endpoint of line>:
enter @5,0 *right-click*
Arc/Close/Halfwidth/Length/Undo/Width/<Endpoint of line>:
enter @0,35 *right-click*
and so on to complete the outline – dimensions given in Fig. 6.14.

8. *Left-click* on **Save As...** in the **File** menu and save the drawing to a suitable filename – e.g. building. It is preferable to save to your own floppy disk in say drive a:. The full filename of your saved drawing is then is *a:\building.dwg;*

   Stage 3 – Adding windows and doors to the front elevation – Fig. 6.15

1. **Command:**
   PLINE From point: *left-click* at 150,190
   Arc/Close/Halfwidth/Length/Undo/Width/<Endpoint of line>:
   enter w (for Width) *right-click*
   Starting width<0>: *enter* 0 *right-click*
   Ending width <0>: *right-click* (to accept)
   Arc/Close/Halfwidth/Length/Undo/Width/<Endpoint of line>:
   enter @20,0 *right-click*
   Arc/Close/Halfwidth/Length/Undo/Width/<Endpoint of line>:
   enter @0,30 *right-click*
   Arc/Close/Halfwidth/Length/Undo/Width/<Endpoint of line>:
   enter @-20,0 *right-click*
   Arc/Close/Halfwidth/Length/Undo/Width/<Endpoint of line>:
   enter c (for Close) *right-click*
   Command:

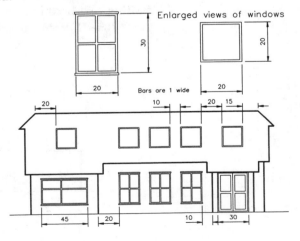

Fig. 6.15 Stage 3 of Example drawing 2

2. **Command:** *enter* o (for Offset) *right-click*
   Offset distance or Through>Through>: *enter* 1 *right-click*
   Select object to offset; *left-click* the pline just drawn
   Side to offset: *left-click* inside the pline
   Side to offset: *right-click*
   Command:

3. Draw plines in a similar manner to construct the bars of the 50 x 30 window. Add the rectangles top and bottom of the window;

4. In a similar manner construct a drawing of the smaller window starting at 90,245

5. **Command:** *enter* cp (for Copy) *right-click*
   COPY Select objects: *enter* w (for Window) *right-click*
   First corner: *pick* above and to left of the 50 x 30 window **Other corner:** *left-click* to the right and below the window
   Select objects: *right-click*
   <Base point or displacement>/Multiple>: *enter* m (for Multiple) *right-click*
   Base point: *left-click* on bottom left corner of the 50 x 30 window **Second point of displacement:** *left-click* at one position for the window in the view
   Second point of displacement: *left-click* at a second position for the window in the view
   Second point of displacement: *left-click* at the third position for the window in the view
   Second point of displacement: *right-click*
   Command:

6. In a similar manner position the smaller windows in the roof of the front elevation;

7. Construct the larger window on the left of the view – with **pline** and **offset**;

8. Construct the doors with **pline** and **offset**.

9. *Left-click* on **Save** in the **File** menu and save the drawing.

Stage 4 – Outline of roof in plan – Fig. 6.16

1. In a manner similar to that in which the outline of the front elevation was constructed, with the aid of **Pline** (set to a width of 0.7), draw the outline of the plan – Fig. 6.17 – commencing at the bottom left-hand corner at coordinate 65,20.

2. *Left-click* on **Save** in the **File** menu and save the drawing.

Stage 5 – Add the end view – Fig. 6.17

1. Construct the end elevation with the aid of **Pline** (set to width of 0.7). The dimensions of the end elevation depend, of course, upon

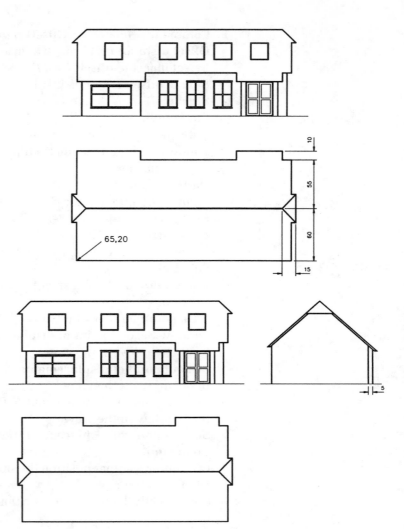

Fig. 6.16 Stage 4 of Example drawing 2

Fig 6.17 Stage 5 of Example drawing 2

the dimensions of the front elevation and plan, apart from the 5 unit dimension given in Fig. 6.18.

2. *Left-click* on **Save** in the **File** menu and save the drawing.

Stage 6 – Add stair and roof and end-elevation windows and door (Fig. 6.18)

1. Details of the stair dimensions are given in a separate drawing. This is drawn with the aid of **Pline**, **Line** and **Offset**;

2. Add the windows in the plan. The sizes must be taken from the front elevation and end elevation by projection, but draw one with the aid of **Pline** and **Offset** and then **Multiple Copy** to other positions;

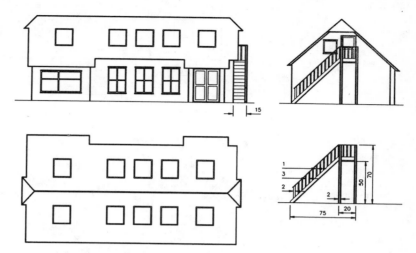

Fig. 6.18 Stage 6 of Example drawing 2

3. Add a door and a window in the End elevation – again with the aid of **Pline** and **Offset**;
4. Project the stair into the front elevation. Remember this will be a view of the rear of the stair. Treads can be drawn with **Offset**;
5. *Left-click* on **Save** in the **File** menu and save the drawing.

Stage 7 – Hatching Fig. 6.19 to 6.21

1. *Left-click* on the **Layer** button in the **Toolbar**. Make **HATCH01** the current layer – Fig. 6.19;
2. With the aid of **Object Snaps** draw lines somewhat like those shown in Fig. 6.20. It is important that the lines coinciding with the on screen drawing fit exactly onto the existing lines – this is why the use of **Osnaps** is necessary. The lines at angles to the current drawing can be placed in any suitable position;

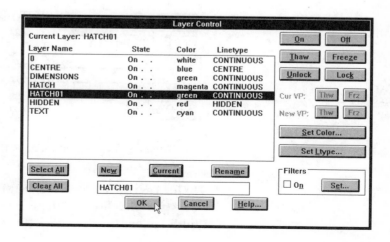

Fig. 6.19 The **Layer Control** dialogue box for Drawing Example 2

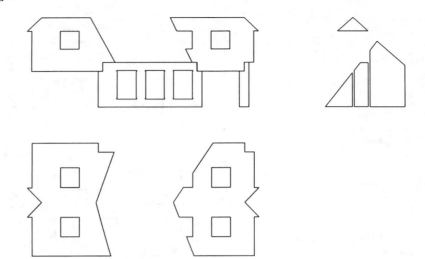

Fig. 6.20 Stage 7 of Example
drawing 2

3. Make the layer **HATCH** current;
4. **Command:** *enter* bh (for Bhatch) *right-click*
   Hatch the areas as shown in Fig. 6.21 using the two patterns:
   For the bricks – **AR-B816** to **Scale 0.025**;
   For the roof tiles – **AR-B88** to **scale 0.025**;
5. Turn layer **HATCH01** off;
6. *Left-click* on **Save** in the **File** menu and save the drawing.

Fig. 6 21 . Stage 7 of Example
drawing 2

Stage 8 – Title – Fig. 6.22

1. **Command:**
   STYLE Text style name(or?)<SIMPLEX>: *enter* italict *right-click*
   New style. Height<>>: *enter* 8 *right-click*
   Width factor<1>: *right-click* (to accept)

Fig. 6.22 Stage 8 of Drawing
Exercise 2

Obliquing angle<0>: *right-click* (to accept)
Backwards<N>: *right-click* (to accept)
Upside-down<N>: *right-click* (to accept)
Vertical<N>: *right-click* (to accept)
ITALICT is now the current text style.
Command:

2. **Command:** *enter* t (for Text) *right-click*
   TEXT Justify/Style/<Start point>: *right-click* (to accept)
   Text: *enter* Suggested design *right-click*
   Command: *right-click*
   TEXT Justify/Style/<Start point>: *right-click* (to accept)
   Text: *enter* for a dining hall *right-click*
   Command: *right-click*
   TEXT Justify/Style/<Start point>: *right-click* (to accept)
   Text: *enter* Extension *right-click*
   Command:

3. *Left-click* on **Save** in the **File** menu and save the drawing.

Example drawing 3 – a flower design – Fig. 6.23

Stage 1 – Fig. 6.24

1. *Left-click* on **New...** in the **File** menu. *Left-click* on **OK** in the **Create New Drawing** dialogue box;
2. Fig. 6.24 shows the method of constructing the flower and leaf part of the design, using **Pline**, **Ellipse**, **Array**, **Arc** and **Mirror**. These commands involve the following prompts:

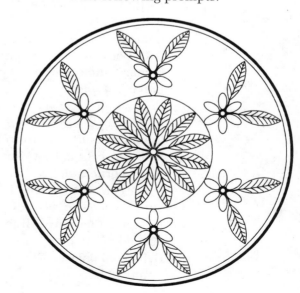

Fig. 6.23 The finished
Example drawing 3

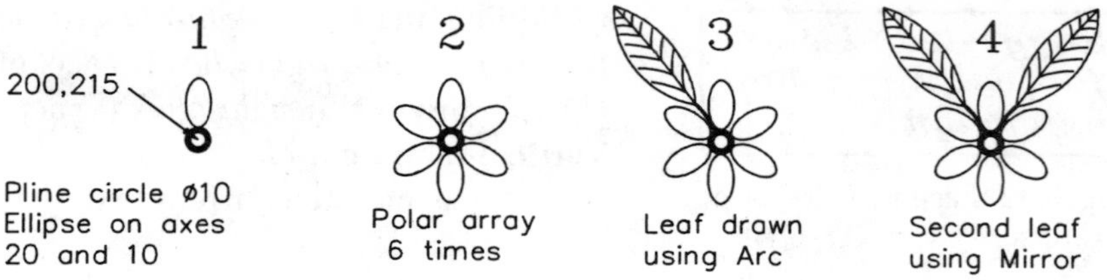

1

200,215

Pline circle Ø10
Ellipse on axes
20 and 10

2

Polar array
6 times

3

Leaf drawn
using Arc

4

Second leaf
using Mirror

Fig. 6.24 Stage 1 of Example
drawing 3

PLINE
Command: *enter* pl (for Pline) *right-click*
PLINE From point: *enter* 195,215 *right-click*
Arc/Close/Halfwidth/Length/Undo/Width/<Endpoint of line>:
enter w (for Width) *right-click*
Starting width<0>: *enter* 2 *right-click*
Ending width <2.0>: *right-click* (to accept)
Arc/Close/Halfwidth/Length/Undo/Width/<Endpoint of line>:
enter a (for Arc) *right-click*
<Endpoint of arc>: *enter* s (for Second) *right-click*
Second point: *enter* 200,220 *right-click*
End point: *enter* 205,215 *right-click*
ELLIPSE
Command: *enter* ellipse *right-click*
<Axis endpoint 1>/Center: *enter* c (for Centre) *right-click*
Center of ellipse: *enter* 200,230 *right-click*
Axis endpoint: *enter* 200,220 *right-click*
<Other axis distance>/Rotation: *enter* 205,230 *right-click*
Command:
ARRAY – see page 58
ARC
Command: *enter* a (for Arc) *right-click*
ARC Center/<Start point>: *pick*
Center/End/Second point>: pick
End point: *pick*
Command:
MIRROR
Command: *enter* mirror *right-click*
Select objects: *enter* w (for Window) *right-click*
Firsts corner: *pick*
Other corner: *pick*
Select objects: *right-click*
First point on mirror line: *pick*
Second point: *pick*
Delete old objects<N>: *right-click* (to accept)
Command:

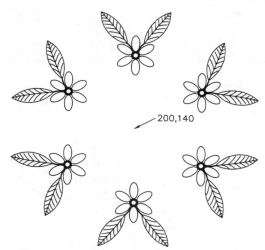

Fig. 6.25 Stage 2 of Example
drawing 3

3. *Left-click* on **Save As...** in the **File** menu and save the drawing with a filename of *a:\design.dwg*.

Stage 2 – Fig. 6.25

1. **Array** the flower and leaves arrangement six times around the centre point – coordinate point 200, 140;
2. *Left-click* on **Save** in the **File** menu and save the drawing.

Stage 3 – Fig. 6.26

1. With the aid of the **Circle** and the **Arc** commands draw the circle (radius 5) and the leaf;
2. Draw circles of centre 220,140 and radii 55 and 125;
3. Draw a **Pline** circle of radius 130 and of width 2;
4. *Left-click* on **Save** in the **File** menu and save the drawing.

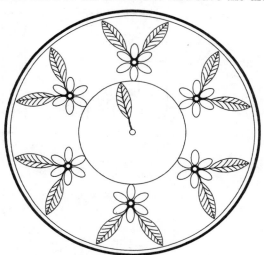

Fig. 6.26 Stage 3 of Example
drawing 3

Stage 4

1. **Polar Array** the leaf pattern 12 times around the centre 220,140;
2. *Left-click* on **Save** in the **File** menu and save the drawing.

Questions

1. Why is the command **Trim** so important in drawing with the aid of AutoCAD for Windows?
2. All CAD software systems will have a **Zoom** command. Why is this?
3. Why should an AutoCAD operator wish to change the acad.pgp file? In which directory is it usually found and how are the changes made?
4. When would you use **Pline** in preference to using **Line**?
5. What happens when the command **Style** is called and what is the purpose of the command?
6. In the Example drawing 2, two extra layers were included in the drawing. Why was this thought to be necessary?
7. What is the difference between a **Polar** and a **Rectangular Array**?

Exercises

1. Figure 6.27. The parts of a small cramp made from steel are shown. Construct a three-view Third angle orthographic projection of the cramp with its parts assembled. Your views should include the sectional view A-A. Fully dimension your drawing and include a title block.

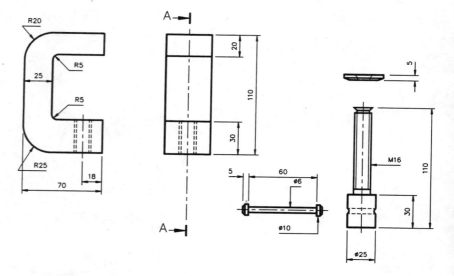

Fig. 6.27 Exercise 1

2. Figure 6.28. A pattern is shown based on dividing an ellipse into 12 parts using a **Block**. Working to dimensions of your own choice construct a similar pattern to that given.

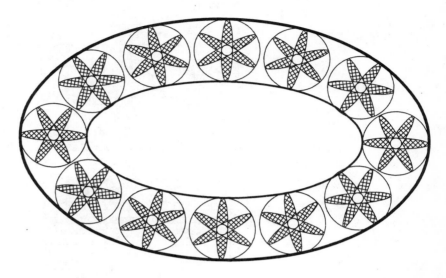

Fig. 6.28 Exercise 2

3. Figure 6.29 is another pattern which has been formed with the aid of **Array**. Construct a similar pattern working to dimensions of your own choice.

Fig. 6.29 Exercise 3

4. Figure 6.30 is a three-view First angle orthographic projection of a small bungalow. Working to the given dimensions, but using any other sizes of your own choice construct a similar three-view drawing.

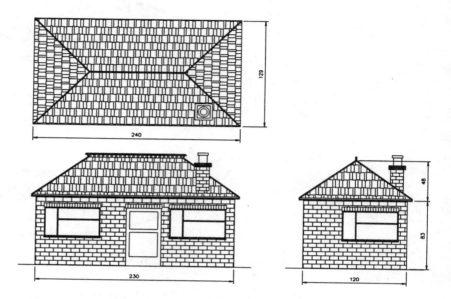

Fig. 6.30 Exercise 4

5. Figure 6.31 shows a two-view First angle projection of a small chest of drawers. Copy the two views, but in Third angle projection.

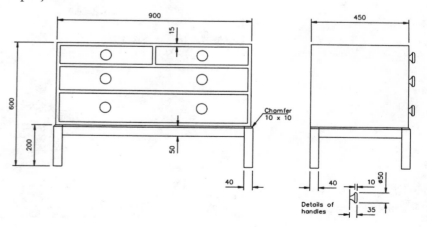

Fig. 6.31 Exercise 5

CHAPTER 7

The View and Edit menus

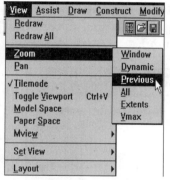

Fig. 7.1 The **View** pull-down menu with the **Zoom** sub-menu

The View pull-down menu and the Aerial View window

The most important command in the **View** menu is **Zoom**. This command allows the operator to construct the smallest details in a drawing in the graphics window and also allows tiny errors to be clearly seen, so that they can be corrected. A *left-click* on **Zoom** in the **Menu bar** brings down the **View** menu. Another *left-click on Zoom* in the menu brings down the **Zoom** sub-menu (Fig. 7.1).

Left-click on the **Aerial View** icon in the **Toolbar** (Fig. 7.2) and the **Aerial Window** (Fig. 7.3) appears in the graphics window. The **Aerial View** window shows a small but complete version of the drawing under construction on the screen. *Left-click* on **Window** in the **Zoom** sub-menu and follow the prompts that appear at the command line:

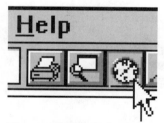

Fig. 7.2 The **Aerial View** icon

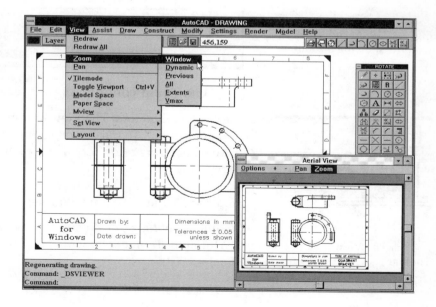

Fig. 7.3 The **Aerial View** window

Command: '_zoom
All/Center/Dynamic/Extents/Left/Previous/Vmax/Window/
    <Scale(X/XP)>:_window
First corner: *pick* Other corner: *pick*
Command:

That part of the drawing enclosed by the **Zoom** window appears in the graphics window and, at the same time, a box with a thick outline appears in the **Aerial View** window showing the area of the drawing covered by the **Zoom** window in the graphics window (Fig. 7.4). This allows the operator to see which part of a drawing is being worked on at the moment. The **Aerial View** window facility is of particular value when working on a drawing constructed within **Limits** larger than those dealt with in this book – as, for example, constructing a drawing to be printed on an A0 sheet (1189 × 841 mm).

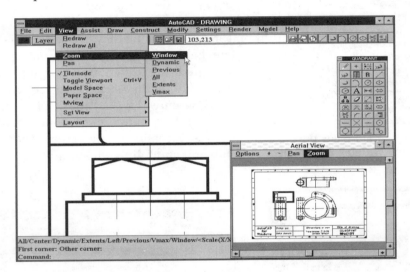

Fig. 7.4 The **Aerial View** window showing a **zoom** window area

The Zoom commands

Fig. 7.5 The **View** icon in the **Toolbar**

Zoom can be called from The **View** pull-down menu; the **View** icon in the **Toolbar** (Fig. 7.5); the on-screen menus – **DISPLAY**, followed by **ZOOM**; by *entering* z (for Zoom) at the keyboard, followed by a *right-click*.

No matter which of these methods is adopted, the following prompts appear at the command line:

Command: *enter* z (for Zoom) *right-click*
    **All/Center/Dynamic/Extents/Left/Previous/Vmax/Window/
    <Scale(X/XP)>:**

These prompts operate as follows:

All: *enter* a (for All) and the whole drawing under construction appears in the graphics window within the area set by the **Limits** command;

Center: *enter* c (for Center) and *pick* a point on screen. The drawing changes so that the *picked* point is central to the graphics window;

Dynamic: *enter* d (for Dynamic) and a thin rectangular outline appears with a cross at its centre. Hold down the left-hand mouse button and an arrow appears up against the left-hand line of the rectangle. Holding down the left-hand button, move the mouse and the rectangle changes size. *Right-click* and only that part of the drawing which was in the selected Dynamic window reappears in the graphics window (Fig. 7.6);

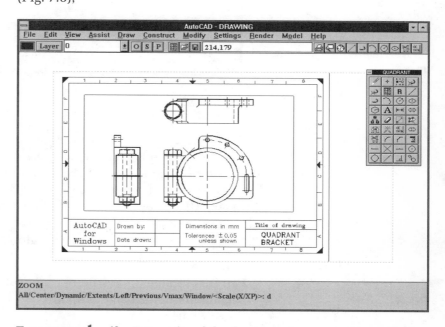

Fig. 7.6 The **Zoom** Dynamic screen

Extents: *enter* e (for Extents) and the drawing changes to fit exactly into the graphics window;

Left: *enter* i (for Left). A prompt appears **Lower left corner point:** select a point on screen and the drawing changes so that the picked point is at the lower left hand corner of the graphics window;

Previous: *enter* p (for Previous) and, if in a zoom window, the drawing reverts to the last called zoom;

Vmax: *enter* v (for Vmax) and the drawing zooms out as far as possible (Fig. 7.7);

Window: *enter* w (for Window) and *pick* the window corners;

Scale: *enter* a fraction (e.g. 1/2) or a decimal (e.g. 0.5) and the drawing re-appears on screen at the stated scale.

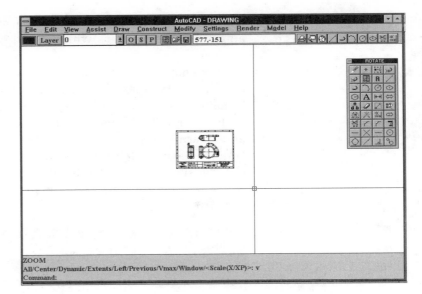

Fig. 7.7 The result of a **Zoom Vmax**

Other View commands

Redraw: A *left-click* on **Redraw** redraws the screen. This is useful to eliminate marks on screen which may occur when erasing, or using other **Modify** commands. Entering r (for Redraw) has the same effect. Only the current viewport is redrawn – see **Layout** later in this chapter;
Redraw All: If several viewports are on screen – see later – all viewports are redrawn;
Pan: A *left-click* on **Pan** brings the following to the command line:

> Command:
> **Pan Displacement:** *pick* point on screen
> **Second point:** *pick* another point
> Command:

and the drawing pans – moves on in the graphics window between the two picked points;
Tilemode, **Toggle Viewport**, **Model Space**, **Paper Space**, **Mview** and **Set View** are all commands associated with 3D (three-dimensional) constructions and so will be dealt with later (page 000 onwards);
Layout: A *left-click* on **Layout** brings down a sub-menu (Fig. 7.8). A *left-click* on **Tiled Viewports** in the sub-menu brings the Tiled Viewport Layout dialogue box on screen. *Left-click* on **Three: left** and the graphics window changes as shown in Fig. 7.9, with three **Viewports**. Viewports are not used to any extent in 2D drawing, but become of importance when constructing 3D drawings (pages 000 onwards).

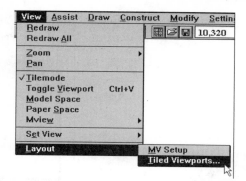

Fig. 7.8 **Tiled Viewports...** from the **View** pull-down menu

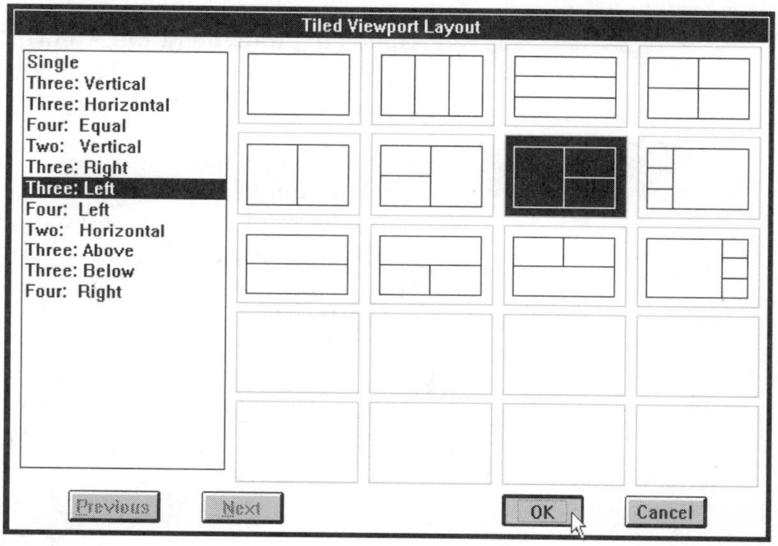

Fig. 7.9 The **Tiled Viewport Layout** Dialogue box

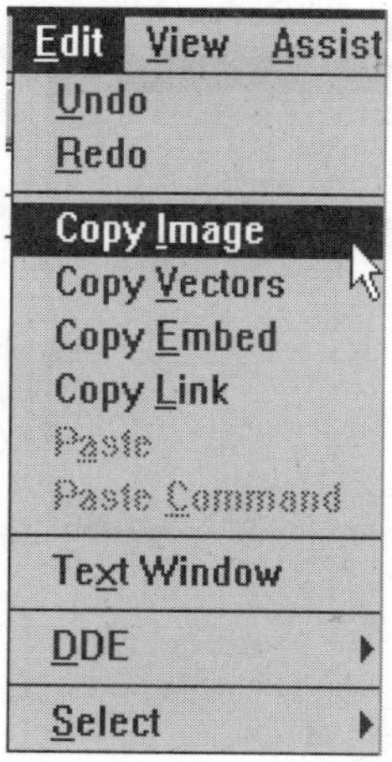

Fig. 7.10 The **Edit** pull-down menu

The Edit pull-down menu

Left-click on **Edit** in the **Menu bar**. The **Edit** menu appears (Fig. 7.10). Selection of the commands in the menu results in the following:
Undo: *Left-click* on this command and the last action taken will be undone. For example, if a line has just been drawn it will disappear from the screen. Repeated *left-clicks* on the command will eventually result in the whole drawing being undone;
Redo: The last feature acted upon by **Undo** will reappear, but note that only one **redo** can take place. If a series of **Undo**s have been called, only the last of them will be **Redo**ne.

The Copy commands from Edit

These all appear to have a similar action, but each really operates differently to produce what appears to be similar results. Before trying out these commands, *Left-click* on the **Clipboard** icon in **Main** window of the Windows **Program Manager** (Fig. 7.11).

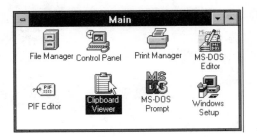

Fig. 7.11 The **Clipboard** icon in the **Main** window

Open any drawing in the AutoCAD for Windows graphics screen. *Left-click* on **Copy Image** in the **View** menu. The command line changes to:

Command:_copy image
Select an area of the screen: a small cross cursor appears. Use the cursor to window an area of the drawing; in the example given (Fig. 7.12) the front view of the drawing has been windowed. The selected area appears on the Windows clipboard.
Command:

Any feature on the clipboard can be pasted into other applications, such as word processing packages, desktop packages or similar applications. This facility allows AutoCAD drawings to be **Pasted** into work sheets, brochures, letters etc.

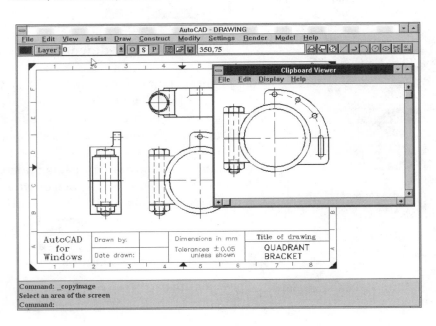

Fig. 7.12 The Windows **Clipboard** with the front view after using **Copy image**

A similar result can be obtained from **Copy Vectors** except that, instead of a raster file being obtained from the copy action, a vector file can be obtained. Whereas a raster file would show lines in a slightly jagged manner when printed, a vector file would show clean lines. This is because AutoCAD drawing are saved as vector-style files.

If the **Copy Link** command is used, the *whole* of the AutoCAD drawing showing in the graphics window is treated as an OLE (Object Linking and Embedding) file, which can be pasted immediately into other applications. An example of a work sheet built up from an AutoCAD drawing pasted from a **Copy Link** AutoCAD drawing and embedded, with added text from the DTP package, is shown in Fig. 7.13.

Note: As stated on page 16, one can switch between applications in Windows by pressing the **Alt** and **Tab** keys. Fig. 7.12 was obtained by using this facility *after* the **Copy Image** command had been called in AutoCAD.

DDE (Dynamic Data Exchange)

Although this AutoCAD facility will not be used to any extent by student readers or beginners learning how to use AutoCAD, the **DDE** command is of interest here. In order to be able to use this **Dynamic Data Exchange** facility, a spreadsheet such as Microsoft Excel must be one of the applications which is available in Windows. The **DDE** command will enable drawing data from an AutoCAD drawing to be

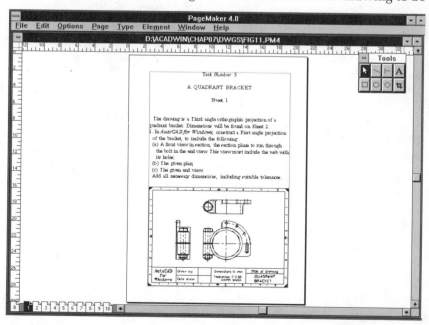

Fig. 7.13 An AutoCAD drawing embedded in a work task sheet in a DTP package

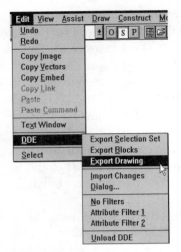

Fig. 7.14 The **Edit** menu with the **DDE** sub-menu

dynamically passed on to a spreadsheet. Figure 7.14 shows the **Edit** menu with the **DDE** sub-menu and with **Export Drawing** selected from the sub-menu. Figure 7.15 shows the data which has been automatically (dynamically) passed from the drawing to the spreadsheet. If you experiment, you will be able to change the data in the spreadsheet, which automatically updates the drawing in AutoCAD. You will also find it possible to change features in the drawing which automatically change the data in the spreadsheet.

Other commands in the Edit menu

Paste: If a previously copied **Image**, **Vector**, **Embed** or **Link** is on the clipboard, it can be pasted into the current drawing, or into another AutoCAD drawing. Remember it is possible to have two AutoCAD graphics windows on screen at the same time and it is possible to copy from one drawing to the other via the clipboard or through **Copy Link**;

Text Window: A *left-click* on this command name brings the AutoCAD Text Window on screen. This shows all the commands used in the current drawing session and other information relevant to the current drawing. The AutoCAD Text Window can also be called by pressing the key **F2**. Press a second time to get back to the AutoCAD graphics window – **F2** toggles between the two windows;

Select: A *left-click* on **Select** and a sub-menu with the selection prompts appears – **Point**, **Window** etc. – these are the same as those seen at the command line when some commands are called – e.g. **Zoom**.

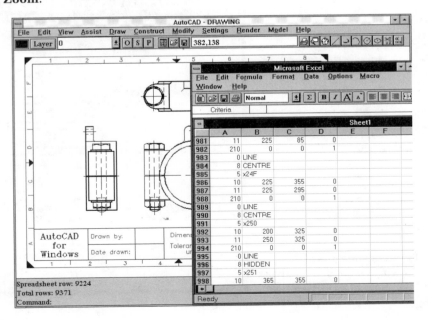

Fig. 7.15 **Excel** spreadsheet with **DDE** data from an AutoCAD drawing

CHAPTER 8

Pictorial drawing

Introduction

Several forms of pictorial drawing are possible in AutoCAD for Windows. Later in this book we will be dealing with 3D drawing, involving coordinates in x, y and z directions. Note that, although the drawing methods described in this chapter appear as if 3D drawings are produced, in fact they are true 2D drawings – they involve coordinates in only the x and y directions.

Before commencing pictorial drawings in AutoCAD **Snap** will need to be set. The setting can be made from the command line. There are four possible settings for **Snap: Standard**, which we have used so far; **Isometric**, which is for isometric drawing; **Aspect**, which allows the vertical snap spacing to be different from the horizontal spacing; **Rotate**, which rotates the snap (and grid) pattern to any angle:

> **Command:** *enter* snap *right-click*
> **Snap spacing or ON/OFF/Aspect/Rotate/Style<0>:** *enter* s (for Style) *right-click*
> **Standard/Isometric<S>:** *enter* i (for Isometric) *right-click*
> **Vertical spacing<0>:** *enter* 5 *right-click*
> **Command:**

and the snap spacing is set to 30 degrees in both directions.

> **Command:** *enter* snap *right-click*
> **Snap spacing or ON/OFF/Aspect/Rotate/Style<0>:** *enter* a (for Aspect) *right-click*
> **Horizontal spacing<0>:** *enter* 5 *right-click*
> **Vertical spacing<0>:** *enter* 10 *right-click*
> **Command:**

and snap spacings are set to 5 units horizontally and 10 units vertically

> **Command:** *enter* snap *right-click*
> **Snap spacing or ON/OFF/Aspect/Rotate/Style<0>:** *enter* r (for Rotate) *right-click*

> **Base point<0,0>:** *right-click* (to accept)
> **Rotation angle<0>>:** *enter* 45 *right-click*
> **Command:**

and snap spacings are rotated at 45 degrees.

Snap positions can always be checked by setting **Grid** on – most easily by pressing the **F7** key.

The second method of setting **Snap** is by a *left-click* on **Settings** in the **Menu bar**, followed by another *left-click* on **Drawing Aids...** in the **Settings** menu. The **Drawing Aids** dialogue box appears in the graphics window (Fig. 8.1). As can be seen in Fig. 8.1, the settings for **Grid**

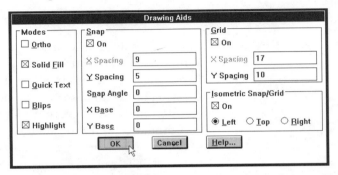

Fig. 8.1 Settings in the
Drawing Aids dialogue box

and **Snap** spacings can be entered in their appropriate boxes, **Grid and Snap** can be set on or off (boxes checked or not checked), the **Snap** angle can be set and a choice can be made between having the **Isometric Snap/Grid** on or off. The final **Isometric** settings – **Left**, **Top** or **Right** – determine the positions of the cursor cross-hairs, whether drawing the right-hand side, the top or the left-hand side of an isometric drawing. These settings refer to the **Isoplane** positions. **Ortho** can also be set in this dialogue box by pressing key **F8**. With **Snap** set for **Isometric** and with **Grid** on, the AutoCAD graphics window will appear as in Fig. 8.2, which includes an isometric drawing. Note the following in Fig. 8.2:

1. The cursor cross-hairs are set to **Top**;
2. **Grid** dots are showing at an isometric angle of 30 degrees.

Isoplane can be set to **Top**, **Right** or **Left** , in that order by pressing the **Ctrl** key followed by pressing the **e** key while **Ctrl** is still pressed. This *toggles* between the three isoplanes. They can also be set at the command line by entering isoplane.

An example of an isometric drawing (Fig. 8.3)

1. Set **Snap** to **Isometric** with a spacing of 5;
2. Set **Grid to a spacing of 10;**

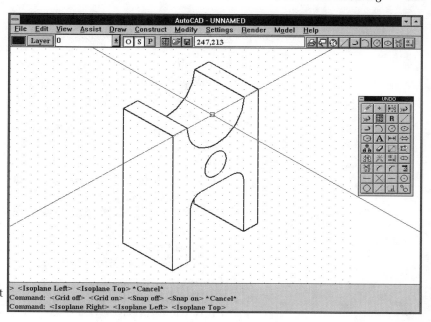

Fig. 8.2 The AutoCAD for Windows graphics window set up for isometric drawing

3. Set **Ortho** on;
4. Set **Isoplane** to **Top**;
5. **Command:** *enter* l (for Line) *right-click* (or *left-click* on the **Line** icon)
   LINE From point: @200<30 *right-click*
   To point: @100<330 *right-click*
   To point: @200<210 *right-click*
   To point: c (for Close *right-click*
   Command:
6. Set **Isoplane** to **Right**;
7. **Command:** *enter* l (for Line) *right-click* (or *left-click* on the **Line** icon)
   LINE From point: *enter* 165,115 *right-click*
   To point: *enter* @90<270 *right-click*
   To point: *enter* @200<30 *right-click*
   To point: *enter* @90<90 *right-click*
   To point: *right-click*
   Command:
8. Set **Isoplane** to **Left**;
9. **Command:** *enter* l (for Line) *right-click* (or *left-click* on the **Line** icon)
   LINE From point: *enter* 78,165 *right-click*
   To point: *enter* @90<270 *right-click*
   To point: *enter* @100<330 *right-click*

To point: *right-click*
Command:

This completes the outline of a "box" which will contain the drawing;

10. Set **Isoplane** to **Top** – preferably by pressing **Ctr/E**;
    Left-click on the **Ellipse** icon in the **Toolbox**;
    Command:_ellipse
    <Axis endpoint 1>/Center/Isocircle: *enter* i (for Isocircle)
    right-click
    Center of circle: *pick* 251,215
    <Circle radius</Diameter: *enter* 20 *right-click*
    Command: *right-click*
    ELLIPSE <Axis endpoint 1>/Center/Isocircle: *enter* i (for
    Isocircle) *right-click*
    Center of circle: *pick* 173,170
    <Circle radius</Diameter: *enter* 35 *right-click*
    Command: *right-click*

11. Set **Isoplane** to **Left**;
    Copy the larger isocircle 15 units down;
    Copy the smaller isocircle 30 units up;

12. With the aid of the **Quadrant Osnap** draw lines between the two
    smaller isocircles;

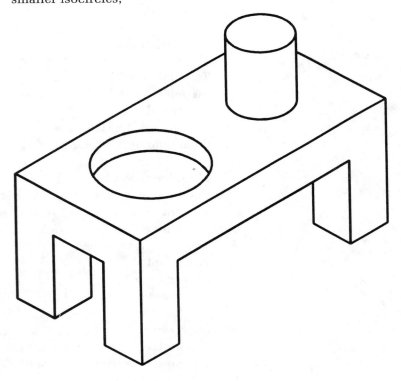

Fig. 8.3 The example isometric
drawing

13. **Trim** unwanted lines and parts of ellipses;
14. Changing **Isoplane** as necessary completes the "legs" of the drawing. The spacings for each part are 30 units.

Notes
1. In the above the *relative coordinate* method has been used with **Line**;
2. The angles in the coordinates are those common to isometric drawing;
3. If keys **Ctrl/D** are pressed, the angular relative coordinates will show up in the coordinate window in the **Toolbar** as the lines are drawn. It may be necessary to press the two keys twice before the numbers show in the window;
4. The setting of the **Isoplane** between **Top**, **Right** and **Left** will need to be carried out repeatedly. This can be done quickly by taking advantage of the keystrokes **Ctrl/E**;
5. When using the **Trim** command for trimming in isometric drawings, you may find it does not work properly because lines which appear to meet at a point are not, in fact, meeting. If this happens, try **Break** instead.

Isometric drawing exercises

1. Fig. 8.4. Copy the given drawing 1 to the dimensions given. Do not attempt the dimensions.
2. Fig. 8.4. Copy the given drawing 2 to the dimensions given. Do not attempt the dimensions.
3. Fig. 8.5. Copy the given isometric drawing to the dimensions given with the drawing.
4. Fig. 8.6. The upper orthographic projections are of an end bracket and a spindle, which are to be assembled as indicated in the lower

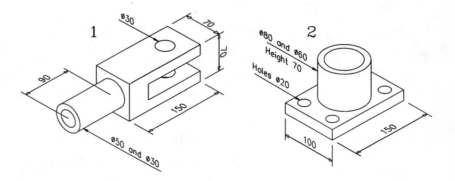

Fig. 8.4 Exercises 1 and 2

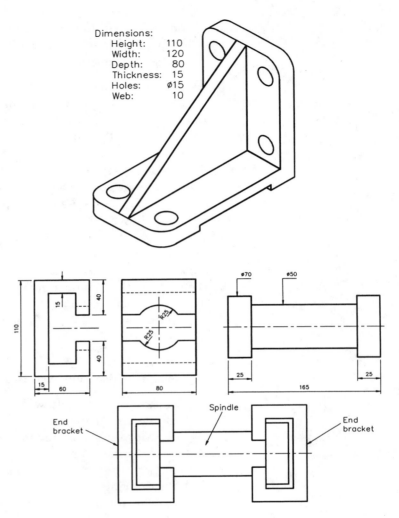

Dimensions:
Height: 110
Width: 120
Depth: 80
Thickness: 15
Holes: ⌀15
Web: 10

Fig. 8.5 Exercise 3

Fig. 8.6 Exercise 4

drawing. The spindle is placed between two of the end brackets. Construct an isometric drawing of the assembled parts, working to the given dimensions.

5. Fig. 8.7. Two parts of an assembly are shown in orthographic projections – Part B, which is made from a plastic material can be stretched to clip over Part A, which is made from cast zinc. Construct an isometric drawing of the two parts when assembled in the position shown by the assembly view.

Exploded isometric drawing

In an exploded pictorial drawing each part of an assembly is drawn as if pulled out from the part into which it fits. The "explosion" is

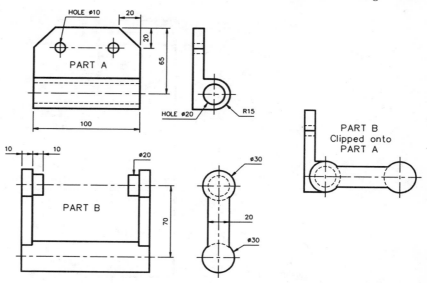

Fig. 8.7 Exercise 5

normally shown as if it has taken place in a straight line. Figure 8.8 is an example of a simple exploded isometric drawing which has been constructed in AutoCAD for Windows. This example is of a jointing method such as might be used in furniture making.

Figure 8.9 is a First angle orthographic projection of a corner of a frame jointed with a double mortise and tenon joint. Working to the given dimensions, construct an exploded isometric drawing of the joint with the rail pulled out from the upright.

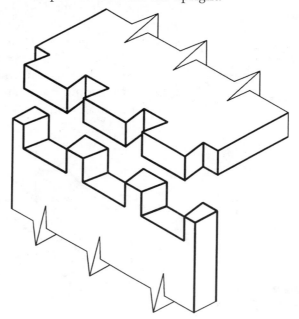

Fig. 8.8 A simple exploded isometric drawing of a dovetail joint

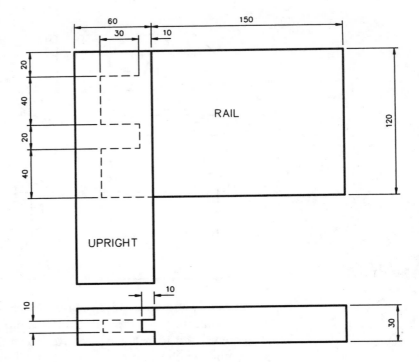

Fig. 8.9 Exercise 6

Cabinet drawing

Cabinet drawing is a particular type of *oblique* drawing. In general, to construct a cabinet drawing, draw a front view of the article. Then draw lines at an angle of 45 degrees from each corner of the front view. If drawing to full size, measure along each 45 degree line a distance equal to half the depth of the article. Complete the rear – more or less a copy of the front. The receding lines can be drawn at other angles – e.g. 30 or 60 degrees, but the more usual angle is 45 degrees. The scaling of receding lines can differ from half-scale, but again, half-scale is that most commonly accepted. Figure. 8.10 is an example of a

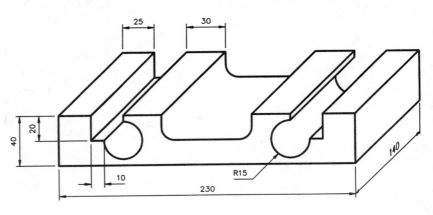

Fig. 8.10 An example of cabinet drawing

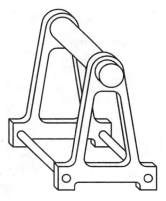

Fig 8.11 An example of cabinet drawing where care must be taken because of receding parts

cabinet drawing of a slider guide. Cabinet drawing is a useful form of pictorial drawing for articles which are have a fairly complicated view from one direction but are of uniform thickness. One problem with cabinet drawing is that the pictorial view tends to look slightly distorted, but they are easily and quickly produced.

Unlike with isometric drawing there is no need to change snap or grid, because the angle of 45 degrees is easily obtained working across the diagonals of the grid and snap settings.

When the front contains receding parts, care is needed to ensure that these are accurately drawn – see the second example, Fig. 8.11.

Planometric drawing

Planometric drawings can be easily constructed in AutoCAD by setting Snap Rotate to an angle of either 45 degrees or 30 degrees. This can be carried out either by entering 45 (or 30) in the **Snap Angle box** of the **Drawing Aids** dialogue box (Fig. 8.1) or from the command line:

> **Command:** *enter* snap *right-click*
> **Snap spacing or ON/OFF/Aspect/Rotate/Style<0>:** *enter* r (for Rotate) *right-click*
> **Base point<0,0>:** *right-click* (to accept)
> **Rotation angle<0>>:** *enter* 45 *right-click*
> **Command:**

A graphics window with **Snap** (with **Grid** on) with a planometric drawing under construction is shown in Fig. 8.12. In planometric drawing, a plan of the required drawing is first drawn on the 45 degree (or 36, 60 degree) axes. Verticals are taken at necessary points and details added as required. Using keys **F8** and **F9** to toggle between **Ortho** on and off and **Snap** on and off makes your work easier when constructing in planometric.

Figure 8.13 is a drawing of a house in planometric based on 45 degree axes. Door and windows were constructed with the aid of **Offset**. Details of roof tiles and wall cladding have been added with the aid of **BHatch**. The drawing has been incorporated in a planometric drawing of a proposed building site as shown in Fig. 8.14. The following commands were used in constructing Fig. 8.14:

Snap – set to rotate 45;
Insert – to insert the house drawing into the new drawing;
Scale – to scale the house to 0.25 of its original size;
Copy (Multiple) – to copy the three right-hand houses;
Mirror – to mirror two houses to the left-hand side of the window;
Fillet – to draw the arc of the pavement;

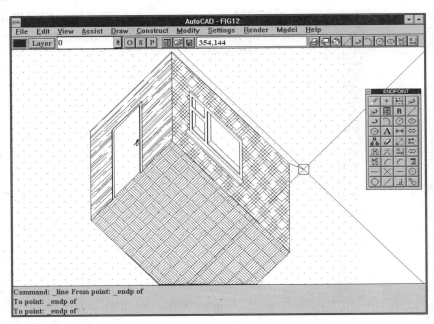

Fig. 8.12 A planometric drawing under construction in AutoCAD for Windows

Offset – to draw the height of the pavement;
Array – to draw the lines of the fencing;
Bhatch – to hatch the pavements;
Pline – of width 1, to draw the outline in which the drawing is set.

Note: Fig. 8.14 required a fair amount of memory and disk space to complete. When the file for the drawing was examined it was found to occupy 3.4 Mb of disk space. This was reduced to 0.3 Mb by purging unnecessary parts of the file as follows:

First save the drawing and re-open it, because the **Purge** command will only work on a newly opened drawing:

> **Command:** *enter* purge *right-click*
> **Purge unused Blocks/Dimstyles/LAyers/LTypes/SHapes/STyles/**
>   **All:** *enter* a (for All) *right-click*

Unnecessary parts will be purged from the file.

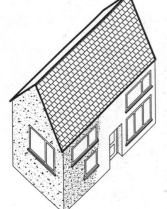

Fig. 8.13 A planometric drawing of a house

Questions

1. How is the AutoCAD graphics window set up for constructing isometric drawings?
2. At which angle is it usual to draw receding lines when constructing a cabinet drawing?
3. By how much are receding lines scaled in cabinet drawing?

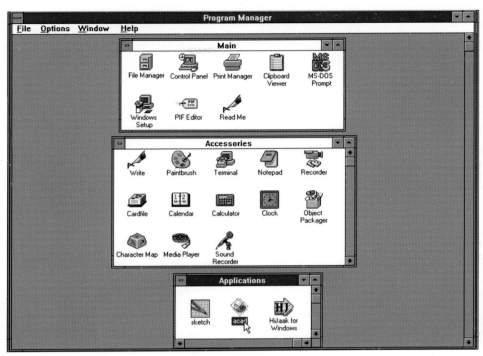

Plate I A **Program Manager** window of Windows 3.1

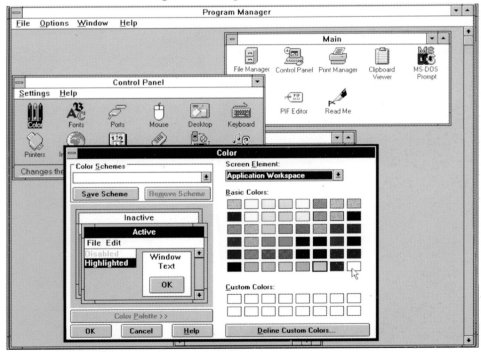

Plate II Setting the colours for the various parts of the windows for applications in Windows 3.1 from the **Color** dialogue box

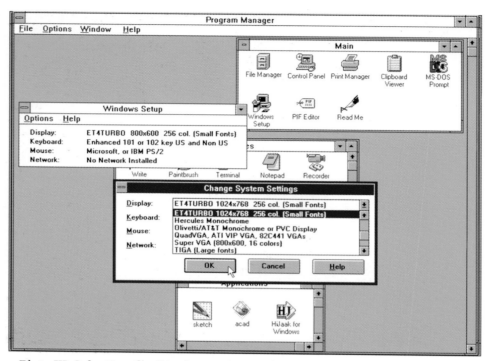

Plate III Selecting the Display setting in the Windows 3.1 **Windows Setup** dialogue box

Plate IV A three-view 2D orthographic projection of a building in an AutoCAD for Windows graphics window

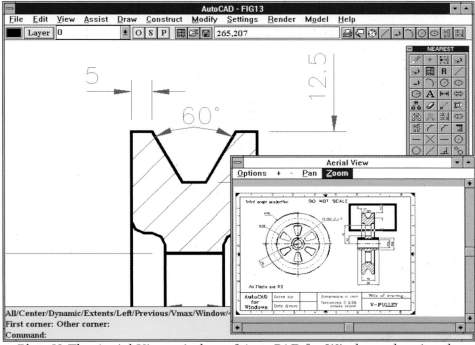

Plate V The Aerial View window of AutoCAD for Windows showing the area of the drawing which has been zoomed

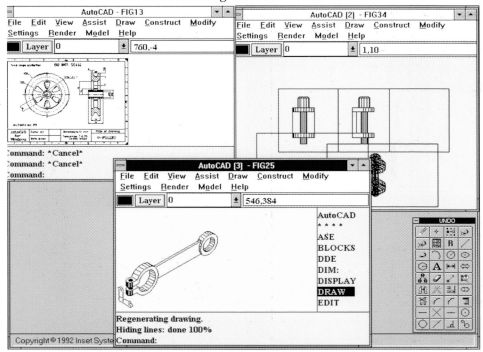

Plate VI   Three separate AutoCAD for Windows graphics windows on screen at the same time

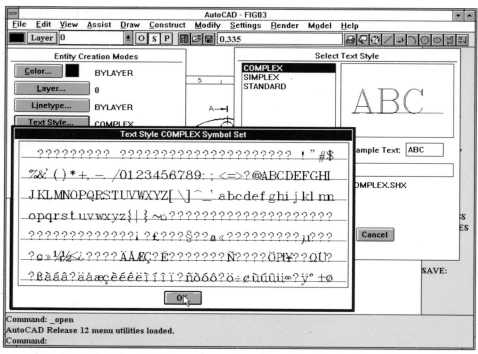

Plate VII The **Text Style** message box from the **Entity Creation Modes** dialogue box

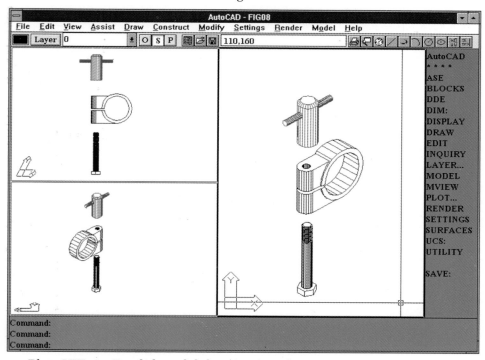

Plate VIII A 3D solid model drawing in a three-viewport AutoCAD for Windows graphics window

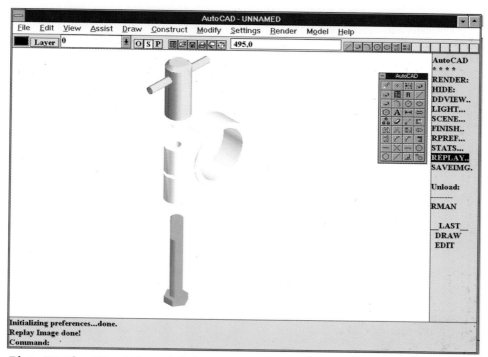

Plate IX The 3D solid model shown in Plate VIII after rendering in AutoCAD Render

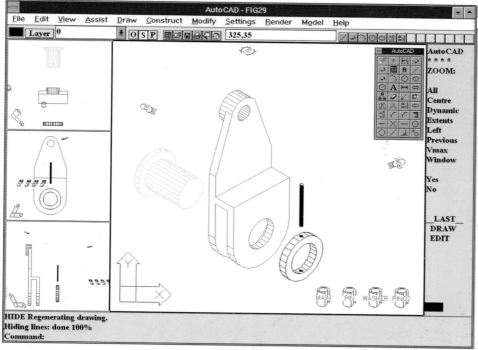

Plate X A four-viewport AutoCAD window of a 3D solid model after finishes have been applied and before rendering

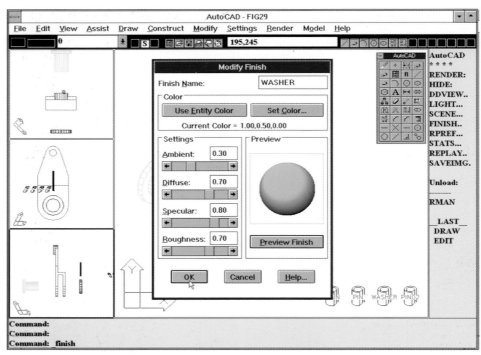

Plate XI The **Preview Finish** sphere for one of the finishes to be applied to the 3D model shown in Plate X

Plate XII A completed rendering of a 3D solid model

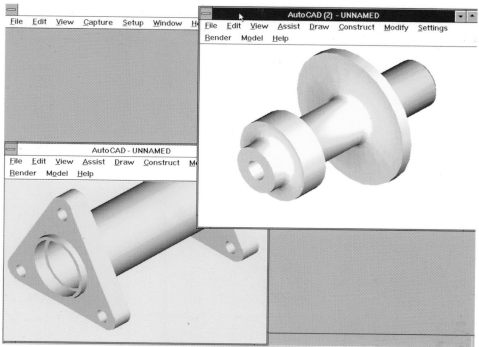

Plate XIII Two AutoCAD graphic windows with a different rendering
appearing in each

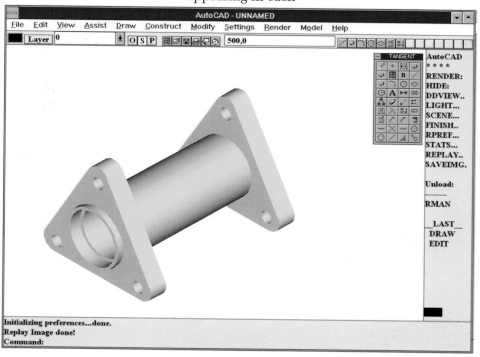

Plate XIV A rendered 3D solid model of a spacing device made from copper

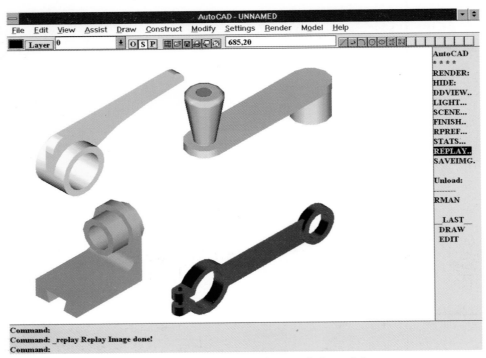

Plate XV Four rendered 3D solid models

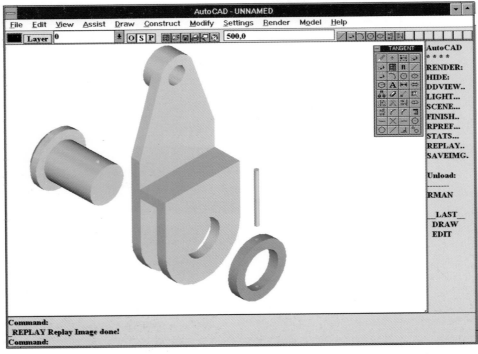

Plate XVI An exploded 3D model rendered in AutoCAD Render

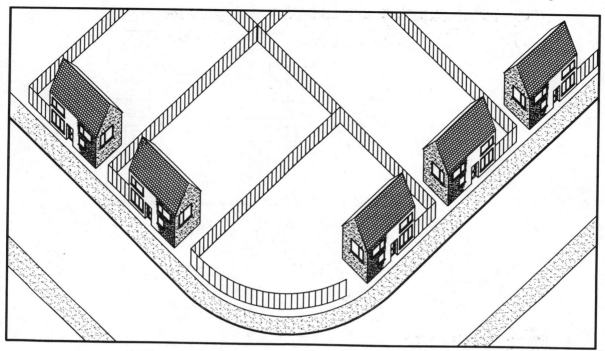

Fig. 8.14 The drawing of a house of Fig. 8.13 incorporated in a planometric drawing of a proposed building site

4. How is the AutoCAD graphics window set up for constructing planometric drawings?
5. For what type of pictorial drawing would you use the planometric method?

Exercises

7. Construct a planometric drawing of a house similar to that given in Fig. 8.13. Work on **Snap** rotated at either 30 or 45 degrees.
8. Figure 8.15 is a first-angle orthographic projection of a slide. Construct a cabinet drawing of the slide.
9. Figure 8.16 is a third-angle orthographic projection of a counter-weight. Construct a full-scale cabinet drawing of the counter-weight.
10. Figure 8.17 is a third-angle orthographic projection of a tensioner. Construct a cabinet drawing of the component.

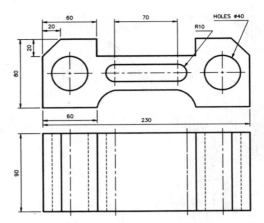

Fig. 8.15 Exercise 8

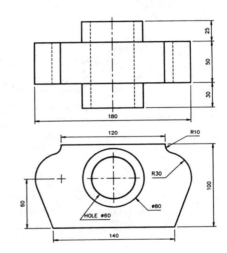

Fig. 8.16 Exercise 9

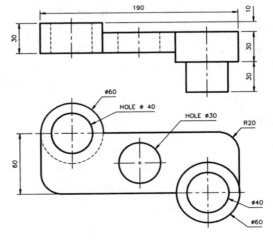

Fig. 8.17 Exercise 10

CHAPTER 9

Text and dimensions

Introduction

A large number of different styles of text can be included in drawings constructed in AutoCAD. There are three commands associated with the adding of text in AutoCAD:

Style – for selecting the font style, its height and other features associated with the text;
Text – text appears at the command line, but does not appear in the graphics window until *Return* is pressed or a *right-click* of the mouse;
Dtext – or dynamic text. Text appears in the graphics window as it is being entered at the keyboard.

The style of font selected will also affect the text and figures included with dimensions.

Style

When the command **Style** is entered:

> **Command:** *enter* style *right-click*
> **STYLE Text style name (or?)<STANDARD>:** *right-click*
> **Existing style.**

and the **Select Font Style** dialogue box appears (Fig. 9.1). It will be seen that, in the **List Files of Type** box, two types of files – those ending with the extensions ***.shx** and ***.pfb** – are listed in the list box of the dialogue box:

*.shx are shape files for AutoCAD fonts;
*.pfb are Postscript files.

Double-click on the name of the font style required – e.g. **simplex**. Further prompts appear at the command line:

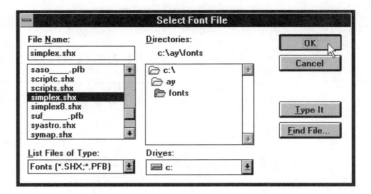

Fig. 9.1 The **Select Font Style**
dialogue box

> **Command:** *enter* style *right-click*
> **STYLE Text style name (or?)<STANDARD>:** *right-click*
> **Existing style. Height:** *enter* 10 *right-click* (for text of height 10
>   units)
> **Width factor<1>:** *right-click* (to accept)
> **Obliquing angle<0>:** *right-click* (to accept)
> **Backwards<N>:** *right-click* (to accept)
> **Upside down<N>:** *right-click* (to accept)
> **Vertical<N>:** *right-click* (to accept)
> **SIMPLEX is now the current text style:**
> **Command:**

Each time the text style is changed these six parameters need setting
– usually it is only the height which will need to be changed.

Text and Dtext

When the style of text has been selected, text can be added to the
current drawing from the command line by calling **Text,** or dynamically in the graphics window as it is entered at the keyboard by calling
Dtext. Text features can be further changed by responses to the
prompts associated with the two commands:

> **Command:** *enter* Text (or dtext) *right-click*
> **TEXT Justify/Style/<Start point>:** *pick* (or enter coordinates)
> **Rotation angle<0>:** *right-click* (to accept)
> **Text:** *enter* required text *right-click*
> **Command:**

Figure 9.2 shows a variety of font styles and different responses to the
various prompts associated with the commands **Style** and **Text** (or
Dtext). These are AutoCAD text styles (from *.shx files) and some
Postscript text styles (from *.pfb files).

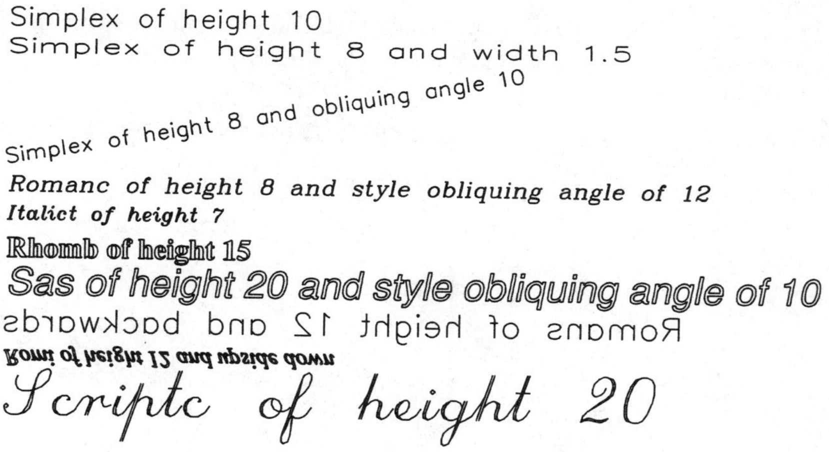

Simplex of height 10

Simplex of height 8 and width 1.5

Simplex of height 8 and obliquing angle 10

Romanc of height 8 and style obliquing angle of 12

Italict of height 7

Rhomb of height 15

Sas of height 20 and style obliquing angle of 10

Romans of height 12 and backwards

Romn of height 12 and upside down

Fig. 9.2 Examples of different **Style** settings

Scriptc of height 20

If the response is j (for Justify), the command line shows:

> **Command:** *enter* Text (or dtext) *right-click*
> **TEXT Justify/Style/<Start point>:** *enter* j (for Justify) *right-click*
> **Align/Fit/Centre/Middle/Right/TL/TC/TR/ML/MC/MR/BL/BC/BR:**

Figure 9.3 shows the results of responses to some of these justification prompts.

Respond with a **?** to the **Style** prompt:

> **Command:** *enter* style *right-click*
> **STYLE Text style name (or?)<SIMPLEX>:** *enter* ? *right-click*
> **Text styles to list<*>:** *right-click*

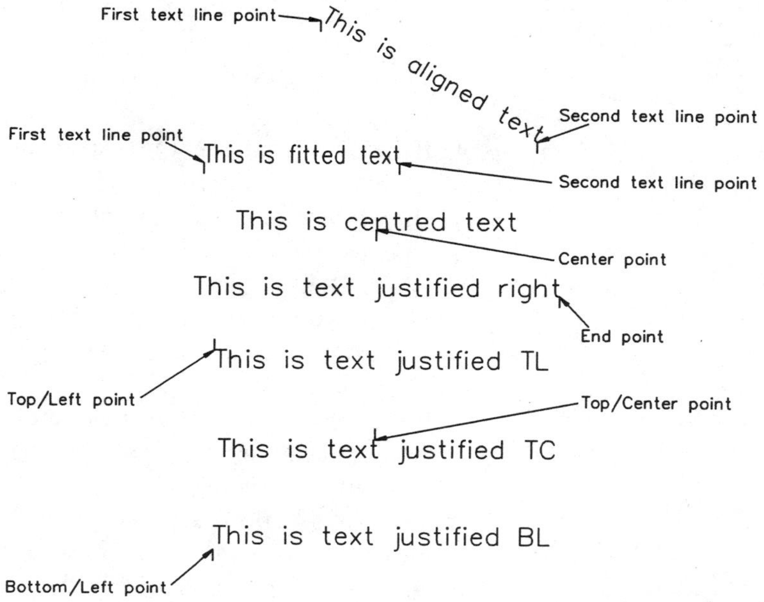

First text line point —— This is aligned text

Second text line point

First text line point — This is fitted text

Second text line point

This is centred text

Center point

This is text justified right

End point

This is text justified TL

Top/Left point

Top/Center point

This is text justified TC

This is text justified BL

Fig. 9.3 Some responses to **Text Justify** prompts

Bottom/Left point

and an AutoCAD text window appears with details of the text styles already in the current drawing – an example is given in Fig. 9.4.

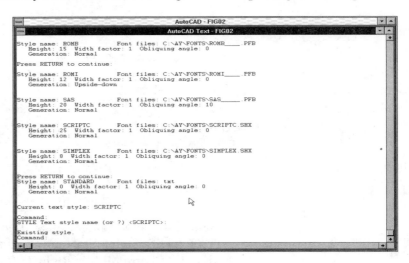

Fig. 9.4 An example of an AutoCAD text window with font style details

Notes on Style, Text and Dtext

1. In Fig. 9.1 it will be noted that my AutoCAD files are held in a directory with the name of AY (my initials). This is because I hold the DOS AutoCAD Release 12 files in the acad directory on my computer;

2. It is not absolutely necessary to use the font style names given in the **Select Font Style** dialogue box. If using several styles in a drawing, abbreviations for each style can be entered at the keyboard, e.g. simplex could be s; romanc could be r; italict could be i, and so on;

3. The selected font styles and the text associated with them are saved in the drawing file;

4. If the **Style** prompt of the text prompts is returned, any style already in the current drawing can be used. If a new style is required, then the **Style** command sequence must be used;

5. The text icon from the **Toolbox** calls up **Dtext**;

6. When **Dtext** is used in place of text, each letter or figure as it is entered appears in the graphics window encased in a square. The square moves on as further figures or letters are entered at the keyboard;

7. Take care when attempting to make text read vertically. All previously placed text of the same style will be placed vertically in the current drawing;

8. Rows of text properly spaced one below the other can be obtained by two *double-right-clicks* or by pressing the *Return* key twice after each line of text has been added to the drawing.

Dimensions

AutoCAD dimensioning is **associative**, i.e. dimensions are added to a drawing with each part – dimension lines, extension lines, arrows and text – associated with each other. Each dimension acts as if it were a single entity – each dimension is, in fact, a block. If one wishes to edit any part of an associative dimension, it must first be exploded with the aid of the **Explode** command.

Dimensioning parameters can be set in the **Dimension Styles and Variables** dialogue box (page 27), which can be called either by a *left-click* on **Dimensions Styles...** in the **Settings** menu or by entering **ddim** at the command line. A variety of types of dimensioning are possible. Examples are given in Fig. 9.5 and 9.6.

As an example of including a dimension in a drawing, add a horizontal dimension as follows:

> **Command:** *enter* dim *right-click*
> **Dim:** *enter* hor (for Horizontal) *right-click*
> **First extension line origin or RETURN to select:** *pick*
> **Second extension line origin:** *pick*
> **Dimension line location (Text/Angle):** *pick*
> **Dimension text<100>:** *right-click* (to accept) or *enter* new figures *right-click*
> **Dim:**

If the *Return* key is pressed in answer to the **or RETURN to select:** prompt, the result will give the horizontal dimension of a selected entity.

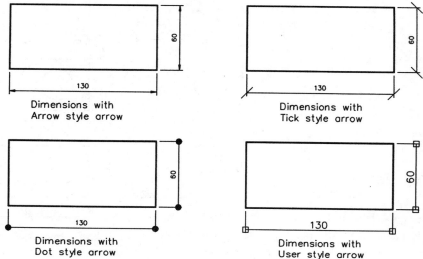

Fig. 9.5 The four types of **Arrow** which can be set in the **Dimension Styles and Variables** dialogue box

Dimensions with
Arrow style arrow

Dimensions with
Tick style arrow

Dimensions with
Dot style arrow

Dimensions with
User style arrow

The Dim variables

To see a list of the dimensioning variables which can be set in AutoCAD for Windows, enter setvar at the command prompt:

Command: *enter* setvar *right-click*
Variable name or ?: *right-click* (to accept)
Variable(s) to list<*>: *right-click* (to accept)

and an AutoCAD text window appears showing the variables and their settings. Scroll through these until you come to the **dim** variables – those beginning with **dim**. You will find quite a number of them and, as you become more expert with AutoCAD, it is worthwhile experimenting with these. The more frequently used variables are set automatically in the **Dimension Styles and Variables** dialogue box, but some have to be set at the command line. In Fig. 9.6 the results of settings for the following four dim set variables are given:

dimtol – set on for dimensions to include tolerances; set off if not required;
dimtp – to set the size of the upper tolerance; include a plus sign if you wish to have it included with the tolerance dimension;
dimtm – to set the size of the lower tolerance; do not include the minus sign – it is included automatically;
dimalt – to set the inclusion of alternative dimensions – in the example given in Fig. 9.6 **units** were set from the command line to give

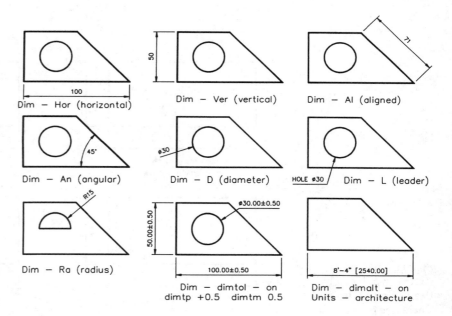

Fig. 9.6 The more common forms of dimensioning

Architectural feet, inches and fractions. The alternative dimensions were millimetres (in brackets). If **dimalt** is set to off, alternative dimensions are not included.

There are many other dim variables, which are not included here because this book is not intended to describe the more advanced dimensioning constructions possible with AutoCAD for Windows.

To set the type of dimensioning units

Command: *enter* units *right-click*

and an AutoCAD text window appears (Fig. 9.7) in which the type of units can be set by entering responses to the prompts which appear in the text window.

A user arrow for dimensions

If you wish to use your own arrow type when adding dimensions to a drawing:

1. Draw the arrow in such a manner that it is only one unit in length (Fig. 9.8). The figure entered in the **Arrow Size** box of the **Dimension Style and Variables** dialogue box will scale your arrow drawing by a scale equal to the figure in the box;
2. Save the drawing as a **block** within the current drawing – to a filename such as **arrow**;

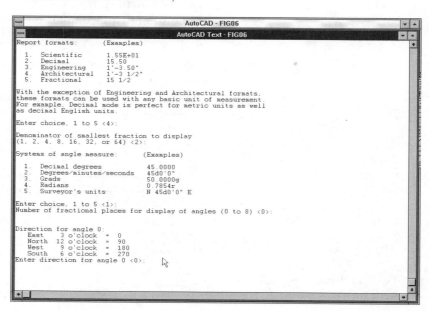

Fig. 9.7 The AutoCAD text window in which units are set

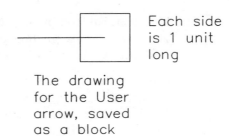

Each side
is 1 unit
long

The drawing
for the User
arrow, saved
as a block

Fig. 9.8 The drawing for a
User arrow

3. Check the circle above the **User** in the dialogue box;
4. Enter the name **arrow** (filename of your arrow) in the **User Arrow** box;
5. *Left-click* on **OK** in both the **Arrows** dialogue box and the **Dimension Style and Variables** dialogue box;
6. Any dimensions now added to your drawing will have your arrow.

The actions of Stretch and Scale on associative dimensions

Figure 9.9 shows the action of **Stretch** and **Scale** on a dimension. Remember that a dimension acts as a single entity. Call Stretch:

> **Command:** *enter* stretch *right-click*
> **Select objects to stretch by window or polygon...**
> **Select objects:** c (for Crossing) *right-click*
> **First corner:** *pick* **Other corner:** *pick* **1 found**
> **Select objects:** *right-click*
> **Base point or displacement:** *pick*
> **Second point of displacement:** *pick*
> **Command:**

If a dimensioned drawing is scaled, not only will the drawing be redrawn to the new scale but all dimensions will be redrawn to the scaled sizes.

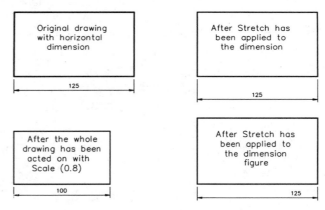

Fig. 9.9 The actions of **Stretch** and **Scale** on a dimension

Questions

1. What is the purpose of the command **Style**?
2. What is the difference between fonts – one held in a file with an extension *.shx and the other held in a file with an extension *.pfb?
3. What is the difference between text set with an obliquing angle within the **Style** command prompts and one set with an obliquing angle within the **Text** command prompts?
4. When **Justify** is the selected response to one of the **Text** prompts, what is the meaning of the resulting prompts **TR**, **ML**, **BL** and **BR**?
5. What is meant by the term **Associative dimensioning**?
6. What is the effect of the command **Stretch** on a dimension?
7. What is the effect of the command **Scale** on a dimension?
8. Describe the steps necessary to ensure that one's own design for arrows is used when dimensioning a drawing.

Exercises

1. Construct a three-view Third angle isometric projection of the block shown in Fig. 9.10 and fully dimension your drawing.

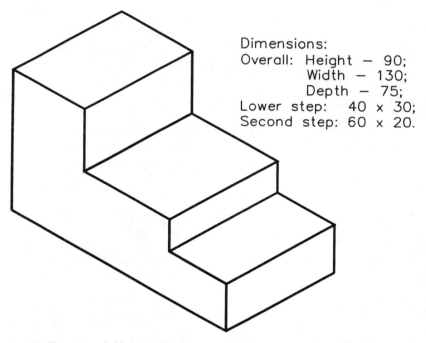

Dimensions:
Overall: Height — 90;
          Width — 130;
          Depth — 75;
Lower step: 40 x 30;
Second step: 60 x 20.

Fig. 9.10 Exercise 1

2. Construct a full-size three-view Third angle orthographic projection of the block given in Fig. 9.11 and fully dimension the three views.

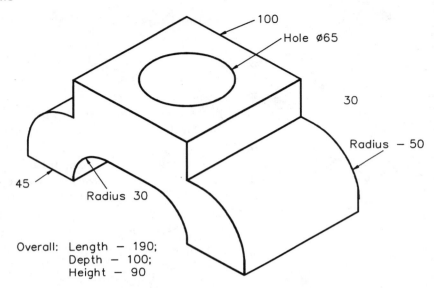

Fig. 9.11 Exercise 2

3. Figure 9.12 is an orthographic projection of a hanging spindle support. Redraw Fig. 9.12 in Third angle projection, with the end view in section. Fully dimension your drawing, to include tolerances of ±0.05 mm for every dimension. **Note:** you will have to set **Units** in the **Units Control** dialogue box to two decimal places in order to be able to include the tolerances. Complete your drawing with a suitable title block.

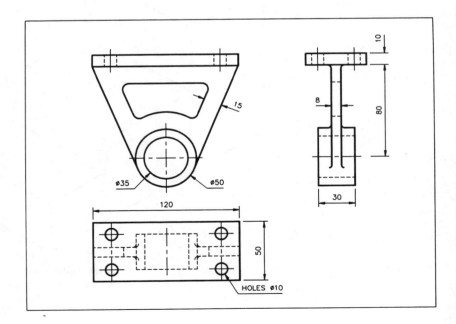

Fig. 9.12 Exercise 3

4. Figure 9.13 is a sectional view through a bush plate. Without including the grid lines, construct a full-size copy of the drawing and add all necessary dimensions, including tolerances of +0.05 mm.

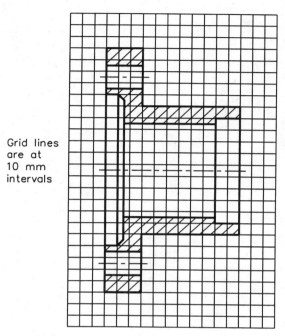

Grid lines are at 10 mm intervals

Fig. 9.13 Exercise 4

5. Figure 9.14 is a front view of a small single-storey house. Copy the given view, including the dimensions. Add any further dimensions you consider necessary.

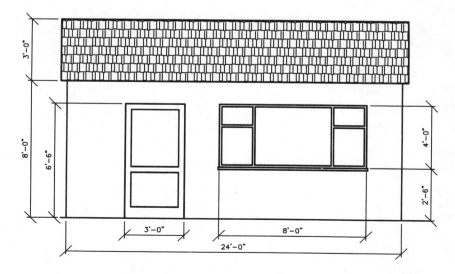

Fig. 9.14 Exercise 5

6. Figure 9.15. For this exercise set **Units** to **Architectural** (from the keyboard); **Limits** to 200,150; **Grid** to 12: **Snap** to 6. Grid and Snap are set as indicated because the dimensions are in feet and inches and there are 12 inches to each foot. With these settings, each coordinate unit will represent 1 inch, therefore 12 coordinate units represents 1 foot. Note the way in which coordinates show in the coordinate box in the **Toolbar**. When using architectural units, all length figures must be entered in feet and inches, e.g. 36'-6" or 48'. Otherwise AutoCAD will only recognize the figures as coordinate units – in this example representing inches.

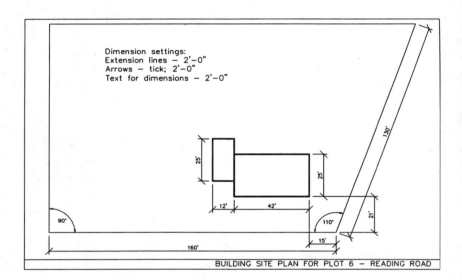

Fig. 9.15 Exercise 6

CHAPTER 10

Wblock, Insert and circuit drawing

Introduction

Any AutoCAD drawing can be "inserted" into any other AutoCAD drawing with the aid of the **Insert** command. An inserted drawing is in the form of a "block" – it is as if it were a single entity, although it may originally have been made up from a number of individual entities. An inserted block can be "exploded" into its separate entities by the action of the **Explode** command. Any part of a drawing can be saved as a separate drawing file with the aid of the **Wblock** command. When so saved, the resulting file is an AutoCAD drawing file with the *.dwg extension.

Insert

We have already had an example of an AutoCAD drawing which could be inserted into another in Fig. 6.4, reproduced in this chapter as Fig. 10.2. This drawing is an example of the type of layout sheet which might be found in an the design office of an engineering firm. Take as an example Fig. 10.1, a drawing of a flange. When the drawing has been

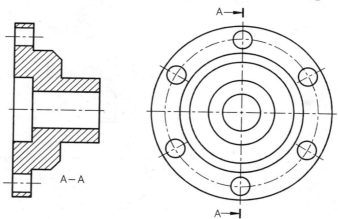

Fig. 10.1 A two-view orthographic projection of a flange

completed it could be placed in the drawing layout sheet (Fig. 10.2) as follows; the result is shown in Fig. 10.3

The procedure for the insertion from the command line is:

Command: *enter* insert *right-click*
Block name (or?): *enter* chap06\fig05 *right-click*
Insertion point: *enter* 5,5 *right-click* (or *pick* a point in the graphics window)
X scale factor<1>/Corner/XYZ: *right-click* (to accept)

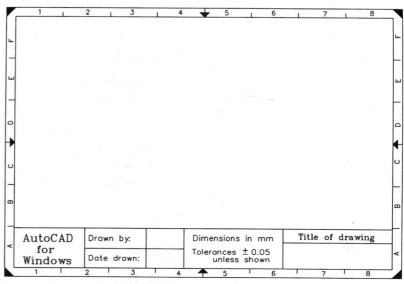

Fig. 10.2 The drawing sheet layout from Fig. 6.4

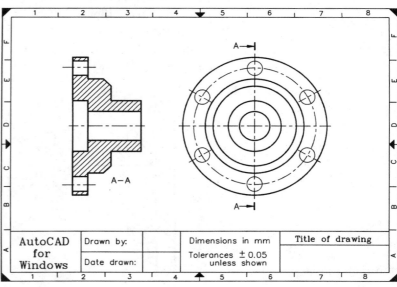

Fig. 10.3 The drawing sheet layout inserted into the flange drawing of Fig 10.1

Y scale factor (default=X): *right-click* (to accept)
Rotation angle<0>: *right-click* (to accept)
Command:

and the sheet layout is inserted into the graphic window (Fig. 10.3).

A title and other details could be entered in the title block at this stage.

Explode

The inserted block can be exploded into its constituent entities as follows:

Command: *enter* explode *right-click*
Select objects: *left-click* on any part of the inserted block **1 found**
Select objects: *right-click*
Command:

and the inserted block drawing will explode into its original entities. Before the action of the **Explode** command, the inserted drawing could be acted upon by any **Modify** command (e.g. **Move** or **Erase**) as if it were a single entity. After the action of the **Explode** command, each entity in the drawing can be acted upon by a **Modify** command.

Ddinsert

If, instead of entering the command name **Insert** at the command line, **ddinsert** is called, the **Insert** dialogue box appears (Fig. 10.4). The dialogue box can also be called by a *left-click* on **Insert...** in the **draw** pull-down menu. Entering the file name in the **File...** box will have the

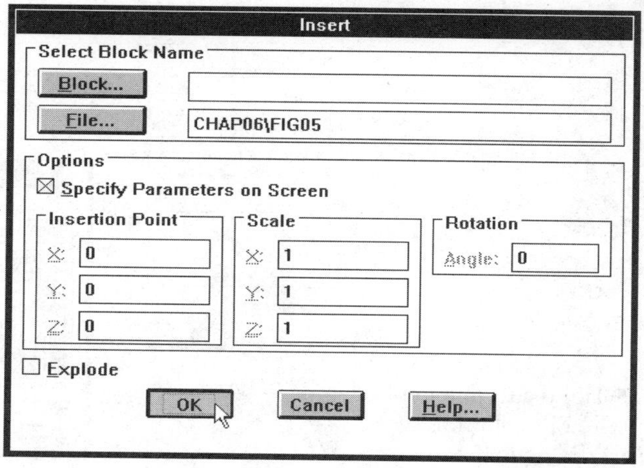

Fig. 10.4 The **Insert** dialogue box

same result as entering the name at the command line after calling **Insert**. A *left-click* on the **File...** button brings the **Select Drawing File** dialogue box on screen, from which the required file can be selected (Fig. 10.5).

When the drawing to be inserted has been selected, then the prompts associated with the **Insert** command appear at the command line:

> **Insertion point:** *enter* 5,5 *right-click* (or *pick* a point in the graphics window)
> **X scale factor<1>/Corner/XYZ:** *right-click* (to accept)
> **Y scale factor (default=X):** *right-click* (to accept)
> **Rotation angle<0>:** *right-click* (to accept)
> **Command:**

Note: If a drawing is inserted into another through the **Insert** dialogue box, the drawing can be exploded before being inserted by checking the **Explode** box in the **Insert** dialogue box.

Blocks

It will be seen in Fig. 10.5 that one of the buttons in the **Insert** dialogue box is labelled **Block...** If blocks have been saved **IN THE DRAWING** then a *left-click* on the **Block...** button will bring the **Blocks Defined in this Drawing** dialogue box on screen. An example is given in Fig. 10.6, in which a number of electrical and electronic circuit diagram symbols are included with the drawing. Note that the blocks included in the list in the dialogue box cannot necessarily be seen in the actual drawing, although they can be inserted into it.

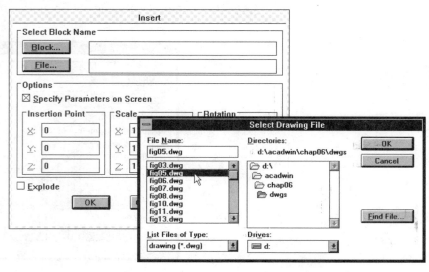

Fig. 10.5 The result of a *left-click* on the **File...** button of the **Insert** dialogue box

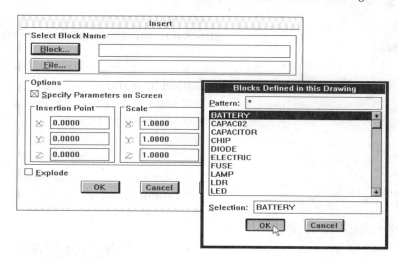

Fig. 10.6 The **Blocks Defined in this Drawing** dialogue box

The Wblock and Block commands

Both these commands use the same prompts, but whereas the action of **Wblock** results in a drawing file saved apart from the current drawing, the action of **Block** creates a drawing saved within the current drawing. When a drawing has been created with **Wblock**, it can be opened as can any other AutoCAD drawing, but a **Block** can only be recalled within the drawing in which it has been saved. The prompts associated with the commands are:

> **Command:** *enter* wblock *right-click*

In the case of **Wblock** the **Create New Drawing File** dialogue box appears; a file name for the wblock is entered in the **File Name** box of the dialogue box – e.g. in the example (Fig. 10.7) lamp. Then:

> **Block name:** *right-click* (accept the name entered in the dialogue box)
> **Insertion base point:** *pick* the required point (or *enter* coordinates)
> **Select objects:** *window* the objects
> **Select objects:** *right-click*
> **Command:**

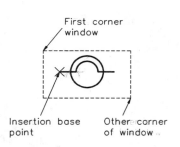

Fig. 10.7 A lamp symbol saved as a **Wblock** (or **Block**)

The objects selected within the window disappear from the screen, but they can be brought back by:

> **Command:** *enter* oops *right-click*
> **Command:** and the objects re-appear

In the case of **block** the dialogue box does not appear but the following prompts (which are similar) appear:

Command: *enter* block *right-click*
Block name (or?): *enter* a filename (in the example given (Fig. 10.7) lamp)
Block name: *right-click* (to accept the filename)
Insertion base point: *pick* or *enter* coordinates
Select objects: *window* the objects
Select objects: *right-click*
Command:

The objects can be brought back on screen with **oops**.

If a number of blocks are saved within a drawing, responding with a **?** to the prompt **Block name (or?):** brings up an AutoCAD text screen with the names of all the blocks within the drawing (Fig. 10.8).

Fig. 10.8 An example of part of the AutoCAD text screen which appears when the **?** response is given to **Block name (?):**

The drawing of circuits

The insertion of blocks (as **blocks** or **Wblocks**) is of particular value when constructing circuit diagrams – electrical, electronic, pneumatic etc. It is possible to build up a library of drawings of circuit symbols on a disk, with the aid of the **Wblock** command, and then to **Insert** the symbols from such libraries into drawings of circuit diagrams. Disks containing libraries of this type are also sold commercially, but for the purposes of the examples given here, the libraries can be built up by the reader. Examples of small libraries of such symbols are given in Figs. 10.9, 10.10 and 10.11.

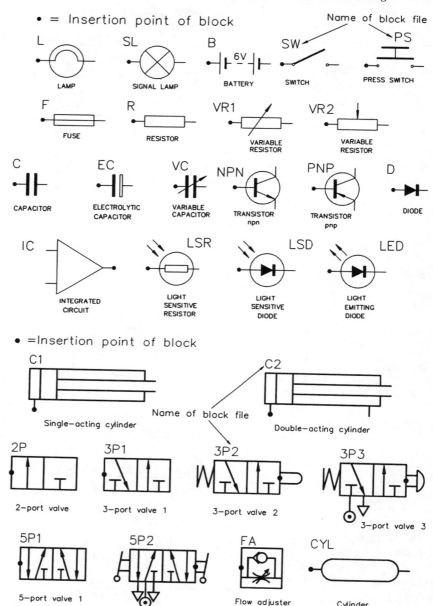

Fig. 10.9 A small library of electrical and electronics symbols

Fig. 10.10 A small library of pneumatics symbols

Constructing a circuit diagram using insertions

Stages in the construction of a simple electronics circuit diagram are given in Fig. 10.12. The symbol drawings for insertion were chosen with the use of the **ddinsert** command and then selecting from the **Insert** dialogue box which appears when the command is entered at the command line. The stages as given in Fig. 10.12 are:

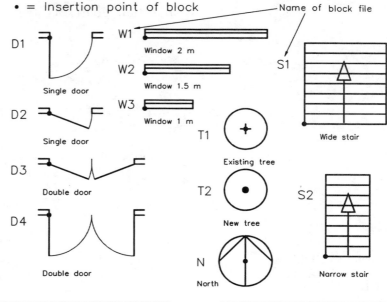

Fig. 10.11 A small library of building drawing symbols

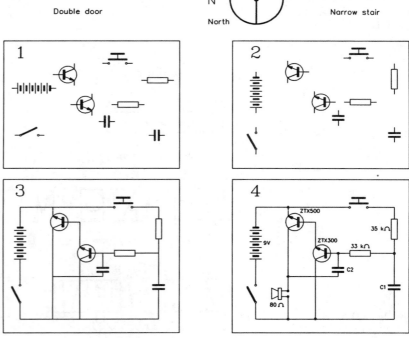

Fig. 10.12 Stages in constructing an electronics circuit diagram by the insertion of symbols from a library

1. Insert each symbol into the graphics window in an approximate position. Some of the symbols will not be lying in the correct vertical or horizontal position;

2. **Move** and **Rotate** the symbols until they are in the desired position in the circuit diagram. If the symbol drawings are inserted without being exploded, they can each be moved or rotated as if they were single entities;

3. Join the symbols with lines (or, if wished, polylines). Any slight changes in position that may be necessary can be carried out with the **Move** command, using **Osnaps** to make sure that conductor lines and symbols meet accurately;

4. Complete the circuit diagram by adding symbols which are not in your library (in the example given, the loudspeaker). Add donuts at each conductor intersection. Add a title if thought necessary (Fig. 10.13).

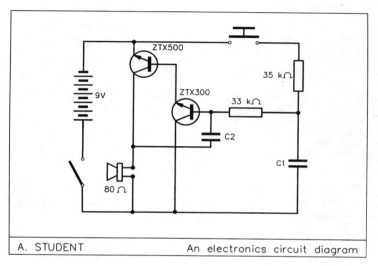

Fig. 10.13 The completed circuit diagram

Types of file format in AutoCAD for Windows

AutoCAD graphics windows can be saved to a number of different file formats. Among these are:

*.dwg	the AutoCAD drawing file format;
*.dxf	the Drawing Interchange File format;
*.dxb	DXF files saved to a binary format;
*.bmp	bitmap files;
*.clp	Windows Clipboard files;
*.eps	Postscript files;
*.sld	AutoCAD slide files
*.wmf	Windows metafiles;
*.tga	to save 3D models as rendered files (see page 197).

DXF (Drawing Interchange Files) format

To exchange drawing files between different CAD systems, Autodesk have developed the DXF file format, which has been largely accepted as the industry standard. DXF files are used as follows:

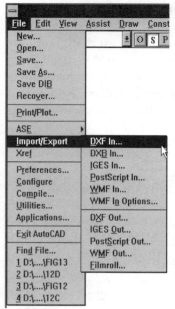

Fig. 10.14 The **File** pull-down menu with **DXF In...** selected from the **Import/Export** sub-menu

1. In a CAD system which has the necessary facility, a drawing is saved as a file with the extension *.dxf*;
2. The file can be opened in AutoCAD for Windows, provided it is opened into a graphic screen which has not previously had any settings saved with it. This can be achieved by a *left-click* on **New...** in the **File** menu, which opens up the **Create New Drawing** dialogue box. A *left-click* in the box next to **No Prototype** followed by a *left-click* on **OK** results in a graphics window with no previously saved settings ;
3. *Left-click* on **Import/Export** in the **File** menu, followed by a *left-click* on **DXF In...** (Fig. 10.14). This opens the **Select DXF File** dialogue box (Fig. 10.15), from which any DXF files previously saved can be opened into the graphics window;
4. If the *acad.dwg* file is opened as a **Prototype** graphic screen for a DXF file, only part, if any at all, of the DXF file can be opened.

Figure 10.16 is an example of a number of **Clip_Art** files from AutoSketch for Windows which have been opened in AutoCAD for Windows via the DXF facility. AutoSketch files are saved with the extension *.skd*, but AutoSketch drawings can also be saved as DXF files with the extension *.dxf*. Fig 10.16 was created in the following manner:

1. Four Clip_Art files (extension *.skd*) were each saved as DXF files in AutoSketch for Windows;
2. Each of the DXF files was opened separately in AutoCAD for Windows in **New** drawings with the **No Prototype** box checked;
3. Because the drawings were Clip_Art blocks they were acted upon by **Explode** before being saved as AutoCAD drawing files with the extension *.dwg*;
4. Each drawing was then **Insert**ed separately into a **New** drawing. As they were inserted blocks, each could be moved or scaled as single entities;

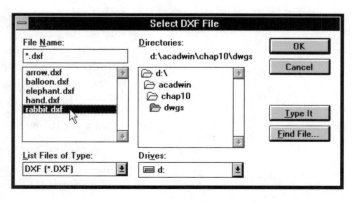

Fig. 10.15 The **Select DXF File** dialogue box

Fig. 10.16 Some Clip_Art files from AutoSketch for Windows, saved as DXF files and inserted into AutoCAD for Windows after being saved as AutoCAD drawing files

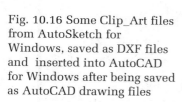

5. Text was added into the balloon. The balloon was also exploded and altered slightly from its original Clip_Art outline.

Notes

1. It is the intention of Autodesk in future releases of AutoSketch to allow drawing files to be saved with the *.dwg* file extension, which will allow AutoSketch 2D files to be opened directly into AutoCAD;

2. Any drawing constructed in other CAD software systems which include the DXF facility can be opened in AutoCAD using a sequence similar to that outlined above.

DIB (Device Independent Files) format

Left-click on **Save DIB** in the **File** menu (Fig. 10.17). The **Save DIB** dialogue box appears (Fig. 10.18). *Enter* a filename in the **File Name** box of the dialogue box, followed by a *left-click* on **OK**. The following parts of the AutoCAD for Windows graphics window are saved as a bitmap file with the extension *.bmp:

The graphics area
The toolbar
The toolbox
The command line area.

An example of the resulting graphics can be seen in Fig. 10.19.

EPS (Encapsulated Postscript File) format

Fig. 10.14 shows that the graphics area can be saved in a Postscript file. In the example given in Fig. 10.22, the saving has been to a file with an *.eps* extension. *Left-click* on **Postscript Out...** in the **File** menu. The **Create Postscript File** dialogue box appears (Fig. 10.20). *Enter* a filename in the **File Name** box of the dialogue box followed by a *left-*

Fig. 10.17 **Save DIB** from the **File** menu

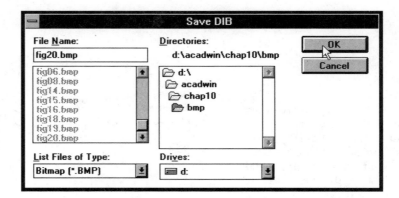

Fig. 10.18 The **Save DIB** dialogue box

Fig. 10.19 An AutoCAD graphics windows saved as a DIB file

click on OK and an AutoCAD text window appears in which the parameters for the required Postscript file are entered in response to a series of prompts. As can be seen from Fig. 10.21, the file has been saved:

In a TIFF format;
Of an image size of 512;
To millimetre unit sizes;
To FIT in the USER size of 115 × 80 mm.

EPS files are of particular value for including AutoCAD drawings into documents produced with the aid of desk editing or word processor applications.

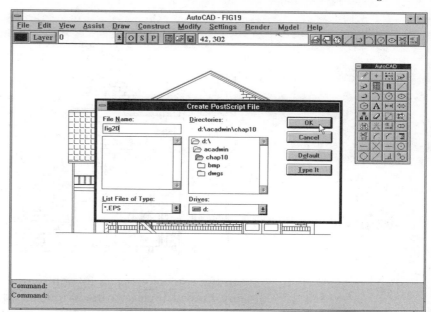

Fig. 10.20 The **Create Postscript File** dialogue box

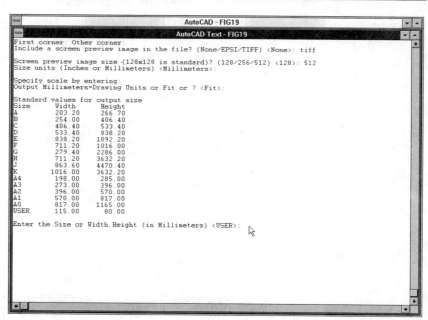

Fig. 10.21 The AutoCAD text window in which the parameters for a Postscript file are entered

Files with the extension *.clp (Clipboard files)

If an AutoCAD drawing is saved to the Windows Clipboard through **Copy Image**, **Copy Vectors**, **Copy Embed** or **Copy Link** from the **Edit** menu, the copying is to the Windows Clipboard. Once copied to the Windows Clipboard, the drawings can then be saved to a named file

Fig. 10.22 The resulting EPS
file

with the extension *.clp*. Examples of an AutoCAD drawing with a
Copy Embed image in the Windows Clipboard, together with the
required **Save Clp** dialogue box are given in Fig. 10.23. Clipboard files
can be **Paste**d into the AutoCAD graphics window.

Other types of file

A *left-click* on **WMF Out...** from the **File** menu allows a drawing in the
graphics window to be saved as a Windows metafile with an *.wmf*

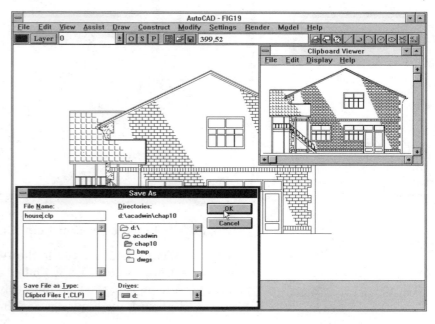

Fig.. 10.23 A Clipboard copy
of an AutoCAD drawing to be
saved with the file extension
*.clp

extension. WMF files can be pasted back into AutoCAD or other Windows applications.

To save a drawing as a slide file with the extension *.sld*:

Command: *enter* mslide (Makeslide) *right-click*

A **Create Slide File** dialogue box appears in which one *enters* the required filename.

Slide files can be quickly recalled to screen by:

Command: *enter* vslide (View slide) *right-click*

A **Select Slide File** dialogue box appears from which a file can be selected.

Slide files look like drawing files, but they cannot be added to or edited in any way. When selected, they appear in the graphics windows overlaying the current drawing. When a redraw or regen is called, the slide disappears from screen to be replaced by the current drawing. Slide files are very useful if one wishes to show a number of drawings one after the other, as in a slide "show". They take up very little disk space, appear on screen very quickly and disappear just as quickly when the next file is loaded.

Questions

1. Explain the difference between a **block** and a **Wblock**.
2. What is the purpose of the command **Explode**?
3. When **ddinsert** is called the **Insert** dialogue box appears in the graphics window. Two buttons are named **Block...** and **File...** . What is the difference between the two dialogue boxes connected with these two buttons?
4. What is the difference between a file with the extension *.dxf* and one with the extension *.dxb?
5. Why are DXF files important when working with several CAD systems?
6. Which parts of the AutoCAD for Windows graphics screen are saved in a DIB file?
7. What is the difference between the two types of AutoCAD files with the extensions *.dwg* and *.sld?
8. What file extension is given to a Windows Clipboard file?

Exercises

1. Figure 10.24 is an outline building plan of the two floors of a two-storey house. Draw and save as blocks within your drawing a

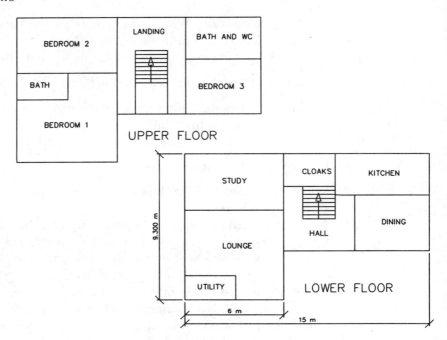

Fig. 10.24 Exercise 1

sufficient number of drawing building symbols from Fig. 10.11 to complete the building plan. Then, working to a scale of 20 coordinate units = 1 metre, copy Fig. 10.24 and add windows and doors as necessary from the blocks you have included in your drawing.

2. Figure 10.25 is an outline drawing for an electronics circuit. Draw and save as many blocks as necessary from Fig. 10.9 within your drawing to complete the circuit. Then, adding blocks from those you have included in your drawing, draw the circuit.

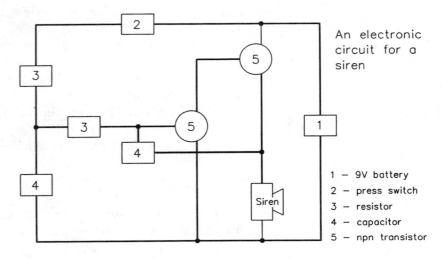

An electronic circuit for a siren

1 — 9V battery
2 — press switch
3 — resistor
4 — capacitor
5 — npn transistor

Fig. 10.25 Exercise 2

3. Figure 10.26 is another outline drawing for an electronics circuit. Draw and save as many blocks as necessary from Fig. 10.9 within your drawing to complete the circuit. Then, adding blocks from those you have included in your drawing, draw the circuit.

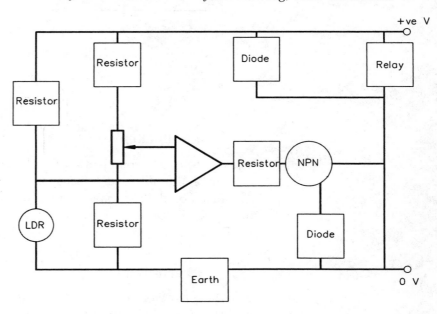

Fig. 10.26 Exercise 3

CHAPTER 11

3D drawings

Introduction

The 3D Surfaces commands of AutoCAD will only be described here to a limited extent, because, with the introduction of the Advanced Modelling Extension (AME) and its updating to AME 2.1 in AutoCAD for Windows, they have largely been superseded by AME 2.1.

3D coordinates

In earlier chapters we dealt only with two-dimensional drawing (2D), in which any point in the graphics window can be referred to in terms of two coordinate unit numbers x and y. When dealing with three-dimensional drawing (3D), a third coordinate is required to determine the height of the drawing above the 2D surface of the screen. This third coordinate is referred to as z. Thus any point in a 3D drawing can be given terms of x,y,z, similar to referring to points in a 2D drawing in terms of x,y.

Figure 11.1 shows the positive and negative aspects of x, y and z units with respect to the origin point (where $x,y,z = 0,0,0$) at the bottom left-hand corner (usually) of the AutoCAD for Windows graphics window. A simple 3D drawing is included in the illustration. It will be seen from Fig. 11.1 that:

+ve x units are horizontally to the right of the origin;
-ve x units are horizontally to the left of the origin;
+ve y units are vertically above the origin;
-ve y units are vertically below the origin;
+ve z units are towards the operator from the graphics window;
-ve z units are away from the operator behind the graphics window.

Note: The term *solid model*, will be used throughout the remainder of this book to refer to 3D drawings created in AutoCAD.

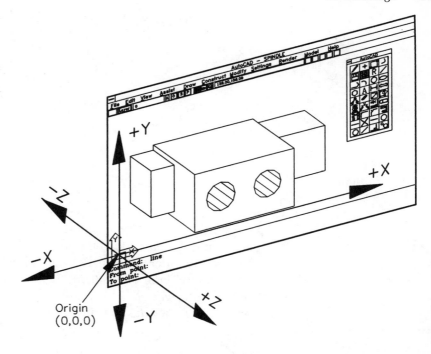

Fig. 11.1 3D coordinates in
AutoCAD for Windows

The command 3DFACE

To create a 3D drawing of a rectangular prism (Fig. 11.3)

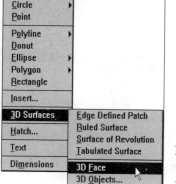

Fig. 11.2 The **Draw** pull-down
menu with **3D Face** selected

Base of prism: Either *left-click* on **Draw** in the **Menu bar** followed by
a *left-click* on **3DFace** (Fig.11.2), or *enter* 3dface at the command line:

Command: *enter* 3dface *right-click*
First point: *enter* 100,200 *right-click*
Second point: *enter* 300,200 *right-click*
Third point: *enter* 300,100 *right-click*
Fourth point: *enter* 100,100 *right-click* **Note** how the rectangle
    3dface closes
Third point: *right-click* to complete the sequence
Command:

Notes:

1. The 3DFace looks like a 2D rectangle, but it is really a 3D surface;
2. 3DFaces can only be drawn as quadrilaterals (4 edges) or as
    triangles (3 edges) – no other form of 3DFace is possible;
3. Further 3DFaces can be drawn by continuing.

Back face of prism
Command: *enter* 3dface *right-click*

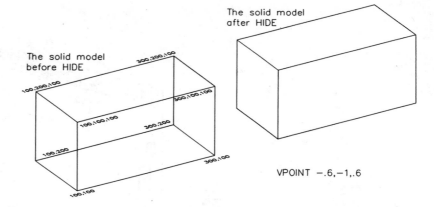

Fig. 11.3 A simple 3D solid
model

First point: *enter* 100,200 *right-click*
Second point: *enter* 300,200 *right-click*
Third point: *enter* 300,200,100 *right-click*
Fourth point: *enter* 100,200,100 *right-click*
Third point: *right-click* to complete the sequence
Command: *right-click* to bring back the 3dface command sequence

Front face of prism
First point: *enter* 100,100 *right-click*
Second point: *enter* 300,100 *right-click*
Third point: *enter* 300,100,100 *right-click*
Fourth point: *enter* 100,100,100 *right-click*
Third point: *right-click* to complete the sequence
Command: *right-click* to bring back the 3dface command sequence

Left-hand end of prism – another method
First point: *enter* 100,100 *right-click*
Second point: *enter* 100,200 *right-click*
Third point: *enter* **.xy** *right-click*
of pick the point 100,200 **(need Z):** *enter* 100 *right-click*
Fourth point: *enter* **.xy** *right-click*
of pick the point 100,100 **(need Z):** *enter* 100 *right-click*
Third point: *right-click* to complete the sequence
Command: *right-click* to bring back the 3dface command sequence

Right-hand end of prism
First point: *enter* 300,100 *right-click*
Second point: *enter* 300,200 *right-click*
Third point: *enter* **.xy** *right-click*
of pick the point 300,200 **(need Z):** *enter* 100 *right-click*
Fourth point: *enter* **.xy** *right-click*
of pick the point 300,100 **(need Z):** *enter* 100 *right-click*

Third point: *right-click* to complete the sequence
Command: *right-click* to bring back the 3dface command sequence

Top of prism
First point: *enter* 100,100,100 *right-click*
Second point: *enter* 100,200,100 *right-click*
Third point: *enter* 300,200,100 *right-click*
Fourth point: enter 300,100,100 *right-click*
Third point: *right-click* to complete the sequence
Command:

This sequence of entries creates a six-sided 3D drawing 200 units long by 100 units wide by 100 units high. Figure 11.3 shows the results of the drawing sequence given above.
Note: a 3D coordinate point vertically above a 2D point can be selected by either:

1. *entering* the *x.y.z* coordinates;
2. *entering* **.xy**, which brings **of** at the command line, followed by *picking* the *x,y* point. **(need Z):** then appears at the command line. *Entering* the *z* coordinate determines the required *x,y,z* point.

Continuing the 3DFace command sequence

If, instead of a *right-click* or pressing the *Return* key when the prompt **Third point:** appears at the command line for a second time, another *x,y,z* coordinate is entered, the prompt **Fourth point:** reappears. *Entering* another coordinate fixes another *x,y,z* point. The whole of the 3D drawing in Fig. 11.3 could have been constructed in this manner. An example of two faces constructed by continuing the sequence is shown in Fig. 11.4, together with the required command line sequence.

The command VPOINT

3D drawings can be viewed from different viewing points with the aid of the command **VPOINT**. Figure 11.5 gives four examples. The command sequence is:

Command: *enter* vpoint *right-click*
Rotate/<View point><0,0,1>: *enter* -1,-1,1 *right-click*
Regenerating drawing.
Command:

and the drawing reappears in the graphics window in its new "pictorial" view.

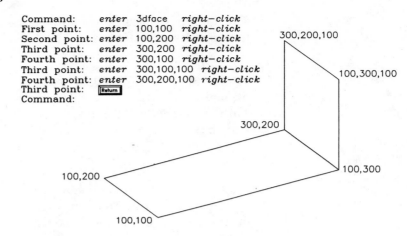

```
Command:        enter  3dface     right-click
First point:    enter  100,100    right-click
Second point:   enter  100,200    right-click
Third point:    enter  300,200    right-click
Fourth point:   enter  300,100    right-click
Third point:    enter  300,100,100  right-click
Fourth point:   enter  300,200,100  right-click
Third point:    [Return]
Command:
```

Fig. 11.4 Continuing the
3DFace command sequence

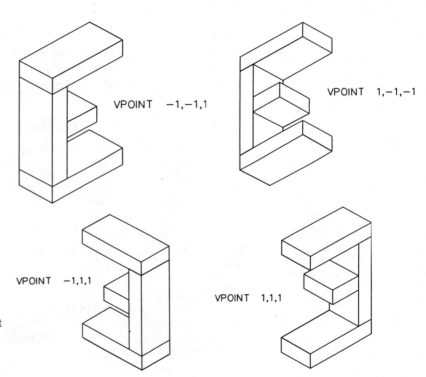

Fig. 11.5 Examples of different
views of a 3D drawing with
the aid of **VPOINT**

Notes

1. The figures **0,0,1** and -1,-1,1 in the above sequence indicate the x,y,z
   coordinate positions of the point from which the view is being
   "seen". These coordinates represent direction only and not the
   distance from the origin. This is because the views resulting from
   VPOINT are in parallel projection and not perspective projections;

2. The x,y,z points are taken with reference to the origin (0,0,0). This results in the following:
VPOINT 0,0,1 is as seen from above – it is the plan view;
VPOINT 0,1,0 is as seen from the right – it is an end view;
VPOINT 1,0,0 is as seen from the left – it is also an end view;

3. In the examples given in Fig. 11.5:
VPOINT -1,-1,1 is as seen from the left, from the front and from above;
VPOINT 1,-1,-1 is as seen from the right, from the front and from below;
VPOINT -1,1,1 is as seen from the left, from behind and from above;
VPOINT 1,1,1 is as seen from the right, from behind and from above.

The command HIDE

Any constructions lying behind 3D surfaces such as those formed with the aid of **3DFACE** can be hidden by calling the command **HIDE**. All that is required is to *enter* hide at the command line followed by a *right-click* or by pressing the *Return* key. The sequence showing at the command line is:

Command:
HIDE Regenerating drawing.
Hiding lines: done 100%
Command:

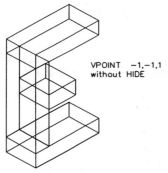

VPOINT -1,-1,1
without HIDE

Fig. 11.6 A 3D drawing created with **3DFACE** without **HIDE**

and lines behind 3D surface faces are hidden.
Examples of the use of **HIDE** are given in Figs 11.1, 11.3 and 11.5. Figure 11.6 shows a **VPOINT** -1,-1,1 view of the 3D drawing of Fig. 11.5 before **HIDE** was called. This model was constructed from a number of 3Dfaces.

3D Objects

A *Left-click* on **3D Objects ...** in the **Draw** pull-down menu (Fig. 11.7) brings the **3D Objects** dialogue box into the graphics window – Fig. 11.8. The required 3D object can be selected from this dialogue box, or alternatively, enter 3d at the command line, which allows a selection to be made by entering the initial letter of the 3D object from a prompt line:

Command:
Initializing ... 3D Objects loaded
Box/Cone/Dish/DOme/Mesh/Pyramid/Sphere/Torus/Wedge: *enter*
p (for Pyramid) *right-click*

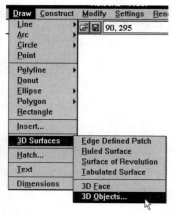

Fig. 11.7 Selecting **3D Objects ...** from the **Draw** pull-down menu

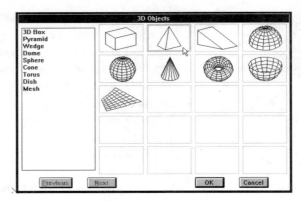

Fig. 11.8 The **3D Objects** dialogue box

and a series of further prompts will be seen asking for dimensional parameters for the selected 3D object.

A simple 3D drawing from 3D Objects – Fig. 11.9

This model was constructed by calling 3d at the command line, rather than by selection from the **3D Objects** dialogue box. The sequence of responses to the command line prompts was as follows:

> **Command:** *enter* 3d (for 3D Objects) *right-click*
> **Initializing ... 3D Objects loaded.**
> **Box/Cone/Dish/DOme/Mesh/Pyramid/Sphere/Torus/Wedge:** *enter* b (for Box) *right-click*
> **Corner of box:** *enter* 100,200 *right-click*
> **Length:** *enter* 200 *right-click*
> **Cube/<Width>:** *enter* 100 *right-click*
> **Height:** *enter* 100 *right-click*
> **Rotation angle about Z axis:** *enter* 0 *right-click*
> **Command:** *right-click* – to get back into the 3D objects prompts
> **3D**
> **Box/Cone/Dish/DOme/Mesh/Pyramid/Sphere/Torus/Wedge:** *enter* DO (for DOme) *right-click*
> **Center of dome:** *enter* .xy *right-click*

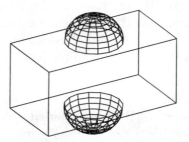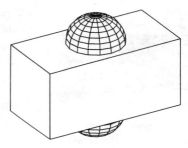

Fig.11.9 A 3D drawing made up of a Box, a Dome and a Dish, before and after **HIDE**

.xy of *pick* the centre of the box **(need Z):** *enter* 100 *right-click*
Diameter/<Radius>: *enter* 40 *right-click*
Number of longitudinal segments<16>: *right-click* – to accept
Number of lateral segments<8>: *right-click* – to accept
Command: *right-click* – to get back into the 3D Objects prompts
3D
Box/Cone/Dish/DOme/Mesh/Pyramid/Sphere/Torus/Wedge: *enter*
d (for Dish) *right-click*
Center of dish: *pick* the centre of the box *right-click*
Diameter/<Radius>: *enter* 40 *right-click*
Number of longitudinal segments<16>: *right-click* – to accept
Number of lateral segments<8>: *right-click* – to accept
Command:

No further examples of the use of the **3D Objects** will be given here because solid models created with the aid of the Advanced Solid Modelling Extension (AME) are not only more easily constructed, but also allow for more complex solids to be drawn (see page 169). However, the reader is advised to experiment with the 3D Objects commands.

<h2 style="text-align:center">3D Surfaces</h2>

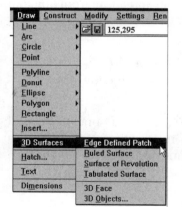

Fig. 11.10 Selecting **3D Surfaces** from the **Draw** pull-down menu

Left-click on **3D Surfaces** in the **Draw** menu (Fig. 11.10). It will be seen that there are four types of 3D Surfaces. These can be selected either from the **Draw** menu or by commands entered at the command line in the form:

Edgesurf for **Edge Defined Patch**;
Rulesurf for **Ruled Surface**;
Revsurf for **Surface of Revolution**;
Tabsurf for **Tabulated Surface**.

The prompts at the command line are the same no matter whether selected from the menu or entered at the command line. Figure 11.11 is an example of a solid constructed with **Edgesurf**. The command line prompts and responses for this solid are as follows:

Construct the outline given in Drawing 1 of Fig. 11.11. Then:

Command: *enter* edgesurf (or *select* from **Draw** menu) *right-click*
Select edge 1: *pick* an edge
Select edge 2: *pick* an edge
Select edge 3: *pick* an edge
Select edge 4: *pick* an edge
Command:

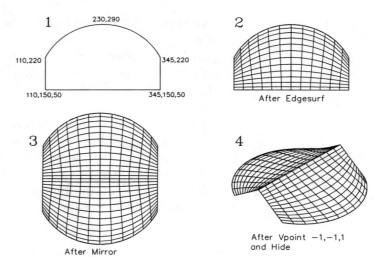

Fig. 11.11 An example of the
use of **Edgesurf**

The surface mesh is formed − Drawing 2. Now **Mirror** the mesh −
Drawing 3 − and view it from **Vpoint** -1,-1,1, followed by **Hide** −
Drawing 4.

Example of solid model constructed with Rulesurf

Draw an arc from 95,230 to 140,150 to 95,50 and a line from 300,330
to 300,80,-100. Then call **Rulesurf**:

   Command: *enter* rulesurf *right-click*
   Select first defining curve: *pick* top end of the arc
   Select second defining curve: *pick* top end of the line
   Command:

The result is as shown in Drawing 1 of Fig. 11.12. If opposite ends of
the two defining curves are picked, as in Drawing 2, the result is
somewhat different, the surfaces of the **Rulesurf** crossing, as shown in
Drawing 2.

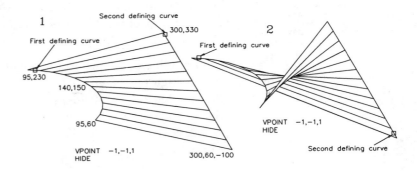

Fig. 11.12 An example of the
use of **Rulesurf**

Example of a 3D drawing constructed with Revsurf

With the **Pline** command draw a suitable outline such as is shown in Fig. 11.13. Add a suitable line for the axis of revolution. Then call **Revsurf**:

> **Command:** *Enter* **revsurf** *right-click*
> **Select Path curve:** *pick*
> **Select axis of revolution:** *pick*
> **Start angle <0>:** *right-click* (to accept)
> **Included angle (+=ccw, -=cw)<Full circle>:** *right-click* (to accept)
> **Command:**

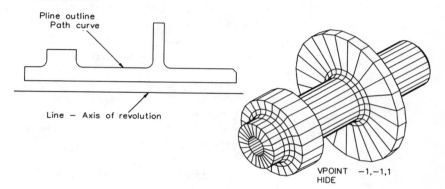

Fig. 11.13 An example of the use of **Revsurf**

Example of 3D drawing constructed with Tabsurf

Draw the arc and line as shown in Drawing 1 of Fig. 11.14. Then call **Tabsurf**:

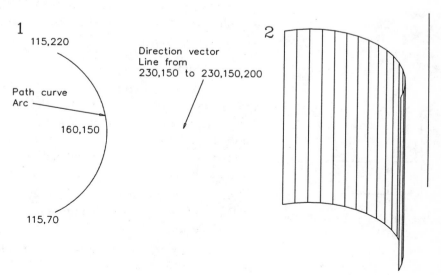

Fig. 11.14 An example of the use of **Tabsurf**

Command: *enter* tabsurf *right-click*
Select path curve: *pick*
Select direction vector: *pick*
Command:

and the tabsurf surface appears.

Surftab1 and Surftab2

All four surface command systems rely on the settings of these two variables, which determine the density of the surface meshes. In the examples given here:

Fig. 11.11 – Edgesurf – **Surftab1** and **Surftab2** set to 12;
Fig. 11.12 – Rulesurf – **Surftab1** and **Surftab2** set to 12;
Fig. 11.13 – Revsurf – **Surftab1** set to 24 and **Surftab2** set to 2;
Fig. 11.14 – Tabsurf – **Surftab1** set to 16 and **Surftab2** set to 2.

Notes
1. When using Revsurf and Tabsurf, the **Surftab2** setting is usually 2;
2. When using the other two surface commands, the setting of the **Surftab** variables will depend upon the model under construction. The reader is advised to experiment.

The User Coordinate System (the UCS)

The **UCS** allows the operator to set the AutoCAD graphics window in coordinate systems in terms of *x,y,z* at any angle other than that which is set when AutoCAD is started up or when a **New** drawing is called – in what is known as the **WCS** (World Coordinate System). When the **UCS** is set to an angle other than the **WCS**, drawings can be constructed in the graphics window as if the plane of the screen is in a position in which the coordinate *z* is at 0, with *x* coordinates reading horizontally and *y* coordinates reading vertically.

The UCS icon

When a **New** drawing is started in AutoCAD for Windows, the graphics window opens with the **UCS icon** at the bottom right-hand corner (Fig. 11.15). The icon shows an X pointing in the *x* +ve coordinate direction, a Y pointing in the *y* +ve coordinate direction and a W showing that the graphics window is in the World Coordinate System (the WCS). The UCS icon can be turned off by:

Command: *enter* ucsicon *right-click*
ON/OFF/All/Noorigin/ORigin/<ON>: *enter* off *right-click*
Command:

The icon can be turned back on by responding with on when the ucsicon call is made.

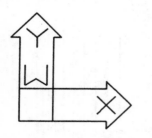

Fig. 11.15 The UCS icon at AutoCAD start-up

The UCS icon can take a variety of forms, among which are those shown in Fig. 11.16.

Note: Whether the icon is on or off, changes in the **UCS** will not take place unless the set variable **UCSFOLLOW** is set to 1 (ON).

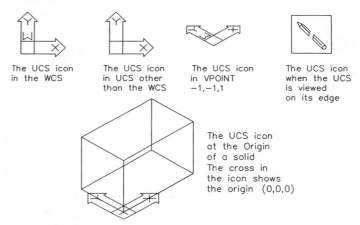

The UCS icon
in the WCS

The UCS icon
in UCS other
than the WCS

The UCS icon
in VPOINT
−1,−1,1

The UCS icon
when the UCS
is viewed
on its edge

The UCS icon
at the Origin
of a solid
The cross in
the icon shows
the origin (0,0,0)

Fig. 11.16 Various types of UCS icon

The set variable UCSFOLLOW

If a new position for the **UCS** is called, there will be no response unless the set variable **UCSFOLLOW** is ON – set to 1 as follows:

Command: *enter* ucsfollow *right-click*
New value for UCSFOLLOW<0>: *enter* 1 *right-click*
Command:

The UCS Orientation dialogue box

Left-click on **UCS** in the **Settings** pull-down menu and the **UCS** sub-menu appears (Fig. 11.17). A *left-click* on **Presets...** in this sub-menu brings the **UCS Orientation** dialogue box into the graphics window (Fig. 11.18). Selections can be made from the dialogue box to set the **UCS**

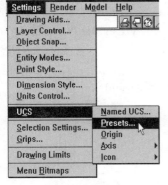

Fig. 11.17 **UCS Presets ...** from the **Settings** menu

Fig. 11.18 The **UCS Orientation** dialogue box

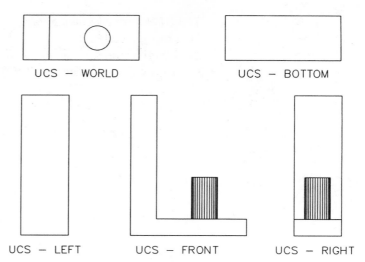

Fig 11.19 Some examples of
UCS orientations

in any position, as if viewing a solid model from the top, from the back, from the left, from the right, and from the bottom. Examples are shown in Fig. 11.19. Figure 11.20 shows the solid model as a 3D drawing.

UCS prompts at the command line

Enter ucs at the command line and prompts appear:

> **Command:** *enter* ucs *right-click*
> **Origin/ZAxis/3point/Entity/View/X/Y/Z/Prev/Restore/Save/Del/?/**
> **<World>:**

Origin: Fig. 11.21 shows the UCS icon at the model origin, which becomes *x,y,z* = 0,0,0. Use the **UCSICON** call as well;

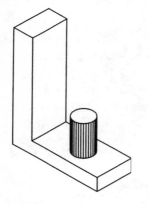

Fig. 11.20 The solid model
shown in Fig. 11.19

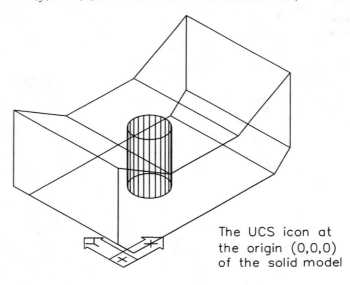

Fig. 11.21 The UCS icon at the
solid model origin

The UCS icon at
the origin (0,0,0)
of the solid model

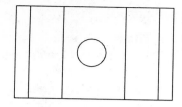

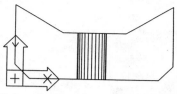

The result of the UCS 3point response

UCS 3point
Origin point: 135,165
Point on positive portion of the X axis: 300,165
Point on positive Y portion of the UCS XY plane: 300,165,1

Fig. 11.22 The results of the 3point response

3point: Fig. 11.22 shows the results of the selection of three points in answer to this prompt;

X/Y/Z: Fig. 11.23 shows the results of a response to the **X**, **Y** and **Z** prompts in turn;

Previous: The response p (for Previous) brings back to the graphics window the UCS previous to the current UCS (if any);

Save: The response s (for Save) brings the prompt: **?/Desired UCS name:** at the command line. Entering a name allows the operator to recall the saved UCS, which can be recalled later by the **Restore** response;

Delete: allows a UCS view to be deleted from the list held in the current drawing. The prompt line will show:

UCS name(s) to delete:

ZAxis: allows a solid model to be rotated around the z axis;

World: *entering* w (for World) in response to the UCS prompts always allows the solid model to revert to the **WCS**.

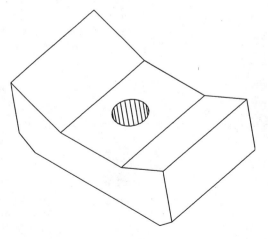

Fig. 11.23 The results of responses to the **X**, **Y** and **Z** **prompts**

View rotated around X 30
around Y 30
around Z 30

Viewports

Fig. 11.24 Selecting **Tiled
Viewports...** from the **View**
menu

Left-click on **Tiled Viewports...** in the **View** pull-down menu (Fig.
11.24). The **Tiled Viewport Layout** dialogue box appears (Fig. 11.25).
Left-click in the **Four: Left** layout box in the dialogue box and the **Four:
Left** viewports appear in the graphics window. An example of a 3D
drawing constructed with the aid of the **Surface** commands is given in
Fig. 11.26. In constructing this solid model:

1. A *left-click* in any one of the four viewports makes that viewport
    active to allow constructions in the selected viewport;
2. While constructing a 3D drawing in one viewport, the construc-
    tions appear in all other viewports;

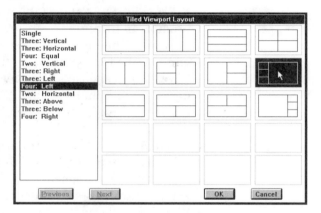

Fig. 11.25 The **Tiled Viewport
Layout** dialogue box

3. With the viewport layout as shown in Fig. 11.26, the constructing
    would normally be carried out in the largest viewport, the other
    viewports being used to indicate to the operator whether his/her
    constructions were correct;
4. In the given example (Fig. 11.26):

    In the large viewport: **UCSFOLLOW** was set to 1 (ON);
    In the other three viewports **UCSFOLLOW** was set to 0 (Off);
    In the upper left viewport **VPOINT** was set to -1,-1,1;
    In the centre left viewport **VPOINT** was set to 1,0,0;
    In the lower left viewport **VPOINT** was set to 0,-1,0;

5. These settings allowed:

    In the large viewport a new **UCS** could be called and the viewport
    would re-set to this new UCS. In all other viewports, new UCS
    settings would be ignored;
    In the upper left viewport a pictorial view would appear;
    In the centre left viewport an end view would appear;
    In the lower left viewport a front view would appear.

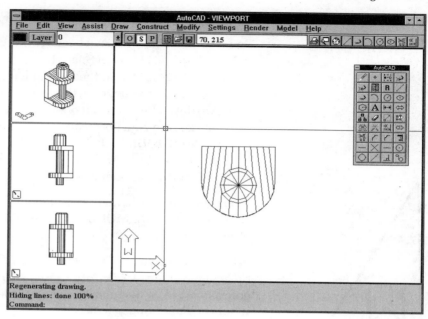

Fig. 11.26 An example of a 3D drawing constructed in tiled viewports

With these settings, the operator can have several views of the model as it is being constructed, allowing him/her to check whether the constructions are correct as they appear in the graphics window. Other settings are, of course, possible if desired.

The 3D drawing was constructed as follows:

1. *Left-click* in each viewport in turn, making it active. Set **UCSFOLLOW** and **VPOINT** as above;
2. *Left-click* in the large viewport and make all constructions in that viewport;
3. Draw the outline of the top face with **PLINE**;
4. In the **UCS Orientation** dialogue box, select **FRONT**;
5. Draw a vertical line 20 units long and **TABSURF** the pline to produce the lower arm;
6. **COPY** the **TABSURF** to its upper position;
7. Go back to the **WCS** – *enter* UCS followed by a w (for World);
8. Construct a **RULESURF** surface for a surface of an arm;
9. In **UCS FRONT** Multiple **COPY** the **RULESURF** surface to both sides of the two arms;
10. In the **UCS FRONT** construct the pin with the aid of **REVSURF**;
11. Go back to the **WCS** and call **HIDE** in each of the four viewports in turn.

Other settings of tiled viewports can be made at the operator's discretion.

Tilemode, Model Space and Paper Space

So far in this book we have been working with the graphics window in **Model Space**. In Model Space the variable **TILEMODE** is ON (set to 1) and the **UCS** icon is at the bottom left-hand corner of the window. When working in viewports, they are set in the graphics window as if laid like tiles – abutting each other edge to edge. In any of the viewport orientations, the viewports cannot be moved from their tiled positions – hence **TILEMODE** is ON.

Tilemode can be turned OFF (or ON), by a *left-click* on **Tilemode** in the **View** pull-down menu (see Fig. 11.24) or by:

Command: *enter* tilemode *right-click*
New value for TILEMODE <1>: *enter* 0 (off) *right-click*
Command:

When **TILEMODE** is **OFF** (set to 0), the UCS icon changes to the Paper Space icon (Fig. 11.27). Any drawing in the previous **Model Space** graphics window disappears, leaving a blank window with nothing in it but the Paper Space icon.

When in Paper Space, a *left-click* on **Tilemode** in the **View** menu takes the graphics window back to **Model Space**, with its viewports – note that there may be only one viewport or there may be several, depending upon how many viewports were in use during the time construction was taking place.

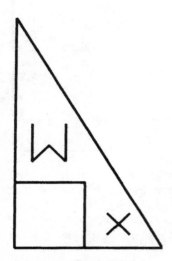

Fig. 11.27 The Paper Space icon

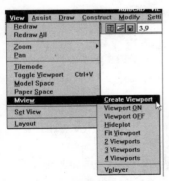

Fig. 11.28 The **Mview** sub-menu from the **View** menu

The command MVIEW

When in Paper Space, *left-click* on **Mview** in the **View** menu (Fig. 11.28), or *enter* mview at the command line:

Command: _mview
ON/OFF/HIDEPLOT/FIT/2/3/4/Restore/<First point>: *enter* r (for Restore) *right-click*
?/Name of window configuration to insert<*ACTIVE>: *right-click* (to accept ACTIVE)
Fit/<First point>: *pick* a suitable window corner point
Second point: *pick* the second window point
Command:

and the construction in the Model Space reappears in the Paper Space window (Fig. 11.29).

The prompts in the MVIEW command

OFF: a *left-click* on any viewport edge erases the whole viewport and its contents;

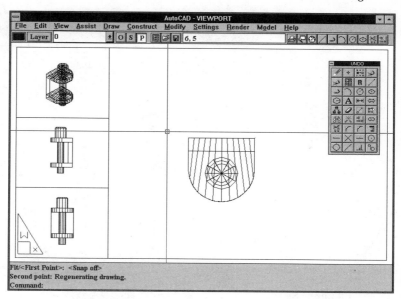

Fig. 11.29 The **Model Space** window restored into the **Paper Space** window

ON: a *left-click* on the edge of a viewport which has been turned OFF brings it and its contents back to the screen;

Hideplot: when printing or plotting the graphics window contents, lines behind 3D surfaces in any selected viewport will be hidden. A *left-click* on an edge of any viewport is effective for this purpose;

Fit: the selected viewports **(from 2/3/4/Restore)** are fitted up to the edges of the Paper Space window;

2: The construction from Model Space is placed in two viewports – a further prompt enables them to be horizontal or vertical;

3: The construction from Model Space is placed in three viewports, with a further prompt allowing them to be placed in a variety of ways;

4: The construction from Model Space is placed in four equal-size viewports;

Restore: Restores the viewports as they were in Model Space.

Re-arranging viewports in Paper Space

Take as an example Fig. 11.29. From **Model Space,** in which the 3D drawing was constructed, and fitting it into four viewports in Paper Space, the graphics window appears as shown in Fig. 11.30. Now switch back to **Model Space** – either *left-click* on **Model Space** in the **View** menu or *enter* mspace at the command line. Even in **Model Space**, the construction is now in four viewports, with all windows holding the same view of the solid (Fig. 11.31).

Although Fig. 11.30 and Fig. 11.31 look similar, the AutoCAD Model and Paper Space windows are very different:

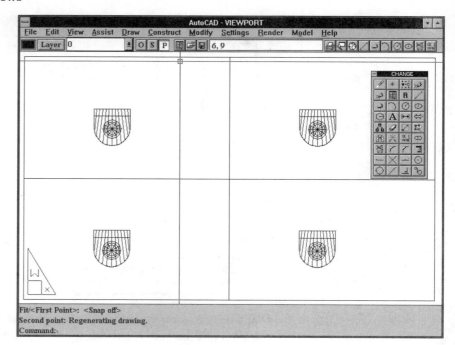

Fig. 11.30 The **Paper Space** window with four viewports

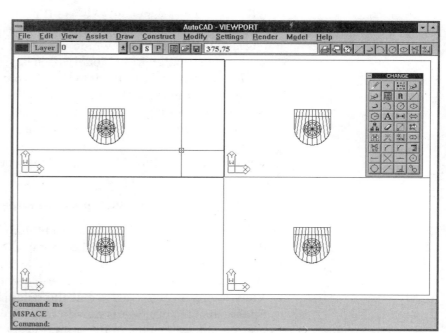

Fig. 11.31 The **Model Space** window showing the same four viewports

1. In **Model Space** only that viewport chosen by a *left-click* within its area, is active;
2. In **Paper Space**, the whole window is active and constructions can be added in any part of the window – for example, text can be added anywhere in the window;
3. In **Model Space** the viewports are tiled and cannot be moved;
4. In **Paper Space** the viewports can be moved, turned off or turned back on. See Figs 11.32 and 11.33 for examples. Both these examples show the possibilities of producing orthographic projections from solid models constructed in AutoCAD with the aid of **Paper Space** viewports.
5. With **Hideplot** the four viewports of Fig. 11.32 can be plotted with hidden lines removed (Fig. 11.34). It should be noted that the viewport boundaries will also be plotted unless they are placed on a different layer and that layer is then turned off.

Note: The use of **Model Space** and **Paper Space** for plotting orthographic drawings will be referred to later in more detail, when dealing with solid modelling with the Advanced Modelling Extension (AME) – pages 169 onwards.

Questions

1. With respect to the AutoCAD graphics window, in which direction would you expect the z axis to be positive?

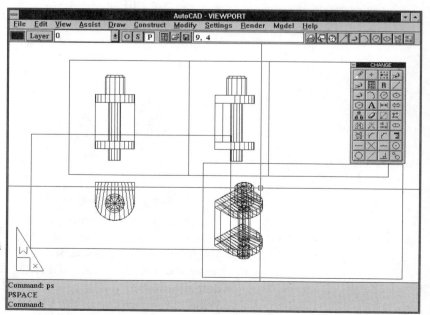

Fig. 11.32 Viewports moved in **Paper Space** to give a three-view First angle orthographic projection with a pictorial view

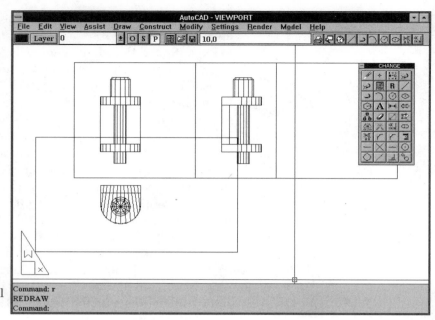

Fig. 11.33 The four viewports of Fig. 11.32 with the pictorial view viewport turned off

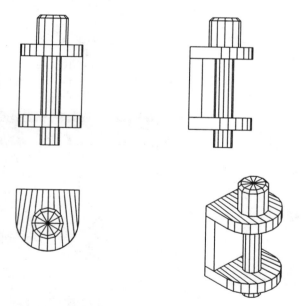

Fig. 11.34 A plot from a **Paper Space** window after using **Hideplot**

2. Which types of polygon can be constructed from a single set of prompts of the command **3DFACE**?
3. What happens if, instead of a *left-click* at the second **Third point:** prompt of the command **3DFACE**, you continue *entering* coordinate numbers?
4. What is the purpose of the **VPOINT** command system?

5. In which position would you expect a 3D drawing to appear when the following **VPOINT** responses are made:

    1,1,1; -1,-1,-1; 1,-1,-1; 2,-1,1; 1,-2,-3?

6. What is the purpose of the command **HIDE**?
7. Name the **3D Objects** which are standard in AutoCAD for Windows.
8. There are four **3D Surfaces** commands. Name them.
9. What does the abbreviation **UCS** stand for?
10. Explain in a few words the purpose of the **UCS**.
11. When can **Viewports** be called – with **TILEMODE** OFF or ON?
12. Why is **TILEMODE** so called?

Exercises

1. Figs 11.35 and 11.36. Construct the 3D drawing to the dimensions and details given.

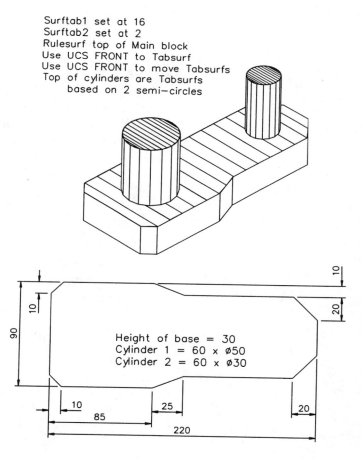

Fig. 11.35 Exercise 1

Fig. 11.36 Dimensions for Exercise 1

2. A command system not mentioned so far is **ELEV**. Follow the sequence:

(i) **Command:** *enter* elev *right-click*
New current elevation<0>: *right-click* (to accept)
New current thickness<0>: *enter* 30 *right-click*
Command:

(Draw a rectangle (line or pline) 220 x 120. View this from VPOINT -1,-1,1. It will be seen that it has height as well as length and width;

(ii) Reset **ELEV** to **Current elevation** of 30 and **Current thickness** of 0;

(iii) Draw a 3dface to the same dimensions as the original rectangle. View this as before, followed by **HIDE**. It will be seen that the rectangle looks like a solid;

(iv) Reset **ELEV** to **Current elevation** of 30 and **Current thickness** of 50;

(v) Draw two circles of diameter 60 and 30 as shown:

(vi) View this as before, followed by **HIDE**. It will be seen that the solid block now has two cylinders on its upper surface.

Figure 11.37 shows the results of this exercise.

3. Fig. 11.38. Working with the command **ELEV** and to the dimensions given with the drawing, construct the 3D drawing shown.

4. Use **REVSURF** to construct the two views of a spindle shown in Fig. 11.39. The **PLINE** of the path curve and the axis of revolution are included with the illustration. Work to any suitable dimensions.

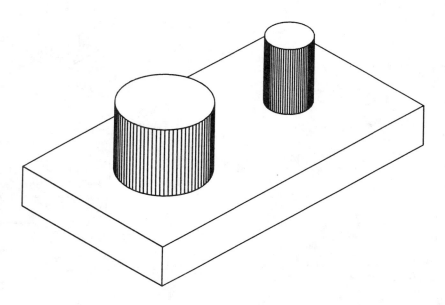

Fig. 11.37 Exercise 2

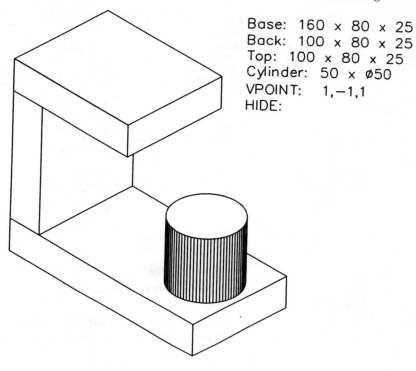

Base: 160 x 80 x 25
Back: 100 x 80 x 25
Top: 100 x 80 x 25
Cylinder: 50 x ⌀50
VPOINT: 1,−1,1
HIDE:

Fig. 11.38 Exercise 3

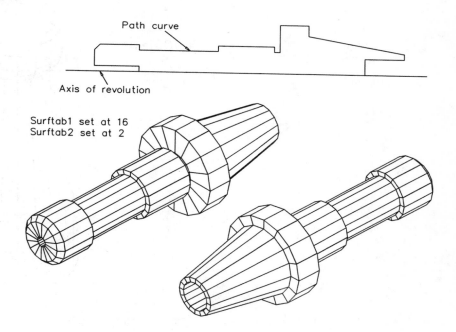

Path curve

Axis of revolution

Surftab1 set at 16
Surftab2 set at 2

Fig. 11.39 Exercise 4

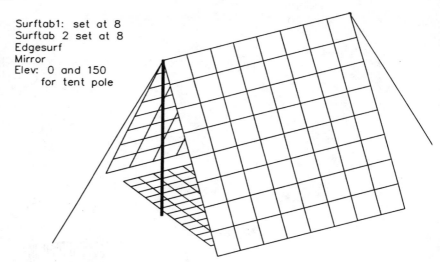

Surftab1: set at 8
Surftab 2 set at 8
Edgesurf
Mirror
Elev: 0 and 150
        for tent pole

Fig. 11.40 Exercise 5

5. Working to any convenient sizes, construct the "tent" shown in Fig. 11.40.

6. Working with the **3D Objects** as stated and to any suitable sizes, construct the 3D drawing shown in Fig. 11.41.

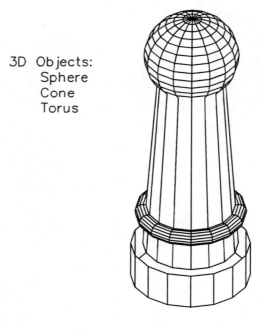

3D Objects:
    Sphere
    Cone
    Torus

Fig. 11.41 Exercise 6

CHAPTER 12

3D solid models with AME

Introduction

The **Advanced Modelling Extension (AME)** is only available with AutoCAD for Windows if the extension software has been purchased with the AutoCAD software. Unlike the 3D drawings constructed with the aid of the **Surface** commands as described in Chapter 11, AME allows the construction of true solid models, the data from which can be transferred to other software products for use in Computer Aided Manufacture (CAM). The solid models are constructed from elements derived from:

1. AME **Primitives** – geometric solids;
2. Solids of revolution formed with the aid of **Solrev**;
3. Extruded solids formed with the aid of **Solext**.

The elements are combined with the aid of three Boolean command systems acting as union, subtraction or intersection:

1. **Solunion**
2. **Solsub**
3. **Solint**.

Other AME commands allow the edges of a model to be filleted or chamfered (**Solfill** and **Solcham**). The model can be sectioned with **Solsect** or cut into parts with **Solcut**. The properties of the solid – volume, mass, centre of gravity etc. – can be determined if required.

The **UCS** is of particular importance when constructing solid models in AME because it allows the model under construction to be placed in a variety of coordinate systems.

The AME Primitives

Left-click on **Primitives...** in the **Model** pull-down menu (Fig. 12.1). The **AME Primitives** dialogue box appears in the graphic window (Fig.

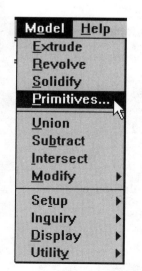

Fig. 12.1 **Primitives** in the **Model** menu

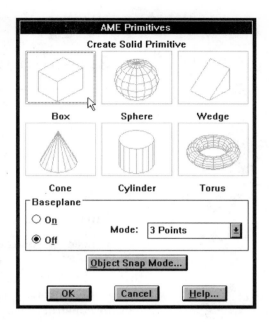

Fig. 12.2 The **AME Primitives**
dialogue box

12.2). As can be seen, there are six AME primitive geometric solids –
Box, **Sphere**, **Wedge**, **Cone**, **Cylinder** and **Torus**. The command systems associated with the primitives can be called either by selection
from the **AME Primitives** dialogue box or by entering the appropriate
command name at the command line. Thus a **Box** can be constructed
either by a *left-click* on the icon in the box labelled **Box,** or:

Command: *enter* solbox *right-click*

the same prompts appear at the command line whichever your choice:

Baseplane/Centre/<Corner of box>: *enter* a coordinate (or *pick*)
    right-click
Cub/Length/<Other corner>: *enter* a coordinate (or *pick*) *right-click*
Height: *enter* a figure for the height *right-click*

A series of messages follow – such as:

Phase I Boundary evaluation begins
Phase II Tessellation computation begins
Updating the Advanced Modeling Extension database
Command:

The 3D box appears in plan on the screen in a plan position (Fig. 12.3).
    Place the solbox in a vpoint viewing position of -1,-1,1 to check that
the solid is correctly drawn (Fig. 12.4).
    Each primitive has its own set of prompts appearing at the command
line, but they all include the set of messages informing the operator of

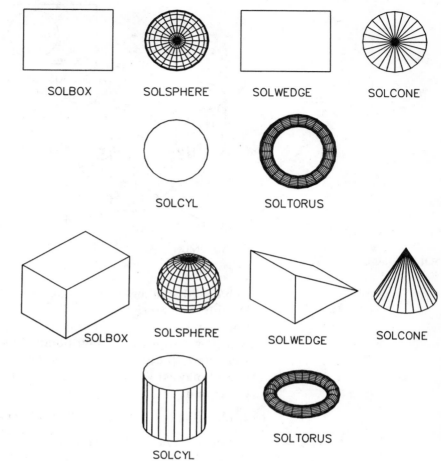

Fig. 12.3 The six **AME** primitives in plan view resting on the *x.y.* plane

Fig. 12.4 The six **AME** primitives in a **VPOINT** -1,-1,1

the evaluation and tessellation procedures. With more advanced constructions in **AME** these operations may take some time, and the messages indicate to the operator that while he/she is waiting the computer is still acting on the data. The sequences of prompts connected with the other primitives will be included in the next few pages.

The AME Boolean operatives – Solunion, Solsub and Solint

Construct two AME primitives – a solbox and a solcyl as shown in Fig. 12.5. The command sequence can be opened either by selecting the primitives for the **AME Primitives** dialogue box or by entering the command at the command line.

Command: *enter* solbox *right-click*
Baseplane/Centre/<Corner of box>: *enter* 50,200 *right-click*

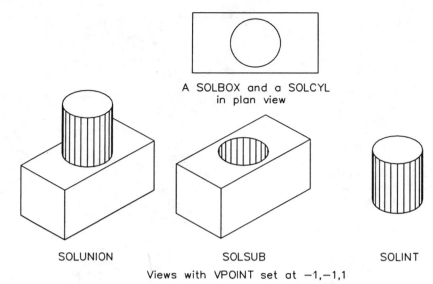

A SOLBOX and a SOLCYL
in plan view

Fig. 12.5 Examples of the
Boolean operatives on a
SOLBOX and a **SOLCYL**

SOLUNION   SOLSUB   SOLINT

Views with VPOINT set at −1,−1,1

Cub/Length/<Other corner>: *enter* 150,150 *right-click*
Height: *enter* 50 *right-click*
Command: *enter* solcyl *right-click*
Baseplate/Elliptical/<Center point: *enter* 100,175 *right-click*
Diameter/<Radius>: *enter* 20 *right-click*
Center of other end/<Height>: *enter* 100 *right-click*
Command:

Now place the two solids in a **VPOINT** set at -1,-1,1 and:

Command: *enter* solunion *right-click*
Select objects: *pick* the solbox **1 found. Select objects:** *pick* the
   solcyl **1 found**
Select objects: *right-click* (to accept)
Command:

Undo the solunion and:

Command: *enter* solsub *right-click*
Select objects: *pick* the solbox **1 found**
Select objects: *right-click* (to accept)
1 solid selected.
Objects to subtract from them... *pick* the solcyl **1 found**
Select objects. *right-click* (to accept)
Command:

Undo the solunion and:

Command: *enter* solint *right-click*
Select objects: *pick* the solbox **1 found**

Select objects: *pick* the solcyl **1 found**
Select objects: *right-click* (to accept)
2 solids selected.
Command:

Note that the use of **SOLINT** results in the interference surfaces of the two solids – which in this example will be the surface of the cylinder. Another example of **SOLINT** is given in Fig. 12.6 between a cylinder and a cone.

Note: A series of messages will appear at the command line between the acceptance of the selected objects and the action taking place in the graphics window. This is common to all the **AME** command prompt sequences.

Fig. 12.6 A **SOLCYL** and a **SOLCONE** after **SOLINT**

A SOLCYL and a SOLCONE

The SOLCYL and SOLCONE after SOLINT

The AME commands SOLSPHERE, SOLWEDGE and SOLTORUS

These three primitive command prompt sequences follow the pattern:

SOLSPHERE
Command:
Baseplane/<Center of sphere><0,0,0>: *enter* a coordinate *right-click* or *pick* a point
Diameter/<Radius>: *enter* a coordinate *right-click* or *pick* a point
Command:

and the sphere appears in the graphics window.

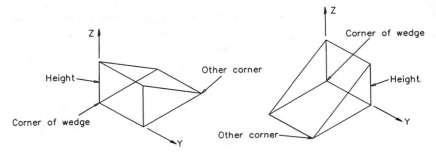

Fig. 12.7 The back of a
SOLWEDGE is in the YZ
plane

SOLWEDGE (Fig. 12.7)
Command: *enter* solwedge *right-click*
Baseplane/<Corner of wedge>:<0,0,0>: *enter* a coordinate *right-click* or *pick* a point
Length/<Other corner>: *enter* a coordinate *right-click* or *pick* a point
Height: *enter* a number for the height
Command:

Note: The back of the wedge so formed – its highest surface – will be in the *y,z* plane in which the **Corner of wedge** point was given (see Fig. 12.7).

SOLTORUS (Fig. 12.8)
Command: *enter* soltorus *right-click*
Baseplane/<Center of torus><0,0,0>: *enter* a coordinate *right-click* or *pick* a point

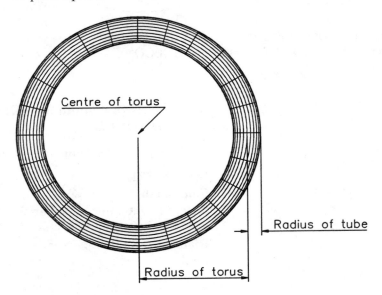

Fig. 12.8 Details of a
SOLTORUS

Diameter/<Radius>: of torus: *enter* a coordinate *right-click* or *pick* a point

Diameter/<Radius> of tube: *enter* the required figures *right-click*

Command:

The prompt Baseplane

The prompt **Baseplane** appears with several of the primitive command prompt sequences. Responses to this prompt can determine the plane of the base for the primitive. As an example, for the torus in Fig. 12.8:

Command: *enter* soltorus *right-click*

Baseplane/<Center of torus><0,0,0>:

Baseplane by Entity/Last/Zaxis/View/XY/YZ/ZX/<3point>: *enter* xy *right-click*

Point on XY plane<0,0,0>: *enter* .xy *right-click*

of *enter* the *xy* coordinate *right-click* **(need Z):** *enter* the z coordinate

Baseplane/<Center of torus><0,0,0>: *enter* a coordinate *right-click* or *pick* a point

Diameter/<Radius>: of torus: *enter* the radius figures *right-click*

Diameter/<Radius> of tube: *enter* the required figures *right-click*

Command:

The torus appears with its base in the stated z plane.

The AME command SOLMESH

When an AME primitive or a solid model formed by the Boolean operatives appears in the graphics window, it will be in the form of a **wireframe** – no 3D surface meshes have been formed. In order to change the wireframes into solid model with 3D surface meshes, the model must be acted on by the command **SOLMESH**. The prompts of this command are:

Command: *enter* solmesh *right-click*

Select objects: 1 found

Select objects:

Updating object

Various messages may appear, followed by:

Surface meshing of current solid is completed

Creating block for mesh representation...

Done

Command:

When the 3D surfaces of a solid model have been meshed, the command **Hide** will cause all hidden lines behind the 3D surfaces to become hidden. If one wishes to change the model back to a wireframe all that is required is:

> **Command:**
> **Select object:** *pick* the solid model **1 solid selected.**
> **Command:**

The AME commands SOLFILL and SOLCHAM

To add a fillet to an AME solid model (Fig. 12.9):

> **Command:** *enter* solfill *right-click*
> **Pick edges of solids to be filleted (press ENTER when done):** *pick*
>   1 edge selected
> **Diameter/<Radius> of fillet <0.00>:** *enter* 10 *right-click*

Various messages may appear, followed by:

> **Updating the Advanced Solid Modeling database**
> **Command:**

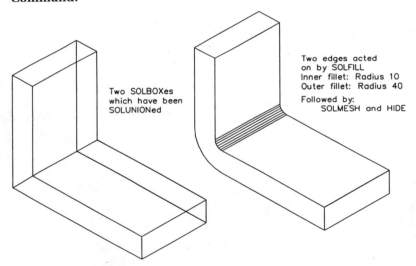

Two SOLBOXes which have been SOLUNIONed

Two edges acted on by SOLFILL
Inner fillet: Radius 10
Outer fillet: Radius 40

Followed by:
    SOLMESH and HIDE

Fig. 12.9 An example of the action of **SOLFILL**

To add a chamfer to an AME solid model (Fig. 12.10):

> **Command:** *enter* solcham *right-click*
> **Pick base surface:** *pick*
> Next/<OK>:
> **Pick edges of this face to be chamfered (press ENTER when done):**
>   *pick* and *right-click*
> 1 edges selected
> **Enter distance along base surface<0.00>:** *enter* 10 *right-click*
> **Enter distance along adjacent surface<10.00>:** *right-click*

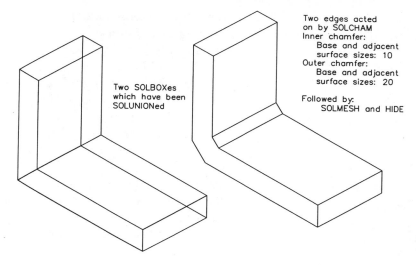

Two SOLBOXes
which have been
SOLUNIONed

Two edges acted
on by SOLCHAM
Inner chamfer:
    Base and adjacent
    surface sizes: 10
Outer chamfer:
    Base and adjacent
    surface sizes: 20

Followed by:
    SOLMESH and HIDE

Fig. 12.10 An example of the
action of **SOLCHAM**

Various messages may appear, followed by:

**Updating the Advanced Solid Modeling database
Command:**

Notes

1. It is not possible to include a fillet or a chamfer if the AME solid is
   meshed. If the attempt is made, the following message will appear
   when an edge is selected:
   **PMESH selected. Change to a WIREFRAME for feature to be
   selected?<Y>:**
   A *right-click* confirms the **<Y>** and the solid is changed back to a
   wireframe;
2. When using the command **SOLCHAM**, the selected base surface
   will highlight by changing to a surface surrounded by dotted lines.
   If a base surface has been selected which is not the desired surface,
   enter n (for Next) and another surface highlights. Continue if
   necessary until the required surface highlights.

A worked example of an AME solid model construction

The following example of a simple 3D solid model worked with the aid
of AME is included here to show how **Primitives** can be formed with
the aid of the Boolean operatives **Solunion** and **Solsub** into a solid
model representing a small engineered component.

Note the use of the **User Coordinate System (UCS)** to reposition the
model in a new UCS for some of the operations. When constructing
many AME solids a number of different *x,y* planes will probably be
required, set with the aid of the **UCS**.

1. Construct a **SOLBOX** 250 by 80 by 15 high
2. **Command:** *enter* ucs *right-click*
   Origin/ZAxis/3point/Entity/View/X/Y/Z/Prev/Restore/Save/Del/?/<World>:
   enter o (for Origin) *right-click*
   Origin point <0,0,0>: *left-click* at 100,200
   The box plan enlarges to window extents.
3. **Command:** *enter* z (for Zoom) *right-click*
   All/Center/Dynamic/Extents/Left/Previous/Vmax/Window/<Scale (X/XP)>:
   enter 1 (previous full size) *right-click*
   The box plan reverts to its original size.
4. **Command:** *enter* ucsicon *right-click*
   ON/OFF/All/Noorigin/ORigin<ON>: *enter* or (for Origin) *right-click*
   Command:
   The **UCS** icon moves to the selected point in the graphics window. The window origin (0,0,0) is now at the bottom top left corner of the 3D box (Fig. 12.11).

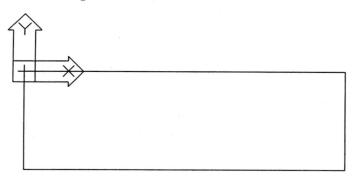

Fig. 12.11 The **USC** icon at a new origin

5. Construct another SOLBOX 40 by 20 by 15 at the centre of each end of the base already constructed;
6. Construct two **SOLCYL**s at the centres of the inner ends of the two small solboxes, each of radius 10 and height 15;
7. **SOLUNION** the two smaller solboxes with its solcylinder;
8. **SOLSUB** the two cylinder and solbox unions from the main base solbox;
9. Construct a **SOLCYL** at the centre point of base solbox of radius 30 and height 40, with its base 15 units above the *x,y* plane
10. Add another **SOLCYL** centred at the same centre point, but without a *z* coordinate – radius 22.5, height 55;
11. **SOLUNION** the base solbox and the outer solcyl;
12. **SOLSUB** the inner solcyl from the main union;

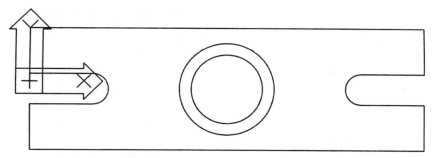

Fig. 12.12 The **UCSICON** in its reset position

13. Reset the **UCS** icon at the position shown in Fig. 11.12;
14. **ZOOM** to 1;
15. Bring up the **UCS Orientation** dialogue box and *left-click* on **UCS FRONT**, **Relative to Current UCS** and **OK**;
16. **ZOOM** to 1;

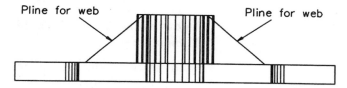

Fig. 12.13 The plines for the two webs

17. Draw plines as in Fig. 12.13;
18. **SOLEXT** the plines 10 high;
19. **UCS** World to check that the pline extrusions are OK;
20. **SOLUNION** the extrusions to the rest of the solid;
21. **VPOINT** -1,-1,1;
22. **SOLFILL** the base corners to a radius of 15;
23. **SOLFILL** the join between the outer solcyl and the base to a radius of 5, not forgetting the rear part of the fillet behind the ribs. Use **ZOOM** as necessary for this;
24. **SOLMESH** the solid model;
25. **HIDE**.

The completed solid model is shown in Fig. 12.14.

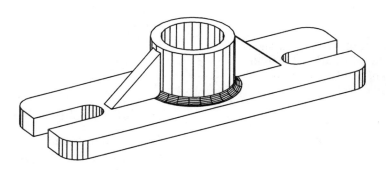

Fig. 12.14 The completed AME solid model

The AME command SOLEXT

In the given example it will be noted that a command **SOLEXT** was used to change the plines for the webs into solids with a thickness of 10 units. Any pline outline can be extruded into an AME solid with the aid of this command. The command **Extrude** can be called from the **Model** pull-down menu or by entering solext at the command line. The prompts are:

> **Command:** *enter* solext *right-click*
> **Select regions, polylines and circles for extrusion...**
> **Select objects:** *pick* **1 found**
> **Select objects:** *right-click*
> **Height of extrusion:** *enter* 50 *right-click*
> **Extrusion taper angle<0>:** *enter* 15 *right-click*

Various messages may appear, followed by:

> **Updating the Advanced Solid Modeling database**
> **Command:**

Examples of extrusions are given in Fig. 12.15. These were taken from the pline outlines given in Fig. 12.16. The bottom right-hand corner example is of two extrusions taken from plines, with the inner pline extruded at a height of 10 and an angle of 30, followed by the use of **SOLSUB** to subtract the inner extrusion from the outer.

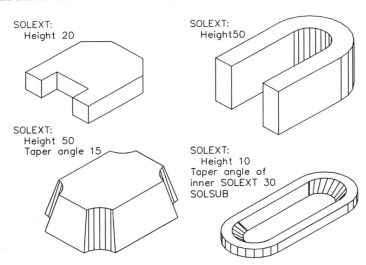

SOLEXT:
Height 20

SOLEXT:
Height 50

SOLEXT:
Height 50
Taper angle 15

SOLEXT:
Height 10
Taper angle of
inner SOLEXT 30
SOLSUB

Fig. 12.15 Some examples of AME solids formed with the aid of **SOLEXT** from plines

The AME variable SOLWDENS

The density of the wireframe in primitives and extrusions involving circular parts is set from 1 to 12 by calling the variable **SOLWDENS**,

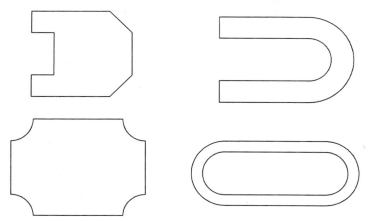

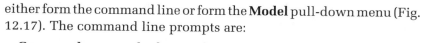

Fig. 12.16 The pline outlines from which the solids shown in Fig. 12.15 were extruded

either form the command line or form the **Model** pull-down menu (Fig. 12.17). The command line prompts are:

Command: *enter* solwdens *right-click*
Wireframe mesh density (1 to 12) <1>: *enter* 6 (for example *right-click*
Command:

and the wire density is set. In examples shown in this chapter **Solwdens** has been set at 6.

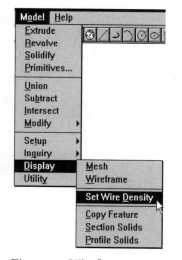

Fig. 12.17 **Wireframe Density** (Solwdens) from the **Model** pull-down menu

The AME command SOLREV

This command will form a solid of revolution. An example is given in Figures 12.18 and 12.19. The prompts associated with the command are:

Command: *enter* solrev *right-click*
Select region, polyline or circle for revolution...
Select objects: *pick* **1 found**
Select objects: *right-click* (to accept)
Axis of revolution – Entity/X/Y/<Start point of axis>: *pick*
End point of axis: *pick*
Command:

and the solid of revolution is formed.

If an angle other than **<full circle>** is entered, the result will be partial solids of revolution. Examples are given in Fig. 12.20. This shows solids of revolution when the responses to the prompt **Angle of revolution<full circle>:** have been 180, 90 and 60, giving a half solid of revolution, a quarter solid of revolution and a one-sixth solid of revolution respectively. In the example of a half solid of revolution, a keyway was included by the use of **SOLBOX** and **SOLSUB** to subtract the box from the solid.

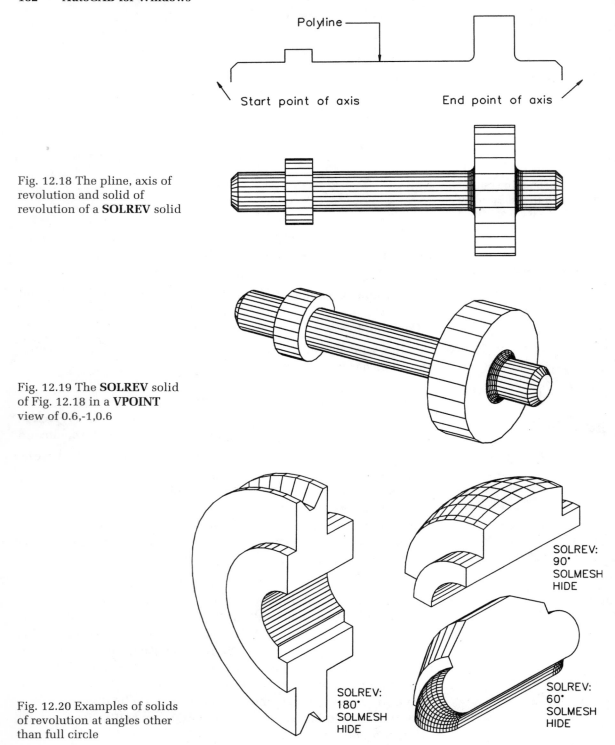

Fig. 12.18 The pline, axis of
revolution and solid of
revolution of a **SOLREV** solid

Fig. 12.19 The **SOLREV** solid
of Fig. 12.18 in a **VPOINT**
view of 0.6,-1,0.6

Fig. 12.20 Examples of solids
of revolution at angles other
than full circle

In all the examples of solids of revolution shown in Figs 12.18 to 12.20, **SOLWDENS** was set to 12.

Questions

1. What does the abbreviation AME stand for?
2. When is it easier to use an extrusion rather than to union several primitives?
3. Name the six primitives in a standard AutoCAD for Windows package.
4. Can you give the version number of the AME included with AutoCAD for Windows?
5. What are the name of the commands giving the three Boolean operators?
6. What does the **SOLWDENS** command control?
7. Why is the **UCS** so important when working in AME?
8. When a solid is first constructed in AME it is in a wireframe form. How is the wireframe changed to a 3D solid with surface meshes?
9. Why is it important to move the **UCSICON** to a new origin when changing the **UCS** during the construction of a solid model in AME?
10. What is the purpose of the AME command **SOLREV**?

Exercises

1. Fig. 12.21. Sequence of construction:
   (a) **SOLEXT** two semicircles, one of radius 50, the other of radius 60, to a height of 150;
   (b) Two **SOLBOX**es, each 140 x 70 x 10;

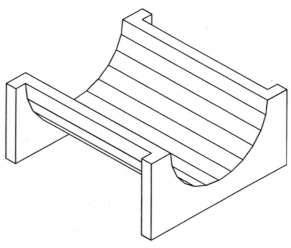

Fig. 12.21 Exercise 1

(c) Change the **UCS** if necessary to move the solboxes to their correct positions;

(d) **SOLUNION** the larger solext to the two solboxes;

(e) **SOLSUB** the smaller solext from the solunion.

Note: SOLWDENS is set to 6

2. Fig. 12.22. Sequence:

(a) Draw the pline outline of the arm – 260 long and 60 high to a suitable shape;

(b) **SOLEXT** the arm 15 high;

(c) Two **SOLCYL**s, each 55 high, one of radius 30, the other of radius 40;

(d) Change the **UCS** to a suitable position and move the **SOLEXT** centrally to the two solcyls;

(e) **SOLUNION** the solext and the larger solcyl;

(f) **SOLSUB** the smaller solcyl from the solunion.

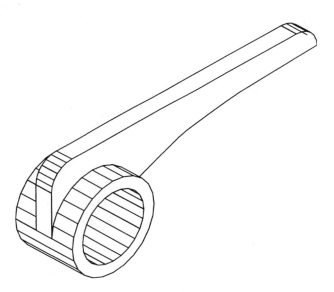

Fig. 12.22 Exercise 2

3. Fig. 12.23. A simple **SOLEXT** solid from a pline outline. Any suitable sizes.

4. Fig. 12.24. Base is 130 x 80 x 30. Bearing outer cylinder is 60 x diameter 60; inner cylinder is 60 x diameter 40; upright is 90 x 80 x 15. Fillet is radius 15. Dovetail slide a **SOLEXT** of suitable size. Bearing protrudes 15 in front of upright.

5. Fig. 12.25. Mostly constructed with **SOLEXT**, but also **SOLCYL**, **SOLUNION** and **SOLSUB**. Sizes: larger end – radii 35 and 25 and height 20; smaller end – radii 30 and 20 and height 15; arm 170 x 40 x 5; holes in clip diameter 7; clips of a suitable size.

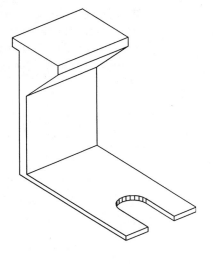

Fig. 12.23 Exercise 3

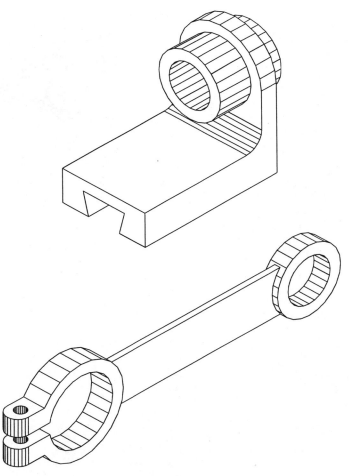

Fig. 12.24 Exercise 4

Fig. 12.25 Exercise 5

6. Fig. 12.26. Here is a more difficult solid constructed from a **SOLCYL** – the table top – and a number of **SOLREV**s – the vase and the legs and rails of the table. Several **UCS** settings will be needed to ensure that the parts are in a correct position in relation to each other.

Fig. 12.26 Exercise 6

CHAPTER 13

More about AME

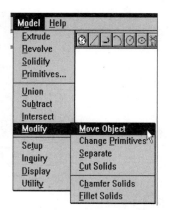

Fig. 13.1 The **Move Object** command from the **Model** pull-down menu

Introduction

Those AME command systems most often used when constructing elementary solid models were described in Chapter 12. In this chapter, other AME commands are introduced. These are for modifying solids constructed mainly with the aid of the command systems described in Chapter 12. Once again it must be emphasized that this book is for students and beginners with AutoCAD, and not all of the many commands and variables to be found in AME are described here.

The AME command SOLMOVE

The **SOLMOVE** command enables the operator to the move or rotate an AME solid along or around one of the x, y or z axes. The command can be called by selection from the **Model** pull-down menu (Fig. 13.1) or by entering solmove at the command line. The following gives the prompts and a sample response to the **SOLMOVE** command.

Command: *enter* solmove *right-click*
Select objects: *pick* the solid
Select objects: *right-click* **1 selected**
?/Motion description: *enter* f (for Face) *right-click*
Select face to define coordinate system: *pick* a face
Next<OK>: *right-click* (to accept the face on which coordinate arrows appear)
FACE coordinates
?/Motion description: *enter* tx50 *right-click*
Command:

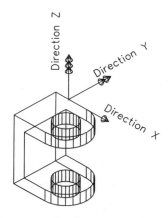

Fig. 13.2 The direction arrows appearing when a face is selected in **SOLMOVE**

Notes
1. Either a face (f) or an edge (e) can be the response to the **Motion description:** prompt. If an Edge is selected the coordinate arrows (Fig. 13.2) appear at the centre of the selected edge;

2. The two main responses (there are others not included here) are to Transfer (t) along the coordinate axes, or to rotate (r) around the coordinate axes;
3. When a transfer movement is requested the distance moved is given in coordinate units;
4. When a rotate movement is requested, the rotation is given in degrees;
5. Figure 13.3 shows transfer movements in each of the three coordinate axis directions *x*, *y* and *z*;
6. Figure 13.4 shows rotation movements around each of the coordinate axes *x*, *y* and *z*.

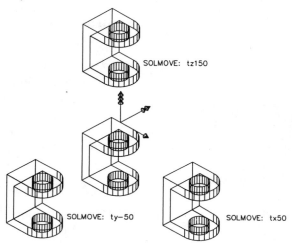

Fig. 13.3 The actions of the **SOLMOVE** responses tx, ty and tz

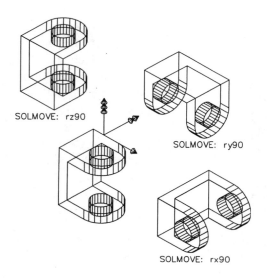

Fig. 13.4 The actions of the **SOLMOVE** responses rx, ry and rz

The AME command SOLCHP

If you wish to change features of the primitives making up an AME solid, use the command **SOLCHP** – the sizes or colours can be changed and a primitive can be deleted, moved or replaced with the aid of this command. The prompts and some sample responses are given below and in Fig. 13.5.

> **Command:** *enter* solchp
> **SOLCHP Select a solid or region:** *pick* the solid
> **1 solid selected.**
> **Select primitive:** *right-click*
> **Color/Delete/Evaluate/Instance/Move/Pick/Replace/Size/eXit:**
>   *enter* s (for size) *right-click*
> **Length along X axis<45>:** *enter* 80 *right-click*
> **Length along Y axis<60>:** *right-click* (to accept)
> **Length along Z axis<15>:** *right-click* (to accept)
> **Color/Delete/Evaluate/Instance/Move/Pick/Replace/Size/eXit:**
>   *enter* m (for Move) *right-click*
> **Base point of displacement:** *pick*
> **Second point of displacement:** *pick*
> **Color/Delete/Evaluate/Instance/Move/Pick/Replace/Size/eXit:**
>   *right-click*
> **Updating the Advanced Modeling Extension database.**
> **Command:**

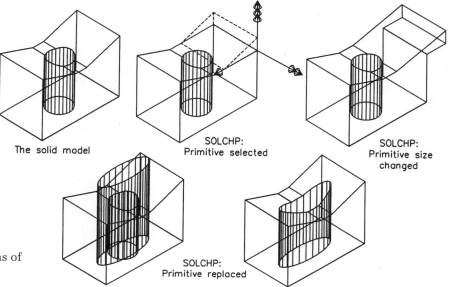

Fig. 13.5 Two of the actions of **SOLCHP**

The solid model

SOLCHP:
Primitive selected

SOLCHP:
Primitive size
changed

SOLCHP:
Primitive replaced

The AME command SOLSEP

Using this command separates out the primitives in an AME solid, according to the stages of the original Boolean operatives. Figure 13. 6 shows the two separations required to change a solid which was first acted upon by **SOLUNION**, then by **SOLSUB**. The **SOLSUB** was the last of the Boolean operations, so it becomes the first of the separations.

Command: *enter* solsep *right-click*
Select objects: *pick* **1 found**
Select objects: *right-click*
Series of messages, ending with
Updating the Advanced Modeling Extension
Command:

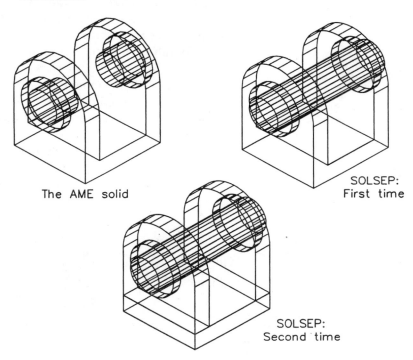

The AME solid

SOLSEP:
First time

SOLSEP:
Second time

Fig. 13.6 The action of
SOLSEP

The AME command SOLPROF

The use of this command changes an AME solid into a profile-only drawing. In order to use this command, a good knowledge of **Tilemode**, **Paper Space** and **Model Space** is necessary – see pages 158 to 164. AME models are constructed in **Model Space**. Unless one has already changed to **Paper Space**, the command line prompts sequences follow the pattern:

Command: *enter* solprof *right-click*
This command is not available in tilemode.
Command:

If this happens, set tilemode off (0), either from the **View** pull-down menu or by entering tilemode at the command line. This puts the graphics window into Paper Space. To obtain the best results I follow the following sequence:

1. Make a new layer VP of colour yellow, from the **Layer Control** dialogue box (Fig. 13.7) or from the command line. Make the layer VP current;

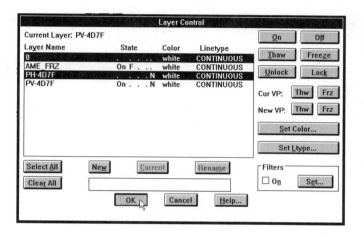

Fig. 13.7 The **Layer Control** dialogue box showing the layers to turn off when using **SOLPROF**

Fig. 13.8 The results of using **SOLPROF** on Fig. 12.26

2. **Command:** *enter* mview *right-click*
ON/OFF/Hideplot/Fit/2/3/4/Restore/<First point>: *enter* f (for Fit) *right-click*
Regenerating drawing
Command:
and the solid model reappears within a yellow-bounded viewport;
3. **Command:** *enter* mspace *right-click*
MSPACE
Command:
and the solid model is now back in model space, but with **Tilemode** off;
4. **Command:** *enter* solprof *right-click*
Select objects: *pick* a solid **1 found**
Select objects: *pick* a solid **1 found** in Fig. 13.8 two solids are being profiled;
Select objects: *right-click*
Display hidden profile lines on separate layers?<Y>: *right-click*

Project profile lines onto a plane?<Y>: *right-click*
Delete tangential edges?<Y>: *right-click*
Series of messages to show processing of computation
Command:

5. *Left-click* on the **Layer** button in the **Toolbar**. Figure 13.7 shows the resulting dialogue box which appears in the graphics window;

6. In the **Layer Control** dialogue box, make the layer(s) with the title **PV-???** current, turn layer(s) with the title **PH-???** off. *Left-click* on **OK** in the dialogue box; the profiled solid model drawing appears in the graphics window (Fig. 13.8). Figure 13.9 shows exercises from Chapter 12 that have been acted on by **SOLPROF**.

Notes

1. Drawings produced with **SOLPROF** are profiles only. Attempts to place them in a new viewing position with **VPOINT** will only result in distorted views;

2. If necessary much of the disk space taken up with the files saved from solid models which have been profiled with **SOLPROF** can be reduced by turning off the layer(s) **PV-??** and then erasing all that is left in the graphics windows. Then make the layer(s) **PV-???** current, followed by calling **SOLPURGE**. This erases the solid model drawings but leaving the profile. If the *.bak file is then examined and compared with the *.dwg file of the profile drawing, it will be seen that considerable disk space has been saved. **WARNING**: be careful not to erase such solid model drawings with non-profiled drawings, although **SOLPURGE** can be used in other ways.

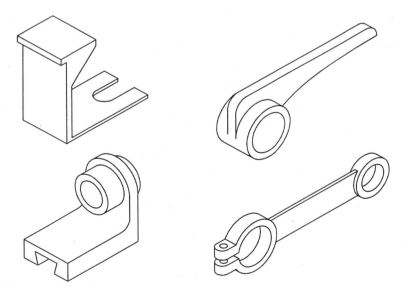

Fig. 13.9 Some exercises from Chapter 12 which have been acted upon by **SOLPROF**

The AME commands SOLCUT and SOLSECT

These two commands are used when constructing sectional views through an AME solid model drawing, although **SOLCUT** also can be used for other purposes. As an example of the way in which the two commands are used, take the component shown in Fig. 13.10 – a spacing device from a machine. This solid model was constructed in a four-viewport graphics window, as shown in Fig. 13.11.

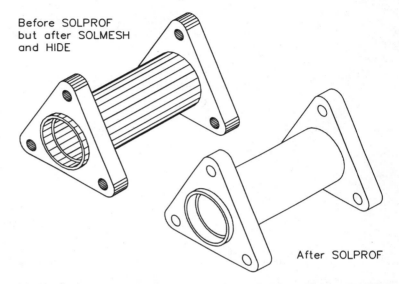

Fig. 13.10 The example solid model to demonstrate **SOLCUT** and **SOLSECT**

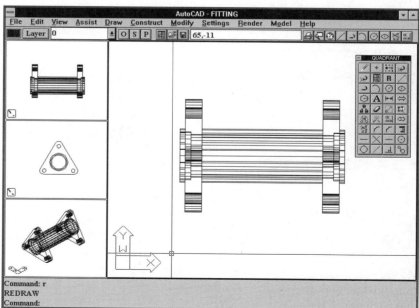

Fig. 13.11 The method by which the example Fig. 13.10 was constructed – in a four-viewport graphics window

When the model had been constructed from a **SOLEXT** and several **SOLCYLs**, and with the Boolean operators **SOLUNION** and **SOLSUB**, it was cut with the aid of **SOLCUT** (Fig. 13.12):

Command: *enter* solcut *right-click*
Select objects: *pick* **1 selected**
Cutting plane by Entity/Last/Zaxis/View/XY/YZ/ZX/<3 points>: *right-click*
First point on plane: *pick* **Second point on plane:** *pick* **Third point on plane:** *enter* .xy *right-click*
of *pick* First point again **(need Z):** *enter* 1 *right-click*
Both sides/<Point on desired side of plane>: *pick*
Series of messages showing progress of computation
Updating the Advanced Modeling Extension database...
Command:

Fig. 13.12 The action of
SOLCUT

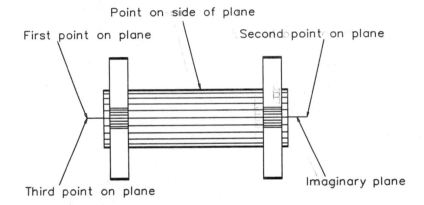

The solid after SOLCUT

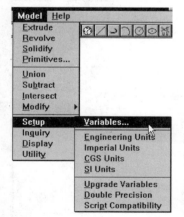

Fig. 13.13 **Variables...**
from the **Model** pull-
down menu

To section the solid after it has been cut, *left-click* on **Variables...** in the **Model** pull-down menu (Fig. 13.13). In the dialogue box which appears, *left-click* on the **Hatch Parameters...** button to bring up the **Hatch Parameters** dialogue box (Fig. 13.14). Enter the required parameters; in the example shown these are:

Name (of hatch pattern): U
Angle: 45
Size: 3

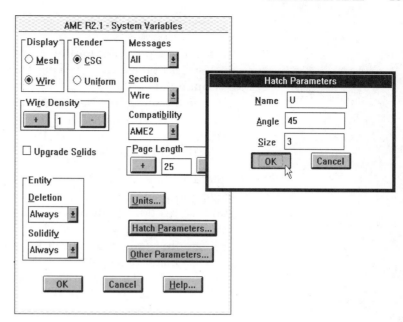

Fig. 13.14 The **AME System Variables** dialogue box and associated **Hatch Parameters** dialogue box

These parameters will give a standard engineering section hatching of parallel lines at an angle of 45 degrees and 3 units. To section the example solid model (Fig. 13.15), proceed as follows:

1. Make a new layer **HATCH**, colour red;
2. Call the command **SOLSECT**:
   Command: *enter* solsect *right-click*
   Select objects: *pick* the solid **1 selected**
   Select objects: *right-click*

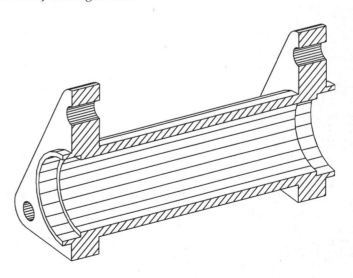

Fig. 13.15 A view of the cut solid showing the hatched surface

Section plane by Entity/Last/Zaxis/View/XY/YZ/ZX/<3 points>:
   right-click
pick three points as for the solcut
A series of messages showing the computation
Command:
The cut surface is now section hatched, as shown in Fig. 13.15.

   The solid, with its hatched surface, could now be acted upon by
SOLPROF as shown in Fig. 13.16 and used as part of an orthographic
projection (Fig. 13.17).

Note: The three-view orthographic projection of Fig. 13.17 is in Third
angle. It is made up from views of the example solid inserted into the
graphics window. Centre lines, hidden detail and dimensions could
be added to this drawing if needed. There are other ways of producing
orthographic projections from solid models, which will be briefly
discussed later (page 197).

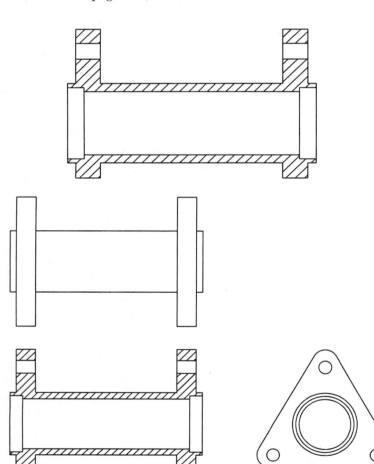

Fig. 13.16 The solid after
SOLPROF, with the hatched
surface at the front

Fig. 13.17 An orthographic
projection including a section
built up from inserted
SOLPROFed views

The AME command SOLUCS

When detail must be added to a sloping surface of a solid model, the surface can be set as a new **UCS** with the aid of the command **SOLUCS**. Figure 13.18 includes an example of its use. The command line prompts are:

Command: *enter* solucs *right-click*
Select objects. *pick* **1 found.**
Edge/<Face>: *pick* the required face
Next/<OK>: *right-click*
Command:

When a face (or an edge) is picked it highlights. If the wrong face is picked, *enter* n (for Next) and another face is highlighted. Continue entering n until the required face is highlighted. Then a *right-click* and the solid moves into a position such that the selected face is on a new **UCS** with the z coordinate at 0 (zero).

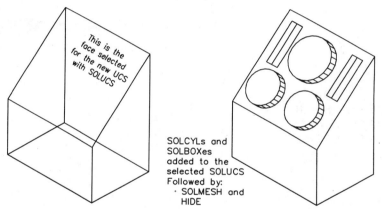

This is the face selected for the new UCS with SOLUCS

SOLCYLs and SOLBOXes added to the selected SOLUCS Followed by:
· SOLMESH and HIDE

Fig. 13.18 An example of the use of **SOLUCS**

Orthographic projections from AME solids

There are several methods by which orthographic projections can be formed from AME solid models. Such projections have the advantage that, if the model is correct, then the views from the solid must also be correct. The first method has already been shown in Fig. 11.34 (page 164) when dealing with 3D drawings constructed with the surface commands. This same method is repeated here for an AME solid model (Fig. 13.19). The projection (Fig 13.20) was constructed as follows:

1. Construct the solid model in MSpace;
2. Turn **Tilemode** off – now in PSpace;
3. Make a new layer – VP, colour yellow;

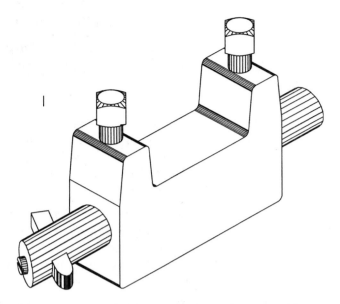

Fig. 13.19. The solid model from which Fig. 13.20 is derived

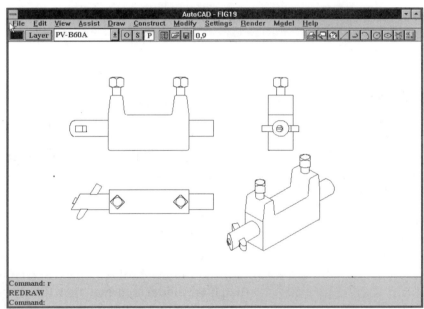

Fig. 13.20 An example of an AME solid in orthographic projection views

4. **Mview** to **Fit** in four viewports;
5. **MSpace**;
6. Set viewports in turn to **UCSFOLLOW** = 0;
7. Set viewports to **VPOINT**s:
   Top left 0,-1,0;
   Top right -1,0,0;
   Bottom right -1,-1,1;

8. **SOLPROF** each viewport in turn;
9. Turn off all layers beginning with **PV-** and also turn off layer **0**;
10. **PSpace**;
11. Move viewports to achieve a good layout;
12. Turn off the layer VP.
Note: The projection is in First angle.

The second method has been demonstrated in Fig. 13.17 on page 196. A third method involves the use of the command **SOLVIEW**. **SOLVIEW** is not part of AME, but is an AutoCAD Development System (ADS) file. It must therefore be loaded by:

> **Command:** *enter* (xload"solview")
> **"solview"**
> **Command:**

Only a bare outline of the possibilities available with this command is included here, the reader is advised to experiment. The AME solid model in Fig. 13.21 is the basis for the examples given here.

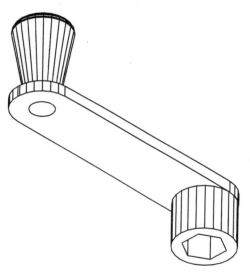

Fig. 13.21 The AME solid model used as an example for showing the uses of **SOLVIEW** and **SOLDRAW**

1. Place the solid model in the **Front UCS**;
2. Set **Tilemode** to off (0), which sets up the **PSpace** window;
3. **MVIEW**. Fit the solid in a viewport (Fig. 13.22);
4. **Command:** *enter* solview *right-click*
   Ucs/Ortho/Auxiliary/Section/<eXit>: *enter* o (for Ortho) *right-click*
   Pick side of viewport to project: *pick* side of viewport
   View center: *pick* a point for the centre of the new view

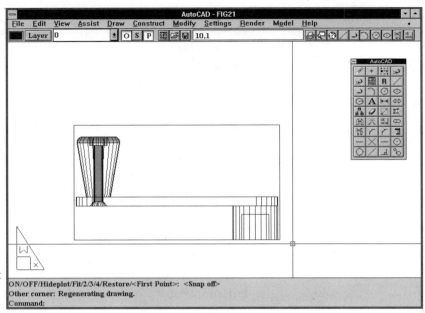

Fig.13.22 **SOLVIEW**. The front view in an **MVIEW** viewport in PSpace

View center: *right-click*
View name: *enter* end *right-click*
Ucs/Ortho/Auxiliary/Section/<eXit>: *right-click*
Command:
This creates an end view with the view name **end** (Fig. 13.23);

5. In a similar manner create a plan view with the view name **plan**;

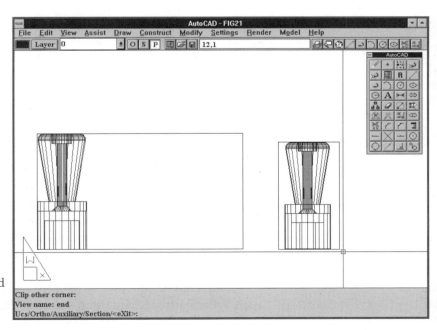

Fig. 13.23 **SOLVIEW**. The end view created and saved with the name end

6. Set **Tilemode** to 1 and **Viewports** to 4;
7. *Left-click* in the top left viewport;
   Command: *enter* view *right-click*
   ?/Delete/Restore/Save/Window: *enter* r (Restore) *right-click*
   View name to restore: *enter* end *right-click*
   Command:
8. Repeat to place the view plan in the bottom left-hand viewport;
9. In the bottom right viewport **VPOINT** -1,-1,-1;
10. **ZOOM** to 1 in each viewport in turn (Fig. 13.24).

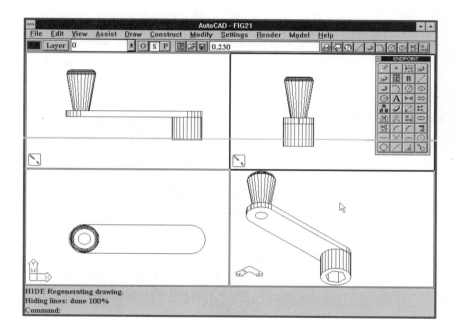

Fig. 13.24 **SOLVIEW**. The views in an MSpace four-viewport graphics window

Notes on AME solid models

1. When saved, AME solid models occupy large areas of space on the disk. For example, on my machine, Fig. 13.15 takes up nearly 250,000 bytes (0.25 Mb). Much of this disk space can be saved by using the two commands **SOLPURGE** and **PURGE**. The second of these commands – purge – can only be called when a drawing is first opened. It will purge from memory unused blocks, junk AME solids, unused layers and unused text styles. **SOLPURGE** will remove unwanted AME solids from memory and will also remove other data, but proceed with care. Used unwarily, solpurge can result in destroying the handles of the file and, if this happens, the drawing is no longer an AME solid model.

2. It will readily be seen from reading Chapters 12 and 13 that there is much more to AME than described here. There simply is not space in a book of this nature to describe all the AME commands, prompts and responses, or all the AME set variables. When the reader becomes more expert with using AME, he/she will find that the interest such expertise arouses will lead on to further exploration with this excellent solid modelling tool.

3. The **UCS** is necessarily often changed when working in AME. When changing the UCS from the **UCS Orientation** dialogue box, check whether the change is taking place **Relative to Current UCS** or **Absolute to WCS**. Unless the correct box against these messages is checked, the results may not be as desired.

Questions

1. What is the action of **SOLPURGE**?
2. Have you decided yet whether you prefer calling commands by selection from a pull-down menu, from an icon in the toolbox or by entering the command name or abbreviation at the command line?
3. Can you call AME commands from the toolbox?
4. What is the purpose of the command **SOLCHP**?
5. Can you give a reason why it is better to move an AME solid with the aid of the command **SOLMOVE** rather than with the command **MOVE**?
6. What is the best way of erasing an AME solid?
7. Why is it not advisable to erase the base primitives from an AME model?
8. What settings to variables must be made before using the **SOLSECT** command?
9. Regions are not described in this book. Find out about regions from the AutoCAD AME manual.

Exercises

1. Figure 13.25. Construct an AME solid model to the details given. Then **SOLPROF** the model.
2. Figure 13.26 is an end view of a garden seat with dimensions of the unit sizes from which an AME solid model of the seat is to be constructed. Figure 13.27 shows the completed solid model after being acted on by **SOLPROF**. Construct the solid model, then **SOLPROF the result.**

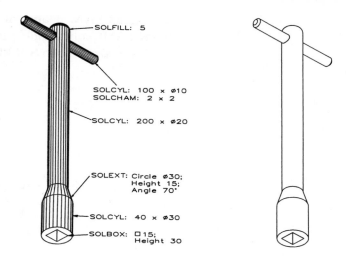

SOLFILL: 5

SOLCYL: 100 × Ø10
SOLCHAM: 2 × 2

SOLCYL: 200 × Ø20

SOLEXT: Circle Ø30;
Height 15;
Angle 70°

SOLCYL: 40 × Ø30

SOLBOX: □15;
Height 30

Fig. 13.25 Exercise 1

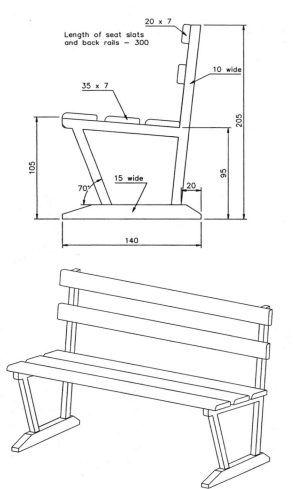

20 × 7

Length of seat slats
and back rails — 300

10 wide

35 × 7

205

95

70°

15 wide

20

105

140

Fig. 13.26 Details of
dimensions for Exercise 2

Fig. 13.27 Exercise 2

3. Figure 13.28 gives details of the coordinate unit sizes for the exploded AME solid model Fig. 13.29. Construct the solid model to the given sizes. Then **SOLPROF** the model.

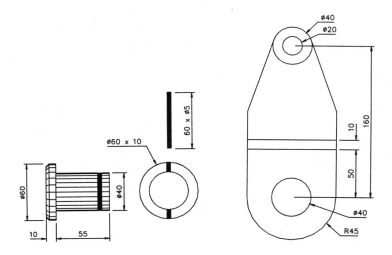

Fig. 13.28 Details of dimensions for parts of Exercise 3

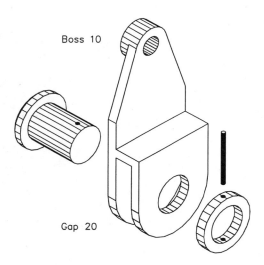

Fig. 13.29 Exercise 3

4. Figure 13.31 is an AME solid model of a garage. The coordinate unit sizes to which the model was constructed are given in Fig. 13.30. The hatch patterns on the roof and front wall of the model were added after placing the solid in a new **UCS** with the aid of **SOLUCS**. Construct the solid. There is no point in using **SOLPROF** on this model as there are no surfaces other than flat ones.

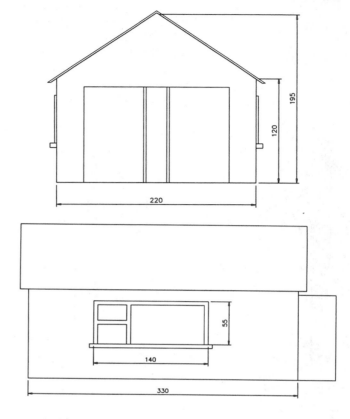

Fig. 13.30 Dimensions for
Exercise 4

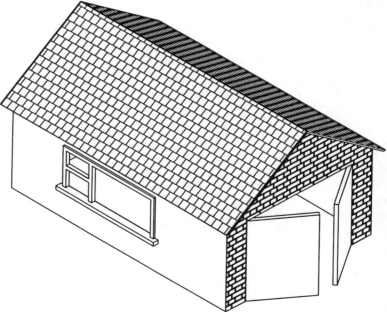

Fig. 13.31 Exercise 4

5. Construct the exploded solid model shown in Fig. 13.32. Details of the dimensions of the clip part of the model are given. Other sizes are left to your judgement. Figure 13.33 shows how the screw part of the bolt was obtained from a **SOLREV**. The head of the bolt was constructed from a **SOLEXT** of a hexagonal polygon.

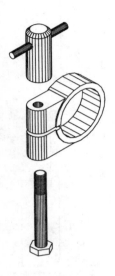

Fig. 13.32 Exercise 5 –
Details of sizes for the clip,
the completed solid and
the solid after **SOLPROP**.

R12
R20

A/F 12 6 DEEP
R10
22
HOLE ⌀6

15
2
20
6

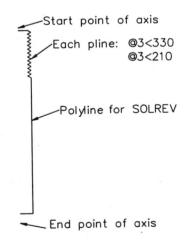

Start point of axis
Each pline: @3<330
             @3<210

Polyline for SOLREV

End point of axis

Fig. 13.33 Details for the
polyline to form the **SOLREV**
of the bolt for Exercise 5

CHAPTER 14

AutoCAD Render

Introduction

AutoCAD Render allows 3D models which have been constructed with the aid of the Surfaces commands or in AME, to be rendered as 3D images. The rendered images convey the form of 3D designs more clearly than the wireframe models from which they are created. The Render program allows:

1. Surface finishes to be added to the model – the finishes can be in any of the colours possible with the computer set-up in use;
2. The surface finishes to be set to defined reflective qualities;
3. Lights to be added to the scene in which the 3D model is situated to increase the realism of the rendered model;
4. The checking of the accuracy of the model which has been designed. This is because a rendered model gives a more realistic impression of a design than is possible with a wireframe model.

Note: AutoCAD Render in AutoCAD for Windows replaces AutoShade, by which 3D models were rendered in earlier releases of AutoCAD.

Two examples of rendering of 3D models constructed with AME from previous chapters will be described. Further examples are shown in colour plates (between pages 112 and 113).

Example 1 – Spacer

1. **Open** the 3D model of the spacer from Fig. 13.10 (Fig. 14.1);
2. *Left-click* on **Render** from the menu bar, followed by a *left-click* on **Finishes...** in the pull-down menu (Fig. 14.2);
3. In the **Finishes** dialogue box (Fig. 14.3) *left-click* on **New...** and enter a name for the finish required in the **Finish name:** box – in this example the name is BRASS;

Fig. 14.1 Example 1 - a 3D
model constructed in AME

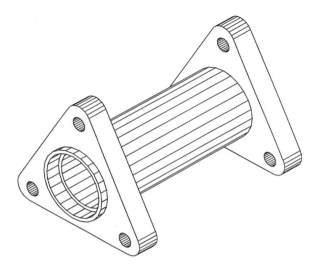

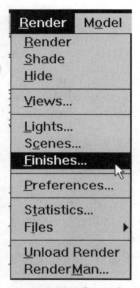

Fig.14.2 **Finishes...** from the
Render pull-down menu

Fig. 14.3 The **Finishes**
dialogue box

4. *Left-click* on **Modify...** in the dialogue box, bringing up the **Modify Finish** dialogue box (Fig. 14.4). In this dialogue box, use the sliders to set the finish reflective qualities as follows:

Ambient: 0.30;
Diffuse: 0.70;
Specular: 0.60;
Roughness: 0.70;

These settings will give a good reflective surfaces quality to the solid;

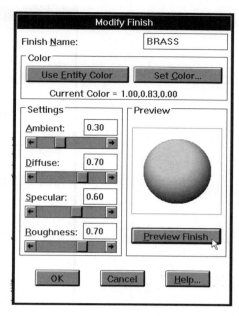

Fig. 14.4 The **Modify Finishes** dialogue box

5. *Left-click* on **Color...** in the dialogue box. The **Color** dialogue box appears. *Left-click* on a suitable colour in the colour wheel. The colour can be adjusted with the aid of the Red, Green and Blue (RGB) slider bars. When satisfied, *left-click* on **OK**;

6. *Left-click* on **Preview Finish** in the **Modify Finish** dialogue box to check whether the finishes as set produce the desired results;

7. *Left-click* on **Preferences... in** the **Render** pull-down menu, followed by a *left-click* in the **Smooth Shading** box in the **Rendering Preferences** dialogue box (Fig. 14.6) to set smooth shading on, followed by a *left-click* on **OK**;

8. *Left-click on* **OK in** the **Modify** dialogue box. The **Finishes** dialogue box re-appears. *Left-click* on **Entities>**, followed by a *left-click* on the solid model – this applies the finish to the model;

9. *Left-click* on **Render** in the **Render** pull-down menu and the solid is rendered. As rendering proceeds a series of messages will appear at the command line indicating the computing procedures taking place.

Fig. 14.7 shows the completed rendering.

Notes

1. With large models, rendering may take a long time;
2. The reader is advised to experiment with the settings;
3. The reflective surface settings given above should be adjusted according to the solid being rendered, but those given for this model will produce reasonably good renderings in most instances.

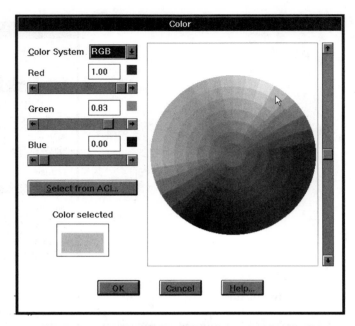

Fig. 14.5 The **Color** dialogue box

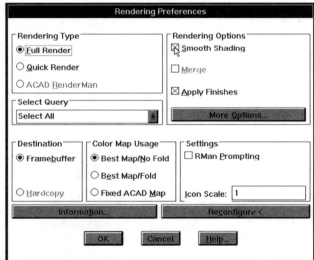

Fig. 14.6 The **Rendering Preferences** dialogue box

4 The **Modify Finish** dialogue box (Fig. 14.4) includes the lighting terms **Ambient, Diffuse, Specular** and **Roughness**:

Ambient lighting refers to the general all-round background lighting of the area in which the model being rendered is placed.

Diffuse lighting is the light which emanates from the model. For example, if the colour for the model is red - set with **Set Color** in the dialogue box - the diffuse colour of the model itself will be a red.

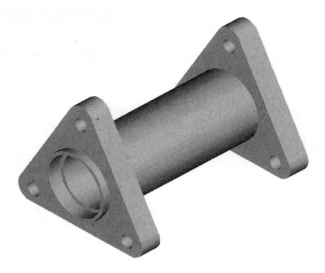

Fig.14.7 The rendered spacer
solid model

Specular lighting is the lighting highlight area of the model. The
size of the highlighted area will show on the **Preview Finish** sphere in
the dialogue box. The spread of the highlight is partly dependant on
the **Roughness** setting.

Roughness. A rougher surface will show a larger spread of the
specular highlight.

Example 2 – Pipe clip

1. **Open** the 3D drawing of a pipe clip from Fig. 13.32 (Fig. 14.8);
2. Following the methods indicated in the previous example and add
   finishes to the model as follows:
   STEEL: of a suitable colour to the bolt;
   NUT: of a suitable colour to the nut;
   CLIP: of a suitable colour to the clip part;
   The reflective surface finishes can be set as for the previous
   example;
3. *Left-click* on **Lights...** in the **Render** pull-down menu. The **Lights**
   dialogue box appears (Fig. 14.9);
4. In the **Lights** dialogue box set up four lights. Each is set by first *left-
   clicking* on **New...**, which brings up the **New Light Type** dialogue
   box (Fig. 14.10). The four lights are set in this dialogue box as:
   BACK: Distant light;
   FRONT: Distant light;
   SIDE: Distant light;
   TOP: Point light;

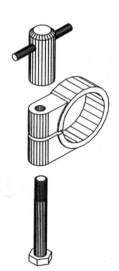

Fig. 14.8 Example 2 - a 3D
model constructed in AME

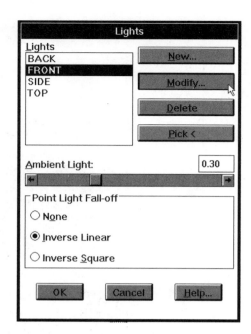

Fig. 14.9 The **Lights** dialogue
box

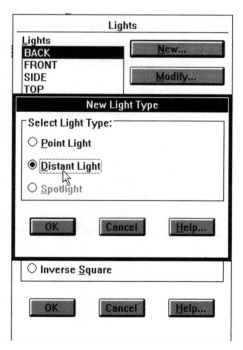

Fig. 14.10 The **New Light
Type** dialogue box

5. Some adjustment of the **Ambient Light** slider may be necessary.
Again, experimentation will help to assess this factor with each
light;

6. Each light can be modified as to its position, intensity and colour in either the **Modify Distant Light** or the **Modify Point Light** dialogue boxes (Fig. 14.11), which are called up from the **Lights** dialogue box by a *left-click* on **Modify...**.
   Figure 14.12 shows the resultant rendering.

Fig. 14.11 The **Modify Distant Light** dialogue box

Fig. 14.12 The completed rendering of Example 2

Notes

1. When finishes or lights have been set, the operator is prompted to place an icon representing the finish or light in the graphic window. Figure 14.13 shows a group of finish icons associated with one of the renderings shown in colour plate ??.

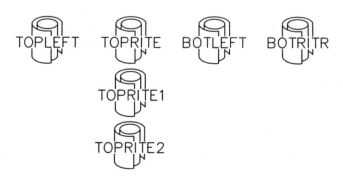

Fig. 14.13 Some finish icons

2. Some practice is necessary before lighting can be set to achieve good results in rendered models. Figure 11.14 shows the principles involved in placing point and distant lights in a general setting – a **Distant Light** pointing from the front and above; a second **Distant Light** pointing from the right (or left) and above; a **Point Light** giving an overall lighting from above;

3. In general **Point** lights give an overall lighting effect in all directions from the position in which they are set, so only the position of the light is needed;

4. **Distant** lights produce beams of lights from the position in which they are set, thus not only is the position of the light necessary but so is the target at which the light is aimed;.

5. When setting lights, it is often necessary to set the z coordinate of their x,y,z positions *entering* **.xy** at the command line, followed by *entering* the z coordinate when **(need Z):** appears at the command line.

Questions

1. What is the purpose of AutoCAD Render?
2. What is meant by surface reflective qualities?
3. Can you explain what is meant by "ambient" light?
4. Can you explain what is meant by "diffuse" light?
5. What is meant by "specular" finish?

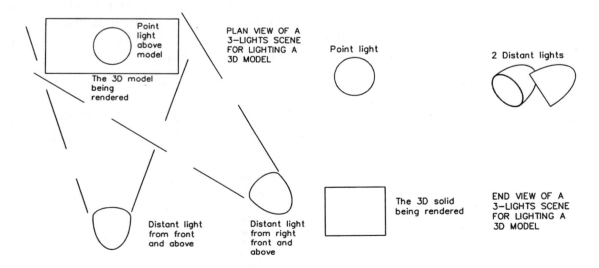

Fig. 14.14 A typical example of a front and end view of a three-lights scene for rendering a 3D model

6. What is meant by "roughness" when the term is applied to a surface finish?
7. What do the letters RGB mean in relation to colour?
8. Check what can be amended in the **Preferences** dialogue box **More Options....**
9. Why has a back light been added to the rendering details of the pipe clip (Fig. 14.8)?
10. What is the difference between a point light and a distant light in AutoCAD Render?

Exercises

The answers to the exercises in Chapters 11, 12 and 13 were mostly 3D models, all of which can be rendered in AutoCAD Render. Open up any of the drawing files you have saved when answering these exercises and render each of them in turn.

APPENDIX A

Windows and MS-DOS

Introduction

When working in AutoCAD on a PC set-up, it is sometimes necessary to have access to the **MS-DOS** command systems in order to manipulate the directories, sub-directories and files which are being developed as drawing proceeds. When using AutoCAD for Windows, there is rarely any need to use **MS-DOS** commands directly from the **C:** prompt; instead, access to the required commands can be made through the **File Manager** window of Windows.

When a drawing has been constructed in AutoCAD, it is saved to disk with a filename ending with the file extension **.dwg**. Drawing files are usually saved in directories or sub-directories. As an example, when constructing the drawings for this book, all drawings were saved to a hard disk partition d:\. in a directory **acadwin** – full name **d:\acadwin**. All of the drawings in any one chapter were saved in a sub-directory of **d:\acadwin** e.g. **d:\acadwin\chap14**. Drawings were saved in a sub-directory of **d:\acadwin\chap14** as **d:\acadwin\chap14\dwgs**. Each drawing file was given its figure number. Figure 14.3 was saved in sub-directory **d:\acadwin\chap14\dwgs** as **d:\acadwin\chap14\dwgs\fig03.dwg**.

The Windows File Manager

A variety of windows can be called onto the monitor screen from the Windows **Program Manager** (Fig. A.1). All through this book are examples of the AutoCAD for Windows graphics window. One such window is the **File Manager**, in which the names of all directories, sub-directories and files can be seen when required. The window also allows calls to be made directly to those **MS-DOS** commands which are of value in the manipulation of directories and files. To call the **File Manager**, *double-left-click* on its icon in the **Program Manager** as indicated in Fig. A.1. The **File Manager,** window appears (Fig. A.2).

Left-click on the button labelled **c** in the menu bar of the window. All the directories contained on the hard disk partition **c:** appear in the window. One such directory is **c:\acad**. A *left-click* on name **acad** in the window brings up all sub-directories and all files in that directory. A *left-click* on the sub-directory name **support** brings up all the files held in that sub-directory. Figure A.2 shows the **File Manager** window

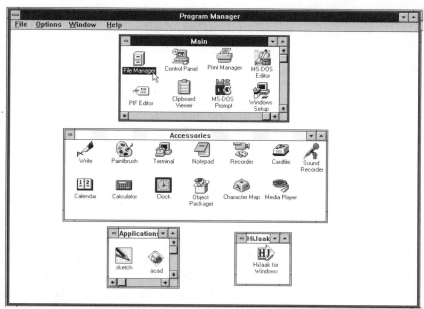

Fig. A.1 The **Program Manager** window of Windows 3.1

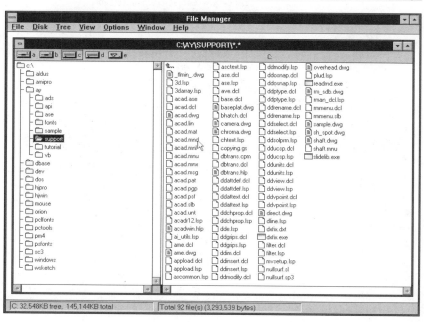

Fig. A.2 The **File Manager** window of Windows 3.1

with all the files held in **c:\acad\support**. Figure A.3 shows some of the files held in c:\acad\support in a table form. There are many files other in the sub-directory **support** of the directory **acad**.

Directories, sub-directories and files

Figure A.3 shows eight of the many files in the sub-directory **support** of the **c:\acad** directory, which is the directory holding the AutoCAD for Windows files on my computer. The full name of any one file in the sub-directory is made up from:

1. The name of the hard disk partition holding the files – **c:**;
2. The name of the directory – **acad**;
3. The name of the sub-directory – **support**;
4. The name of the file – e.g. **acad**;
5. The filename extension showing the type of file – e.g. **.dwg**;
6. Back-slashes (\) between the hard disk name, the directory name, the sub-directory name and the file name;
7. A fullstop (.) between the filename and its extension.

Filename extensions

The filename extension indicates the type of file. We have become accustomed in this book to seeing the extension **.dwg,** indicating that the file is an AutoCAD drawing file. Other types of file in AutoCAD have extensions such as:

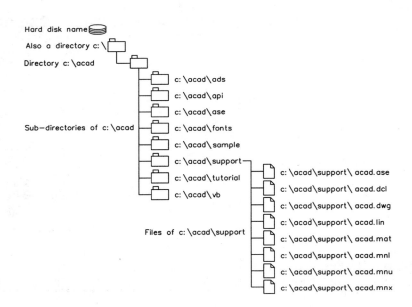

Fig. A.3 Some files in the directory **c:\acad**

bak – backup file formed automatically on disk, when a drawing is saved a second time;

dxf – drawing interchange files – for exchanging CAD files between CAD systems;

mnu – the AutoCAD menu file – details of the screen menus;

mnx – the AutoCAD menu file from which the **.mnu** files are compiled;

sld – an AutoCAD slide file.

There are many others not included in this short list.

MS-DOS commands from the File Manager

Left-click on **File** in the **File Manager** menu bar. The **File** pull-down menu appears (Fig. A.4). *Left-click* on any of the names appearing in the menu which end with three full stops (**...**) and a dialogue box will appear in the window. Figure A.5 shows the **Create Directory** dialogue box. In this dialogue box, entering the name of the required new directory in the **Name** box followed by a *left-click* on **OK** creates the

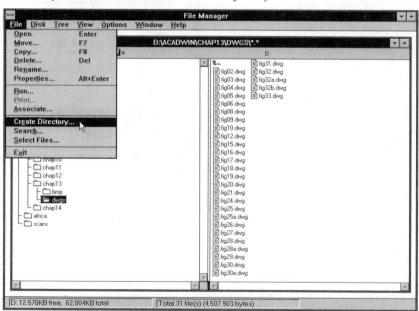

Fig. A.4 The **File** pull-down menu in the **File Manager** window

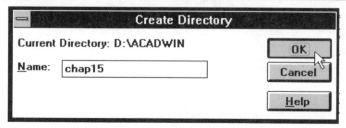

Fig. A.5 The **Create Directory** dialogue box

Fig. A.6 The **Disk** pull-down menu

directory (or sub-directory) as required. Its name will appear in the lists in the window. Other **MS-DOS** commands can be called and operated in a similar manner. Figure A.5 shows the **Disk** pull-down menu which gives access to **MS-DOS** commands associated with disk operations such as formatting. A *left-click* on **Format Disk...** (Fig. A.6) brings up the **Format Disk** dialogue box (Fig. A.7), which allows the formatting of any floppy disks used in the computer.

Other pull-down menus in the **File Manager** window allow rearrangements of the window layout and a number of ways in which files can be seen in the window.

The reader is advised to look at the various commands available in the **File Manager**, taking care all the time that directories or files are not erased or changed in any way. It is very easy, for example, to erase or rename a file, which may cause other users a great deal of trouble in attempting to find a file on a disk.

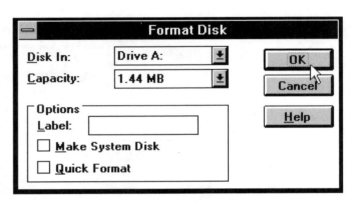

Fig. A.7 The **Create Directory** dialogue box

Printing/Plotting

Printing or plotting of AutoCAD for Windows drawings can be carried out directly from the graphics window or from a plot file. Printing and plotting for anything from any application window in Windows 3.1 is carried out through the Windows **Print Manager**. This includes AutoCAD for Windows. To print or plot any drawing loaded in the AutoCAD graphics window, either *enter* plot at the command line or *left-click* on **Print/Plot** in the **File** pull-down menu. The **Plot Configuration** dialogue box appears - Fig. B1. Printing or plotting is carried out by the selection of parameters from this dialogue box. A *left-click* on the **Device and Default Selection...** button allows the printer or plotter which is to be used to be selected. A *left-click* on the **Size...** button allows the size of the print or plot to be selected or set. A *left-click* on the **Window...** button brings the **Window Selection** dialogue box into the graphics window, to allow a window area for plotting to be *picked* with the aid of the selection device. *Left-click* on **Preview** and the area to be plotted can be seen, either as a rectangle or as a full drawing. Lines can be hidden by ensuring that the **Hide** box is checked. Other parameters for plotting can be set by using the buttons in the **Print Configuration** dialogue box. If the **Plot to File** box is checked, the

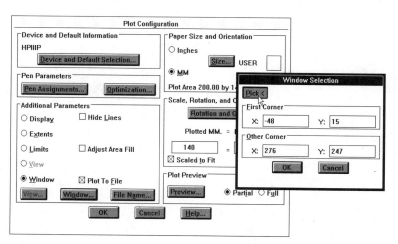

Fig. B1 - The **Plot Configuration** dialogue box

drawing will be saved to a file with a filename extension *.plt*. The drawing can be printed or plotted from this file from the **DOS** prompt, as in the following examples for the plotting of the drawing with a filename dwg01:

C: *enter* print c:\dwgs\dwg01.plt *Return*
or:
C: *enter* type c:\dwgs\dwg01.plt>plt1 *Return*

provided the printer/plotter is configured as being connected to port PLT1.

Glossary

This glossary contain some of the more common computing terms.

Application – the name given to software packages that perform tasks such as word processing, desktop publishing, CAD etc.

ASCII – american national standard code for information interchange. A code which assigns bits to characters used in computing.

AT – advanced technology. Applied to PCs which have an 80286 processor (or better).

Autodesk – the American company which produces AutoCAD and other CAD software packages.

BASIC – beginner's all-purpose symbolic instruction code. A programing language.

Baud rate – a measure of the rate at which a computer system can send and receive information (measured in bits per second).

BIOS – basic input/output system. The chip in a PC that controls the operations performed by the hardware (e.g. disks, screen, keyboard etc.)

Bit – short for binary digit. Binary is a form of mathematics that uses only two numbers: 0 and 1. Computers operate completely on binary mathematics.

Block – a group of objects or entities on screen that have been linked together to act as one unit.

Booting up – starting up a computer to an operating level.

Bus – an electronic channel that allows the movement of data around a computer.

Byte – a sequence of 8 bits.

C – a computer programing language.

Cache – a section of memory (can be ROM or RAM) which holds data that is being frequently used. Speeds up the action of disks and applications.

CAD – computer-aided design. Should not be used as computer-aided drawing.

CAD/CAM – computer-aided design and manufacturing.

CD-ROM – compact disc read only memory. A disk system capable of storing several hundred Mb of data – commonly 640 Mb. Data can only be read from a CD-ROM, not written to it.

Entity – a single feature or graphic being drawn on screen, e.g. a line, a circle, a point, etc. Sometimes linked together with other entities to form a block, where the block then acts as a single entity.

ROM – read only memory. Refers to those chips from which the data stored can be read but to which data cannot be written.

CGA – colour graphic adaptor. A screen display with a resolution of 320 x 200 in four colours. Not used much with modern CAD systems.

Chips – pieces of silicon that have the electronic circuits that drive computers formed from other minerals on their surface.

Clock speed – usually measured in MHz (megahertz) – this is a measure of the speed at which a computer processor works.

Clone –refers to a PC that functions in a way identical to the original IBM PC.

CMOS – complementary metal oxide semiconductor. Often found as battery powered chips which control features such as the PC's clock speed.

Communications – describes the software and hardware that allow computers to communicate.

Compatible – generally used as a term for software able to run on any computer that is an IBM clone.

Coprocessor – a processor chip in a computer that runs in tandem with the main processor chip, and can deal with arithmetic involving many decimal points (floating-point arithmetic). Often used in CAD systems to speed up drawing operations.

CPU – central processing unit. The chip which drives a PC.

Data – information that is created, used or stored on computer in digital form.

Database – a piece of software that can handle and organize large amounts of information.

Directories – the system used in MS-DOS for organizing files on disk. Could be compared to a folder (the directory) containing documents (the files).

Disks – storage hardware for holding data (files, applications, etc.). There are many types; the most common are hard disks (for mass storage) and floppy disks (less storage) and CD-ROMs (mass storage).

Display – the screen allowing an operator to see the results of his work at a computer.

DOS – disk operating system. The software that allows the computer to access and organize stored data. MS-DOS (produced by the Microsoft Corporation) is the DOS most widely used in PCs.

DTP – desktop publishing. DTP software allows for the combination of text and graphics into page layouts, which may then be printed.

EGA – enhanced graphics adaptor. A screen display with a resolution of 640 x 350 pixels in 16 colours.

EMS – expanded memory specification. RAM over and above the original limit of 640 Kb RAM in the original IBM PC. PCs are now being built to take up to 64 Mb RAM.

File – a collection of data held as an entity on a disk.

Fixed disk – a hard disk that cannot usually be easily removed from the computer; as distinct from floppy disks which are designed to be easily removable.

Floppy disk – a removable disk that stores data in magentic form. The actual disk is a thin circular sheet of plastic with a magnetic surface, hence the term 'floppy'. It usually has a firm plastic case.

Formating – the process of preparing the magnetic surface of a disk to enable it to hold digital data.

Giga – means 1,000,000,000. In computer memory terms 1000 Mb (megabytes) – actually 1,073,741,824 bytes because there are 1024 bytes in a kilobyte (K).

GUI – graphical user interface. Describes software (such as Windows) which allows the user to control the computer by representing functions with icons and other graphical images.

Hardcopy – the result of printing (or plotting) text or graphics on to paper or card.

Hard disk – a disk, usually fixed in a computer, which rotates at high speed and will hold large amounts of data, often up to 1 gigabyte.

Hardware – the equipment used in computing: the computer itself, disks, printers, monitor, etc.

Hz (hertz) – the measure of 1 cycle per second. In computing terms, often used in millions of hertz (megahertz or MHz) as a measure of the clock speed.

IBM – International Business Machines. An American computer manufacturing company – the largest in the world.

Intel – an American company which manufactures the processing chips used in the majority of PCs.

Joystick – a small control unit used mainly for computer games. Some CAD systems use a joystick to control drawing on screen.

Kilo – means 1000. In computing terms 1 K (kilobyte) is 1024 bytes.

LAN – local area network. Describes a network that might typically link PCs in an office by cable, where distance between the PCs are small.

Library – a set of frequently used symbols, phrases or other data on disk, that can be easily accessed by the operator.

Light Pen – stylus used to point directly at a display screen sensitive to its use.

Memory – any medium (such as RAM or ROM chips) that allows the computer to store data internally that can be instantly recalled.

MHz – megahertz. 1,000,000 hertz (cycles per second).

Mouse – a device for controlling the position of an on-screen pointer within a GUI such as Windows.

Microcomputer – a PC is a microcomputer; a minicomputer is much larger and a mainframe computer is larger still. With the increase in memory possible with a microcomputer, the term seems to be dropping out of use.

Microsoft – the American company which produces the Windows and MS-DOS software.

MIPS – millions of instructions per second. A measure of a computer's speed – it is not comparable with the clock speed as measured in MHz because a single instruction may take more than a single cycle to perform.

Monitor – the computer's display screen.

MS-DOS – Microsoft Disk Operating System.

Multitasking – a computer that can carry out more than one task at the same time is said to be multitasking. For example, in AutoCAD for Windows, printing can be carried out 'in the background' while a new drawing is being constructed.

Multiuser – a computer that may be used by more than one operator.

Networking – the joining together of a group of computers, allowing them to share the same data and software applications. LANs and WANs are examples of the types of networks available.

Object – a term used in CAD to describe an entity, or a group of entities that have been linked together.

Operating system – software, and in some cases hardware, that allows the user to operate applications software and organize and use data stored on a computer.

PC – personal computer. Should strictly only be used to refer to an IBM clone, but is now in general use.

Pixels – the individual dots of a computer display.

Plotter – produces hardcopy of, for instance, a drawing produced on computer by moving a pen over a piece of paper or card.

Printer – there are many types of printer; dot-matrix, bubble-jet and laser are the most common. Allows material produced on computer (graphics and text) to be output as hardcopy.

Processor – the operating chip of a PC. Usually a single chip, such as the Intel 80386 or 80486 chip.

Programs – a set of instructions to the computer that has been designed to produce a given result.

RAM – random access memory. Data stored in RAM is lost when the computer is switched off, unless previously saved to a disk.

RGB – red, green, blue.

RISC – reduced instruction set chip. A very fast processor.

ROM – Read Only Memory. Data and programs stored in a ROM chip are not lost when the computer is switched off.

Scanner – hardware capable of being passed over a document or drawing and reading the image into a computer.

Software – refers to any program or application that is used and run on computer.

SQL – structured query language.

UNIX – a multiuser, multitasking operating system (short for UNICS: uniplexed information and computing system).

VDU – visual display unit.

Vectors – refers to entities in computer graphics which are defined by the end points of each part of the entity.

VGA – video graphics array. Screen displays with a resolution of up to 640 x 480 pixels in 256 colours. SVGA (Super VGA) allows resolutions of up to 1024 x 768 pixels.

Virtual memory – a system by which disk space is used to allow the computer to function as if more physical RAM were present. It is used by Windows (and other software), but can slow down a computer's operation.

WAN – wide area network. A network of computers that are a large distance apart – communication is often done down telephone lines.

Weitek – makers of math coprocessor chips for 80386 and 80486 computers. Important for AutoCAD users, because the addition of a Weitek coprocessor speeds up drawing construction processes considerably.

WIMP – windows, icons, mice and pointers. A term that is used to describe some GUIs.

Winchesters – hard disks. Refers to the company which made the first hard disks. An out-of-date term.

Window – an area of the computer screen within which applications such as word processors may be operated.

Workstation – often used to refer to a multiuser PC, or other system used for the purposes of CAD (or other applications).

WORM – write once, read many. An optical storage system that allows blank optical disks to have data written onto them only once.

WYSIWYG – what you see is what you get. What is seen on the screen is what will be printed.

XMS – extended memory specifications. RAM above the 1Mb limit.

XT – extended technology. Was used to refer to the original 8060- or 8088-based computers.

Index